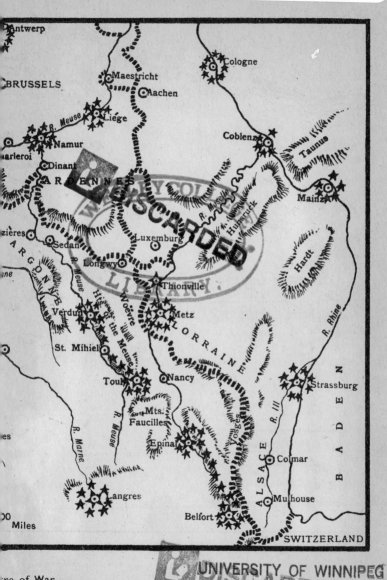

Antwerp

Cologne

BRUSSELS · Maestricht

Aachen

R. Meuse · Liége

Namur

arleroi · Dinant

A R D E N N E S

Coblenz

Taunus

Mainz

zières · Sedan

R. Moselle

R. Hunsruck

Luxemburg

A R G O N N E · Longwy

R. Meuse · Thionville

Hardt

Verdun · Metz

H'ts of the Meuse · Woëvre

L O R R A I N E

St. Mihiel

R. Rhine

Toul · Nancy

Strassburg

B A D E N

Mts. Faucilles

R. Meuse

Osges

R. III

Epinal

R. Marne

Colmar

A L S A C E

Langres

Mulhouse

Belfort

SWITZERLAND

Miles

re of War.

NELSON'S
HISTORY OF THE WAR

VOLUME XIV.

Nelson's History of the War. By
John Buchan.

Volume XIV.   From the Fall of Kut to the
Second Battle of Verdun.

THOMAS NELSON AND SONS, Ltd.
LONDON, EDINBURGH, AND NEW YORK

CONTENTS.

APPENDICES.

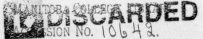

CONTENTS.

LIST OF MAPS.

NELSON'S
HISTORY OF THE WAR.

CHAPTER XCVIII.

THE FALL OF KUT.

Townshend's Position—Beginning of the Siege—Turkish Bom-
bardment during December—The Fight on Christmas Eve—
The Blockade begins—The Relieving Force—Difficulties of
the Undertaking—The River and the Climate—The Turkish
Defences—Aylmer carries Sheikh Saad—Turks driven from
Orah—British held before Umm-el-Hanna—The Rains—The
Inaction of February—The Attack on Es Sinn—Its Failure—
Gorringe succeeds Aylmer—13th Division carry Umm-el-
Hanna and Falahiyeh Positions—Lahore Division advance on
Right Bank—Failure of Attack on Sanna-i-yat—Capture of
Beit Eissa—Gorringe's Last Effort—State of Affairs in Kut—
Growing Famine—Attempt to run the Blockade—Townshend
surrenders—Results of Mesopotamia Expedition—Break-
down of Indian Transport and Medical Service—Suffering of
the Sick and Wounded—A Commission of Inquiry appointed.

WE left General Townshend on December 3,
1915, when he had found sanctuary in Kut
for the remnants of the Bagdad Expedition,
with the enemy closing in around him. He had ap-
proximately 10,000 men, having lost
4,567 in the Ctesiphon fighting and the
subsequent retirement. The wisdom of
that disastrous march up the Tigris has already been
discussed in these pages. General Townshend had

Dec. 3,
1915.

himself pointed out its dangers to his superior commander, but considerations of military etiquette seem to have prevented him from enforcing his views. The responsibility remained with Sir John Nixon and the Government of India. It was an honest mistake in judgment, which indeed had melancholy results; but no campaign was ever conducted without occasional blunders, and it is idle to dwell upon them. Far graver faults were yet to be revealed, for the authorities concerned not only erred in policy, but had made no adequate provision for carrying out any plan to a workmanlike conclusion.

The town of Kut lies inside a loop of the Tigris, where the river, some eighty yards wide, runs roughly due east. The loop is shaped like a Moorish arch, and the opening is to the northward. At its widest it is a mile across, and its length is a little under four miles. The houses are mostly in the loop, but across the river stands a liquorice factory with a few hovels round it. From the south-west corner runs the Shatt-el-Hai, the watercourse which, as we have seen, connects the Tigris with the Euphrates at Nasiriyeh. This gives the squalid little town its importance, for connecting with it a caravan route runs north across the Pushtikuh hills to the Persian border. Its normal population, mostly Arab, was under 4,000, and its narrow, dusty streets and houses, with the plaster peeling from the walls, made up as dreary a scene as could be found in a habitable land. All around it stretched the flat, sun-baked wastes, broken only by an occasional cluster of palms and a clump or two of prickly bush. In the rains the cracked soil became a sea of mire, with the turbid red flow of the Tigris rolling through it like the freshet of a strong river in a tidal estuary.

The position was a good one for defence. There was an entrenched line across the neck of land, with a closed work in it which we called the North Fort. Townshend held also the liquorice factory on the south bank of the river, in the angle of the Shatt-el-Hai. The place was well adapted to resist direct assault, but the task of supplying 10,000 men in that narrow loop would presently become serious. At that date no doubt was felt about the possibility of relief. If Townshend could hold the fort for a couple of months at the most, the relieving force would have ascended the river and dispersed the beleaguering army.

By 5th December the siege had begun in earnest. Four Turkish divisions lay around the town, the chief strength being on the north and south-west. On the 7th Nur-ed-Din summoned the garrison to surrender, and on Townshend's refusal opened a *Dec.* 7. heavy bombardment. Some of the few river craft remaining were set on fire, and the North Fort was temporarily taken. We were compelled also to give up the bridge to the east of the town, which was destroyed, and to draw in our outposts at that point. The bombardment was heaviest on the *Dec.* 10– 10th and 11th, when the Turkish in- 11. fantry also attacked ; but no result was obtained. We had a few hundred casualties, mainly incurred in our sorties, and Townshend estimated the Turkish losses at not less than 1,000.

After that there came a lull. But on the 23rd a new division arrived—the 52nd, from Gallipoli—

and Nur-ed-Din made a furious attempt to carry
Dec. 23. the place by assault. All the morning of the 24th the enemy's fire was
concentrated on the northern defences, and in the
Dec. 24. evening the new division attacked at the
north-eastern corner. During the night
the enemy pierced the position, but was ejected by
the 1st Oxford Light Infantry, reinforced by the 48th
Pioneers and the 2nd Norfolks. The Turks fell
back to trenches 500 yards in rear of their former
first line, with casualties estimated at 700, while our
own were 190. On the 29th the liquorice factory
Dec. 29. on the south bank was bombarded, but
no infantry attack followed. It was the
last of Nur-ed-Din's attempts to blast his way into
the British position. Thenceforth his plan was
blockade.

Meantime the relieving force far down the river
was beginning to move. Their task was far more
complex than would appear from a mere glance at the
geographical distances. Compared with the Tigris,
the Nile, for all its cataracts, was a respectable river.
Interminable windings, endless shifting shoals, and
in normal times a depth too shallow for any but the
lightest craft made the problem of water transport
almost insoluble. To add to this, the rains were
erratic, and when they came the river became a
raging flood and the adjacent desert a lagoon. All
along the banks, separated by any distance from a
hundred yards to several miles, lay wide stretches
of marsh, connected by channels with the river. In
wet weather, therefore, the whole riverine district
was more water-logged than the Yser flats in mid-
winter. When the snow melted in the Armenian

hills the Tigris was well above the level of the surrounding country, and the ill-kept *bunds*, or dykes,
were insufficient to restrain it from spreading in
lakes over great areas. The consequence was that
transport became an incalculable thing, which,
whatever the arrangements at the base, must repeatedly break down in an advance. The only solu-
tion was to follow Lord Kitchener's example in the
Sudan and build a railway at some distance from
the flood region, since the river was wholly un-
trustworthy. Such a course—far cheaper in the
end—was not followed, because the magnitude of
the enterprise and the strength of the enemy were
from the first gravely underrated. It was an instructive lesson in the folly of conducting a campaign with the left hand.

The difficulties did not end with the transport.
There were the trying extremes of the climate to be
reckoned with, the treachery of the Arab tribes, and
the considerable preponderance in numbers of the
Turkish army. Above all, the dead flatness of the
land made attack extraordinarily difficult against an
enemy who thoroughly understood the art of entrenching. There was no natural cover for the
assailant—no villages, hedges, or banks, nothing but
a monotonous level of clay or mud. The innu-
merable marshes gave the Turks excellent flanking
defences, and consequently, by constructing comparatively short trenches between the swamps and
the river, they could block any advance. The alternative—to fetch a wide circuit through the drier
land away from the river—was impossible, because
we had only the Tigris to rely upon for our transport. From start to finish we were compelled to

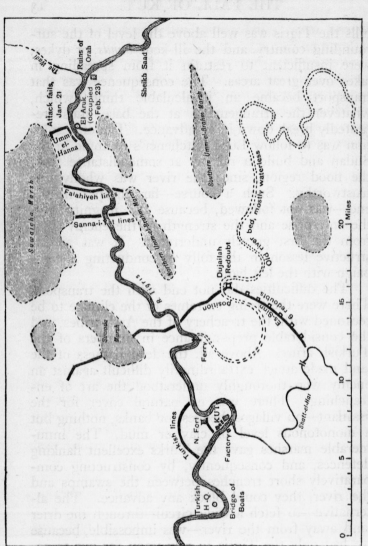

The Turkish Entrenched Positions covering the Investment of Kut (British Operations, January 21 to end of February).

depend upon a precarious and treacherous system
of communication.

Nur-ed-Din drew his lines with the skill of a
master. Having completely invested Kut, he set
himself to bar the road to any relief. His first line
of defence was at Sheikh Saad—about twenty-five
miles due east of Kut, but much longer by the river.
There he had a position on both sides of the stream;
and on his left, since he had no natural obstacle to
rest his flank on, he had a line entrenched at right
angles to his front, very much as he had done at
Ctesiphon. Five miles above Sheikh Saad he had
an intermediate line on the left bank along a watercourse called the Wadi, at a place called Orah or
Owassa, where the Tigris makes a sharp bend to
the south-east. Above Orah the great Suwaicha
marsh flanks the left bank of the river at a distance
of a mile or two. Here there was a series of immensely strong positions, all of the same general
character, astride the river, and resting on swamps
on both wings. From east to west there were the
Umm-el-Hanna position, the Falahiyeh position,
the very formidable lines at Sanna-i-yat, and last of
all, only seven miles from Kut, the Es Sinn position,
the strongest of all, which had its right flank drawn
back almost at right angles from the Dujailah Redoubt to the Shatt-el-Hai. It would appear that
these defences were not wholly ready at the time
when the attack of the relieving force began, but
long ere one position could be carried the alterna-
tives in the rear had been prepared.

Sir John Nixon, the commander-in-chief, was
compelled by ill-health to resign his post, and his
place was taken by Lieutenant-General Sir Percy

Lake, the Chief of the Indian Staff. The relieving force was under General Aylmer, V.C. It consisted of the Lahore division from the Western front, a considerable part of the Meerut division, and some English Territorial battalions which had been brought from India. The van, under Major-General Younghusband, moved out from Ali Gharbi on 4th January, and located the enemy at Sheikh Saad, holding him to his trenches on both sides of the river. On the 6th Major-General Kemball's division came in touch on the right bank. The weather was still dry, but the flat, mud-coloured ground, the haze, and the frequent mirages made reconnaissance a difficult task. Kemball entrenched himself over against the enemy lines, and next day advanced to the attack. An infantry brigade got round the enemy's right flank, and accounted for a whole battalion, taking over 550 prisoners, including sixteen officers. That day, the 7th, General Aylmer's main force came into action on the left bank, and there for two days we fought a costly action. Outflanking was impossible owing to the position of the Turkish left, though our artillery checked an attempt by Turkish cavalry to turn the British right, and the battle was a stubborn infantry frontal attack against a steady and well-directed Turkish fire. On 9th January the enemy, fearing lest our success on the right bank might turn his flank, fell back upon the intermediate position at Orah, where he had the protection of the Wadi watercourse descending from the Pushtikuh hills.

Jan. 4, 1916.

Jan. 6.

Jan. 7.

Jan. 9.

The rains had now begun. The Tigris rose four feet, and a hurricane blew which made navigation a precarious venture. In biting winds and seas of mud the British troops followed up the enemy to the Wadi watercourse. After a long night march on the 12th, Aylmer attacked on the 13th both in front and flank, having concentrated all his force on the northern bank, while *Jan.* 13. monitors from the river bombarded the enemy's right. The position was carried next day, and the enemy retired.

The weather now made reconnaissance hopeless, and any further movement must be very slow. The Turks had only fallen back a mile or two to the Umm-el-Hanna lines, which, as we have seen, were the outermost of the strong positions between the Suwaicha marsh and the river. On 21st January Aylmer attacked them, but failed to carry the ground, and was compelled to *Jan.* 21. entrench himself 1,300 yards from the enemy. Next day there was an armistice for the burial of the dead, and thereafter for more than a month complete stagnation. The Gen- *Jan.* 22. eral Commanding had realized that his force was not sufficient for the task he had set himself, and was waiting on reinforcements. The India Office, by a curious misreading of a telegram, announced that Aylmer was attacking Es Sinn, only seven miles from Kut, when he was only attacking Umm-el-Hanna, twenty-three miles distant, with sixteen miles of fortified ground through which he must force his way before he could join hands with Townshend.

The month of February was one of inaction for Aylmer's army. Early in the month the rains ceased, a cold drying wind blew from the desert, and there was frost at night. It was the right

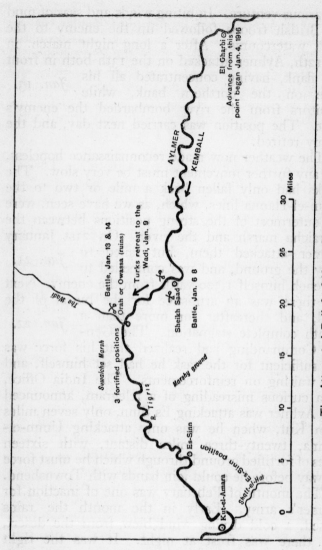

The Attempted Relief of Kut.—Sketch Map of the Earlier Operations.

weather to advance, but he did not consider that he
had the wherewithal to do it. The control of the
expedition had now passed from the Government of
India to the Imperial General Staff at home, and
during the transference operations may have naturally been delayed. There was some skirmishing
with Arab tribes round Nasiriyeh, and on the 23rd
of the month Aylmer pushed out a col- *Feb. 23.*
umn on the right bank of the river to
El Aruk, which enabled him to enfilade the Turkish
position at Umm-el-Hanna. Once again inaction
reigned, till on the evening of 7th March he embarked on the boldest venture of his campaign.

This was no less than to turn the main Turkish
position at Es Sinn by striking straight across the
desert, avoiding the river and the riverine swamps,
against its right flanks at the Dujailah Redoubt. It
was a perfectly sound strategical plan, but it had
to face heavy odds. One difficulty was the night
march across the desert to effect a surprise. Another lay in the fact that there was no water except
in the river, and unless we routed the enemy speedily
and completely we should be hard put to it to support our advanced columns. Our only chance lay in
an immediate success.

The place of assembly on the evening of 7th
March was at the Pools of Siloam, on the right
bank of the river. The force advanced *March 7.*
in three columns over a flat, featureless
desert, between two great belts of swamp, in a direction a point south of west. The night was black as
pitch, and guiding was difficult, for no one had been
over the ground before. " The silence was so profound," wrote Mr. Edmund Candler, who went with

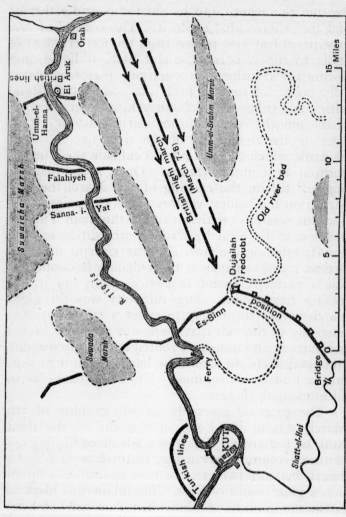

Orah

El Aruk

British lines

Umm-el-Hanna

Swaicha Marsh

Falahiyeh

Sanna-i-Yat

British night march
(March 7-8)

Umm-el-Brahm Marsh

Old river bed

R. Tigris

Suwada Marsh

Dujailah redoubt

Es-Sinn position

Ferry

Bridge

KUT

Turkish lines

Shatt-el-Hai

Miles

The Attack on the Es Sinn Position, March 7-8.

the guides, " that one heard nothing save the howl of a jackal, the cry of flighting geese, and the un-greased wheel of an ammunition limber, or the click of a picketing peg against a stirrup. The instinct to smoke was almost irresistible. A dozen times one's hand felt for one's pipe, but not a match was struck in all that army of thousands of men. Some-times one felt one was moving in a circle. One could swear to lights on the horizon, gesticulating figures on a bank." That night move was brilliantly carried out. Before the first light came we had reached the Dujailah depression, and saw the fires of the Turkish camp. To the west, eight miles away, our men saw also a sight which they were not destined to see again—the flash of Townshend's guns at Kut.

The strategy deserved to succeed, but it failed. We were just too late in starting the attack, and the Turk had his defence ready. Repeatedly *March 8.* during the day we flung ourselves on his breastworks, causing him heavy casualties, and losing singularly few ourselves. But we could not continue the assault on these terms, for we were far from water and supplies; so Aylmer was obliged to fall back to his old position east of Umm-el-Hanna. The beleaguered garrison in Kut had heard with joy the sound of our guns, and waited eagerly to see the familiar khaki on the flats east of the Shatt-el-Hai. But the guns died down, and the rescuers did not come. Once more they were shut off from sight or sound of their kin.

Another month of inaction followed. General Aylmer was superseded in the command by Sir G. P. Gorringe, a soldier with a long record of good service, who had led the expedition to Nasiriyeh in the preceding summer. He had now with him the 13th Division, which, it will be remembered, had done gloriously at Gallipoli in the assault on Chunuk Bair in the preceding August. It was decided to deliver a frontal attack upon the Umm-el-Hanna lines, and to this division the task was entrusted. Meantime we had been hard at work underground. Since there was no cover to screen an advance, it was necessary to push our firing-line close to the enemy's, and no less than sixteen miles of sap work had been completed, which brought us within 100 yards of the Turkish front.

The attack was delivered early on the morning of 5th April. At 5 a.m. the 13th Division rushed

April 5. from the sap-heads, and in one hour had carried the first three lines of the Umm-el-Hanna position. By 7 a.m. they were through the fourth and fifth lines. It was a clear day, and our airplanes warned us that the Falahiyeh lines 6,000 yards farther west, and the Sanna-i-yat line, the same distance beyond them, were being strongly reinforced. The ground in front of us was very open, so General Gorringe deferred the next step till the evening. At 8 p.m. the second advance was made, and the Falahiyeh position fell. It was by far the most successful day in the chronicle of the relief expedition, and the fighting quality which stormed those labyrinths of trenches nine feet deep can scarcely be overpraised. Meanwhile, on the right bank of the river the British left—the Lahore Division * under General Keary, which had to its credit a long year of struggle on the Flanders front

* This was the 3rd (Indian) Division of the *communiqués*. The British 3rd Division never left the Western front.

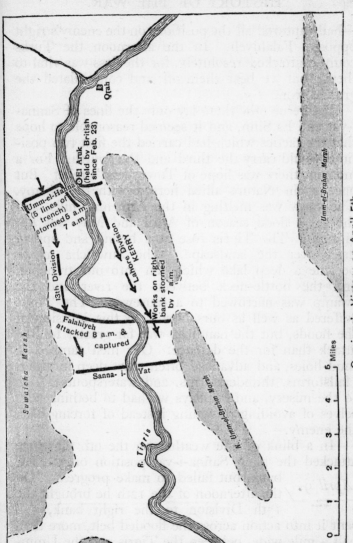

Qrah

El Aruk
(held by British
since Feb. 23)

Umm-el-Hanna
(5 lines of
trench)
stormed 5 a.m.
7 a.m.

Umm-el-Braim Marsh

13th Division

Lahore Division
KERRY

Works on right
bank stormed
by 7 a.m.

Falahiyeh
attacked 8 a.m. &
captured

Suwaicha Marsh

Sanna-i-Yat

N. Umm-el-Braim Marsh

Umm-el-Braim Marsh

R. Tigris

0 1 2 3 4 5 6 Miles

Gorringe's Victory on April 5th.

—had captured all the positions on the enemy's right opposite Falahiyeh. In the afternoon the Turks counter-attacked resolutely, for the loss was vital to them; but we beat them off, and consolidated the ground won.

Before us now there lay only the lines of Sanna-i-yat and Es Sinn, and it seemed reasonable to hope that the tactics which had carried the first two positions would carry the third and the fourth. For a moment there was hope of Townshend's relief. But once again Nature allied herself with the enemy. The snow was melting in the Armenian hills, and the great flood season of April and May was beginning. The Tigris rose at a bound and spread itself over the landscape. The Suwaicha marsh became a deep lake which ran into our trenches, and the bottle-neck between the river and the swamp was narrowed to a causeway. The Turks suffered as well as ourselves from this invasion of the floods, but the handicap was far greater for the attack than for the defence. Our men camped in mud-holes, and advanced often waist-deep in water. Hailstorms, thunderstorms, and waterspouts added to the misery, and for days we had to bethink ourselves of avoiding drowning instead of forcing back the enemy.

In a blink of fine weather on the 9th Gorringe attacked the main Sanna-i-yat position on the left bank, but failed to make progress. On the afternoon of the 12th he brought the 13th Division to the right bank, and sent it into action across the flooded belt, more than half a mile wide, between the Tigris and the Umm-el-Brahm marsh. The attack did not break through,

April 9–12.

but it forced the enemy's right wing back a distance varying from one and a half to three miles. We continued to struggle on the south side of the river, and on 17th April, at seven o'clock in the morning, we carried the strong posi- *April* 17. tion of Beit Eissa, a fort which was within four miles of Es Sinn, and slightly in rear of the Sanna-i-yat lines on the left bank. That same night the Turks launched on us one of the greatest of their counter-attacks. After a heavy bombardment large masses of troops brought from Es Sinn attacked at Beit Eissa between 7 p.m. and 4.30 the next morning. Mr. Candler has described its violence :—

" Six distinct assaults in mass were launched on one bri-gade before two in the morning, as well as sporadic rushes, yet the line was not broken. In spite of the darkness our shrapnel found them. The blaze of the bursting shells disclosed them lying flat, and our infantry poured in a fusillade at ground level. Over 2,000 dead were counted next morning opposite this one brigade alone. So fierce was the persistence of the attack that bodies of the enemy broke through a gap between two battalions, though our line held firm. The Turks who found themselves in the rear of the position were lost ; their line of retreat was cut off, and they were ignorant of the dis-position of our trenches. At dawn they doubled back in confusion on to our line, and were all shot down or captured."

In this action the Turkish losses were 400 prisoners, and it was estimated that 3,000 died. German officers led the attack, and some of them were among the slain. One whole Turkish division was in action, and *April* 18. portions of two others—in all some 10,000 men.

There remained the north bank, where was the main Sanna-i-yat line. On 23rd April we attacked and carried the first and second trenches, but Turkish

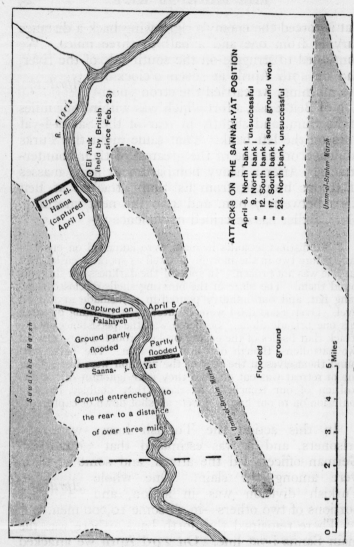

ATTACKS ON THE SANNA-I-YAT POSITION

April 6. North bank | unsuccessful
 "   9. North bank | unsuccessful
 "   12. South bank | some ground won
 "   17. South bank | unsuccessful
 "   23. North bank, unsuccessful

R. Tigris

El Aruk (held by British since Feb. 23)

Umm-el-Hanna (captured April 5)

Suwaicha Marsh

Captured on April 5
Falahiyeh

Ground partly flooded

Sanna-i-Yat

Partly flooded ground

Flooded ground

Ground entrenched to the rear to a distance of over three miles

Umm-el-Brahm Marsh

N. Umm-el-Brahm Marsh

0 1 2 3 4 5 Miles

Gorringe's Operations, April 5-23.

reinforcements drove us out of them. The space
between the river and the swamp was *April* 23.
so narrow that only one brigade could
move in line, and there was no possibility of outflanking. Gorringe had made a gallant effort, but
the weather and the countryside had defeated him.

Let us turn to the state of affairs in Kut itself.
The garrison, it should be remembered, had fought
a most arduous campaign during the preceding
summer, and they had just finished the march to
Ctesiphon, the battle, and the feverish retreat. For
weeks already they had been living on poor rations
and enduring the extreme fatigue of which the
human body is capable. All December they had
been bombarded, and had repulsed repeated attacks.
There were many wounded and much sickness.
But the spirit of the little force never flagged, and
they set themselves to make the best of the wretched
Arab town and their intolerable conditions. On the
ground by the liquorice factory they played a kind
of cricket and hockey, as long as their strength permitted them, and they tried to supplement their
stores by fishing in the river. The gentle art of
Izaak Walton was never pursued under stranger
circumstances.

From the first day of 1916 onward Townshend's
main task was to fight famine. The enemy shelled
the place nearly every night with heavy guns, and
there were destructive bombing raids by Turkish
airplanes ; but starvation was the grimmest foe.
At first there was plenty of horse meat.
On 24th January a large store of grain *Jan.* 24.
was discovered ; but it could not be ground till

millstones were dropped by our aircraft. General Townshend set about planting vegetable seeds to provide some relief from the scurvy that was threat-

Feb. 5.   ening. On 5th February each British soldier was receiving a twelve-ounce loaf of mixed barley and atta, a few dates and gro-ceries, and one pound of horse meat; and each Indian a pound of flour and a small allowance of turmeric, chillies, and ginger. By this time the place had run out of rice and sugar, and there was only milk for ten days in the hospital. In the first week of March the flour ration was reduced, and after Aylmer's failure at Dujailah there was a further

April 8.   reduction all round. On 8th April the mill had to stop working for want of fuel, and hunger began in dead earnest. After 20th April many of the Arabs, with starvation in

April 20.   front of them, tried to escape down the river by swimming. There had all along been a desperate scarcity of tobacco, though ciga-rettes used to be dropped by airplanes, and towards the end men were smoking as substitutes lime leaves, ginger, and baked tea-dregs. Even in January English tobacco was selling at eight shillings an ounce. Soon all the horses and mules had gone. One of the last to be slaughtered was an Indian mule, which had been in three frontier campaigns, and which the butcher twice refused to kill.

On 14th February the King had sent a message of thanks and encouragement to General Town-

Feb. 14.   shend, who had replied cheerfully by wireless. The garrison, almost to the end, believed that they would be relieved. The floods did not affect them greatly, for Kut stands on slightly higher ground than the rest of the plain ; they were even an advantage, since they compelled the Turks to withdraw their lines a considerable distance. But about the middle of April, when all the troops were weak with famine, even the stoutest heart had to recognize that the limits of endurance had been reached. The last effort of Gorringe was to try to break the blockade with a river steamer, the *Julnar*, on 24th April. It was a hopeless task, since the boat had to run the gauntlet *April 24.* of the enemy guns on a winding river against a strong flood, and she went ashore four miles east of the town.

The end came on 29th April. At 11.40 a.m. Townshend sent out a wireless message : " Have destroyed my guns, and most of my munitions are being destroyed ; an offi- *April 29.* cer has gone to Khalil, who is at Madug, to say we are ready to surrender. I must have some food here, and cannot hold on any more. Khalil has been told to-day, and a deputation of officers has gone on a launch to bring food from *Julnar*, ship sent night April 24th, to carry supplies to garrison Kut." A little later he wired : " Have hoisted the white flag over Kut fort and town, and the guards will be taken over by a Turkish regiment, which is approaching. I shall shortly destroy wireless. The troops go at 2 p.m. to camp near Shumvass." It was a very weary and broken force which laid down their arms : the remnant of the historic 6th (Poona) Division, which had begun with a year of unbroken conquests —together with a number of British Territorials. Before surrender the troops occupying the first lines had been too weak to march back with their kits, and had held their position for a fortnight. In all, the garrison at the date of Kut's fall consisted of 2,070 British troops of all ranks, and some 6,000 Indians.

The Turks, after their fashion, behaved with chivalry and decency. Khalil, their commander, treated General Townshend with extreme respect, in view of his gallant resistance. The sick and wounded were sent downstream to Gorringe, and food and tobacco were at once distributed. Townshend and his staff were taken to Constantinople, and the rest to internment in an Anatolian camp.

Kut had resisted for 143 days—a fine record when we consider the condition of Townshend's force at the beginning of the siege. It shared with Przemysl the distinction of being the only place in the war which was taken by blockade ; but, unlike Przemysl, its surrender brought no stigma to the garrison. They resisted to the utmost limits of human endurance, and officers and men shared the same hardships. Its fall was a misfortune, but not a disaster. The temporary loss of 8,000 troops was not a crushing blow to an armed force which now numbered millions. Moreover, the campaign in Mesopotamia, unfortunate as was its immediate issue for Britain, had achieved a real strategic purpose, even in its melancholy later stages. But for the reinforcements sent by the Turks to the Tigris, and their preoccupation with the capture of Kut, it is probable that the Russians in the Caucasus would not have moved so swiftly, and that Erzerum and Trebizond would not have fallen.

These considerations were in the nature of a consolation, and did not touch the question of the fundamental unsoundness of the advance on Bagdad, from which all our troubles had flowed. It should be said, in common justice to the relieving force, that it showed singular gallantry and devotion. All that man could do it did to cut its way through to Townshend. The fault lay in the earlier decision which had created a problem that could not be solved in the scanty time permitted.

But as the news filtered through from Mesopotamia, it became clear to the ordinary man that a mistake in strategy had not been the sole blunder of the Government of India. The transport service from the first had been utterly inadequate; and though the campaign had begun as early as November 1914, the conditions of that appalling country had never been seriously faced. Until February 1916 no special hospital boat had been provided to take down the wounded from the fighting-line, though admirably equipped hospital ships ran between Basra and Bombay. In the same way there was no proper transport from the field to the river. Badly wounded men had to endure agonies in springless carts. There was also a shortage of coolie labour, and far too little attention to sanitation. The British soldier, white or coloured, is an uncomplaining being. He was desperately uncomfortable, but he could joke about it. "They tell me this place was the garden of Eden," said a private. "Well, it wouldn't want no angel with a flaming sword to shift *me* out of it." But even from his lips a cry was wrung. "If you put 500 badly wounded," wrote one officer, "on a paddle steamer in pouring rain, all lying on the hard deck with an awning which does not keep out the rain; give them one doctor, no attendants, no food, scanty blankets, no sanitary arrangements ; leave them there for twelve hours or more, then send them on a twelve hours' journey or more,—it must be trying, to say the least of it. But this is a true picture, and people should know of it." It would be hard from the whole campaign—on the British side, at any rate—to parallel the misery of the severely wounded, lying packed together for hours in pools of water on decks sodden with dirt and animal refuse.

That such conditions should have been possible after a year of war pointed to something very far wrong with the Indian Medical and Transport service. Combined with the strategical blunders, it suggested something very far wrong with the whole Indian military system. The victory which Lord Kitchener had won over Lord Curzon ten years before looked as if it would be dearly paid for, since it had divorced the military side of the Indian Government from all civilian criticism and control. A Commission was appointed to inquire into the whole business ; and though such inquiries in the midst of a war are commonly to be deprecated, this one was justified both by the popular demand and the urgency of the case. The difficulties of Mesopotamian campaigning had been proverbial since the days of Alexander the Great, and those who projected and conducted the river war without allowing for them were gravely lacking in intelligence and public duty.

CHAPTER XCIX.

THE WAR IN THE EASTERN MEDITERRANEAN.

The Situation at Salonika—Changes in the Allied Command—Bulgarians take Greek Forts—Position in Bulgaria—No immediate Chance of Compromise—The Situation in Constantinople—Enver and Talaat—Situation in Egypt—Occupation of Sollum—Defeat of Rebels on Western Frontier—Rescue of the *Tara* Prisoners—The Eastern Frontier—The Fight at Katia—Occupation of Darfur.

DURING the first months of 1916 the stalemate at Salonika continued. Rumours of impending Bulgarian and German attacks were, indeed, assiduously circulated ; but there was small substance behind them. They were not even successful as bluff, for no bluff was needed. Whether the enemy attacked or not, it was imperative that the Salonika occupation once begun should be continued. It was impossible to allow the hesitating neutrality of Greece to be subjected to the pressure of the immediate proximity of the enemy without any Allied force to act as a buffer. It was necessary for political reasons to have a *pied à terre* for the recovery of Serbia. It was especially necessary, in view of the unplumbed chances of the future, to keep the road open for a flank attack on Bulgaria in case the progress of Russia, or the accession of Rumania to the Allies, or the exhaustion of the Turk,

XIV.   3

should put King Ferdinand in peril. The landing at Salonika in October 1915 was not a step which could be easily retraced, for politics and strategy were inextricably commingled in its purpose.

On purely military grounds the stalemate was predetermined. When Sarrail had once completed his lines and blown up the Demir Hissar bridge, he offered an awkward object for attack. The transport problem would be difficult. The Salonika-Monastir railway had no extension to the north, and so could not be used for bringing heavy guns and shells from the Danube. The main railway to Nish had been comprehensively wrecked by the French in its southern section, and the Demir Kapu tunnel especially would take long to repair. The only immediate route by rail was the line from Constantinople and Dedeagatch through Demir Hissar, which was also for the time out of working order. Assuming that these various ways were mended and ready for use, the main Allied position itself was a hard nut to crack. Its eastern half was very strong, and rested on the sea. In the western section only two parts were possible—the twenty odd miles from Lake Langaza to the Vardar, and the eighteen miles of the Vardar valley ; and even there the inducements were small. The Allied entrenchments lay for the most part on northward facing slopes, heavily wired in front, and with seven miles before them of swampy plain over which the invaders must move. It would have been for the attack a second Suvla or Achi Baba. Finally, if the assault had been successful, and Sarrail had been driven to embark, what advantage would have been won ? Some power of coercing Greece, no doubt ;

but, to set against that, a position which must be
held under the perpetual menace of naval attack.

Nor were the Allies better circumstanced for
taking the offensive. There were three possible
directions for an advance. One was on the left,
against Monastir. There the country was open and
easy as far as Verria, which was distant from Monastir only some sixty miles as the crow flies. But
the advance must move along the winding valley
which the railway followed ; the hills as far as
Vodena would have to be captured and held ; and
beyond that a series of narrow defiles must be
traversed. Any such movement would be in
danger of encountering entrenched positions of the
Gallipoli type. A second route lay in the centre
towards Uskub ; but this meant the Vardar valley,
a continuous defile for nearly a hundred miles. An
advance on the right offered better hopes, and there
the enemy seems to have apprehended danger. But
it involved ascending the Struma valley, where there
was no railway, and which led through narrow
passes between the spurs of Rhodope and the
Serbian hills. Moreover, before an advance could
begin, the Vardar valley and the routes from Monastir must be blocked, and the country about Lake
Doiran must be reoccupied. Such a movement
would be costly, laborious, and highly precarious,
and no sane commander would have undertaken it
unless the general diplomatic and military situation
in the Near East had worn a more hopeful com-
plexion than it did in the first month of 1916.

The long spell of inaction at Salonika was employed by the Allies in perfecting their position till
the area of defence was nearly impregnable against

the enemy forces then arrayed before it. These were now almost wholly Bulgarian, for the great attack on Verdun had drawn away most of the remaining divisions with which von Mackensen had fought the autumn campaign. German submarines began to show some activity in the Greek territorial waters of the Salonika Gulf; so, in order to make his own communications secure, General Sarrail, on the *Jan. 28.* morning of 28th January, occupied the Greek fortress of Kara Burun, on the east side of the gulf about fifteen miles from the city. The Greek commandant evacuated the place at the Allies' request, and what might have been the beginning of serious trouble with Greece passed off peacefully, and was soon forgotten. The chief incident of the time was, however, the destruction of a Zeppelin. LZ 85, whose home was at Temesvar in Hungary, had raided Salonika on 1st February, again at the end of the month, and on 18th March. She came again on the night of 7th *May 7.* May, but it was her last trip. She seemed to lose her sense of direction, and wandered over the harbour, under the fire of the shore batteries and the British warships. Finally a shell from a naval gun found a vital part, and she fell a flaming wreck among the swamps at the Vardar mouth.

There was little change for months in the constituents of the Allied army. On 9th May Major-*May 9.* General G. F. Milne succeeded Sir Bryan Mahon as the commander of the British forces. Meantime the remnants of the Serbian army were being refitted and made ready for the field. The capture of Durazzo by the Aus-

trians on 27th February made it necessary to find
some base for refitment inaccessible to the enemy.
Accordingly, French and Italian troops landed at
Corfu, and the use of the island as a Serbian rest
camp began. Then might have been seen the cheer-
ing spectacle of the blue caps of the French Chas-
seurs Alpins amid the rococo splendour of the
Achilleion, that classical villa which the German
Emperor had used as a summer retreat. Some
100,000 Serbian soldiers were assembled at Corfu,
and a considerable part of these were during the
early days of May transferred to Salonika. The
situation seemed to have alarmed the Bulgarian
High Command, who feared an Allied offensive;
so on 26th May Bulgarian forces ad- *May 26.*
vanced on to Greek soil north of Serres
and Drama, and occupied Fort Rupel and one or
two other works which commanded the line on which
they anticipated the Allies might move. The Greek
Government acquiesced, on the ground that the
tolerance which they had already shown to the one
belligerent must be extended to the other. At the
time there was talk in the West of a Bulgarian offensive, to correspond with the Austrian attack on the
Trentino and the German at Verdun. But the incident had no such meaning. It was a defensive
move, to safeguard the roads into Bulgaria, not to
win a stage on the way to Kavala and Salonika.

It was becoming clear that relations between
Bulgaria and her German allies were incompletely
harmonious. The peasants who made up the Bulgarian armies had been promised a short and easy
campaign; they had, on the contrary, suffered
heavy losses, and had been under arms for more

than half a year. Germany was exploiting their land and exporting foodstuffs; their farms were going to ruin, they themselves were badly provisioned, and they detested the overbearing manners of their German colleagues. Among the educated classes there was much irritation at the Prussianizing of the capital, and the intrusion of a horde of Germans into the Government service. Finally, few Bulgarians were perfectly happy in a campaign which arrayed them in opposition to the armies of Russia. On the other hand, Bulgaria had already won much of her desires. She had Uskub and Monastir, and all that part of Macedonia which she had claimed. The only further bribe which Germany could offer her was access to the Ægean at Kavala, and such a prospect had not the same influence on the popular mind as the traditional cry of an unredeemed Macedonia.

In these circumstances it was natural that the thoughts of many among the Allies should turn to the possibility of attaching Bulgaria to their own cause. It was argued with some truth that the talk about " Bulgarian treachery " had been overdone. Apart from the personal misconduct of the egregious Ferdinand and some of his Ministers, there was no reason to label the ordinary Bulgarian with the name of traitor. He had never professed any love for Serbia; he considered that his country had been shamelessly treated in the Balkan wars; he was bitter against his neighbours and those Allied Powers which had befriended them; he fought for what he considered his bare rights, and he accepted any alliance which would assist him to get them. It was argued, further, that the business of the Allies was

Southern Opening of the Struma Valley, showing the approximate
Position of the Greek Forts seized by the Bulgarians.

to beat Germany, and not to punish the moral de-
linquencies of this or that statelet. A friendly Bulgaria would block the Teutonic route to the East,
and put Turkey in the gravest peril. It would at
once release for more fruitful service the quarter of
a million troops now stagnant at Salonika, and turn
the tables on Germany in the East.

Such a view was not without justification ; but
the difficulties before its realization were at the
moment insuperable. The Allies were committed
to a doctrine of nationality, and that was in theory
the policy also of each Balkan state. But it had
never been so in practice. Turkey and Austria between them had displaced and dislocated the Balkan
races. Each little state was oppressed, and was herself an oppressor. Serbia at the outbreak of war saw
people of her own blood in Bosnia, Dalmatia, and
elsewhere under an alien rule ; but she herself
governed large tracts inhabited by Albanian and
Bulgarian races. It was the same with Greece and
the same with Rumania. The Balkan trouble could
only be settled by a complete new delimitation of
territory on racial grounds, and for this a clean
slate and a free hand were needed ; and when the day
for it came it was very certain that those who had
clamoured for it most loudly would raise the gravest
obstacles. " Territory according to nationality "
was all very well as a cry ; but no nation was willing
to give up land which she had won by arms or by
diplomacy, or surrender economic ambitions which
had nothing to do with race. The Allies could only
placate Bulgaria at the expense of Serbia and Greece.
Serbia could not be compensated as she desired until
a complete Allied victory was won, and any attempt to

use her territory to bargain with at a moment when, largely through the fault of the Allies, she was beggared, would have seemed to the world a monstrous dereliction of principle and honour. Further, any bargaining which would outbid Germany at Sofia would be a flat contradiction of what the Allies were professedly fighting for. Germany offered Bulgaria Nish and part of Old Serbia, and during the winter in these districts the familiar practice of Bulgarization had begun in the schools and the local administration. In these districts the population was wholly Serbian. She offered Kavala, where the people were Greek and Turkish, and part of Thrace, where the people were Turkish and Greek. There was no real common ground for dealing between the Allies, with their avowed principles, and King Ferdinand, who had no principles and wanted material gains. Proposals which might have succeeded a year before were simply irrelevant under the changed conditions. Most important of all, the Allies were committed to two aims, both of which were utterly repugnant to Sofia. The first was a greater Serbia; the second was the establishment of Russia on the Bosphorus and Dardanelles. So far the Teutonic League could offer Bulgaria not only a bigger territorial bribe, but a scheme of world policy, not indeed without its dangers, but to the Bulgarian mind a thousandfold less repulsive than the professed objects of the Allies.

Constantinople during the first months of 1916 was in a state of misery and confusion which had not been equalled in the memory of man. At first the evacuation of Gallipoli by the Allies raised its

spirits ; but soon came the fall of Erzerum, which
the Government could not conceal, and presently
the losses of Mush and Bitlis, and the menace to
Trebizond. Starvation laid its hand on the poorer
classes. No supplies could reach the city from
Bulgaria, and but little from Constanza, since the
Russian fleet in the Black Sea barred the Rumanian
voyage to all craft but the smallest schooners and
feluccas. Germany, never loved by the older Turks
or the masses of the people, became highly unpopu-
lar, and all German troops were removed from the
city. There remained numerous German officers
and officials, and several thousand German work-
men in the munition factories ; but to march German
soldiers through the streets of Stamboul would have
provoked a revolution. The ordinary Mussulman
was concerned for the fate of his religion and his
country, and he saw both in the hands of arro-
gant and sacrilegious infidels. Nor was the Young
Turk better regarded. The cooler heads of the
Committee, like Djavid, remained quiet, watching
the tide of affairs ; but Enver and Talaat swaggered
in the limelight, and only the most vigilant espionage
and the most arbitrary police methods saved them
from death. Prince Yussuf-ed-din, the heir to the
throne and no friend of the Committee, was mur-
dered in February by Enver's order, according to
the old fashion of Yildiz, and this barbarous act
roused bitter popular hatred and also widespread
popular fear. Enver's dominance was based wholly
on blood and terror, and had the bullet of some
fortunate assassin found his brain, it is probable that
the whole edifice he had built would have crumbled
in a day, and the Osmanli shaken themselves loose

from their unwelcome fetters. To add to the farce, he and Talaat quarrelled violently. Enver, who, to do him justice, was brave and vigorous, departed to Syria to deal with an Arab rising, and his rival had a brief period of absolute power. The situation can scarcely have been comfortable for the German masters, who found themselves trying to introduce the most modern Prussian methods into a land which seemed to model itself on some swashbuckling Italian city of the Dark Ages.

In these circumstances there was little likelihood of any serious attack on Egypt. Turkey had sent all her Gallipoli army, except some two or three divisions, to the Transcaucasian theatre, and thither went also the big Austrian guns served by Austrian artillerymen. There and in Mesopotamia lay her vital fronts, and she had neither men nor leisure for new adventures. If she mobilized at the start a million men, she had lost not less than 40 per cent. by the end of February. She had no money and little food, and had to content herself with facing the tasks from which there was no escape.

In Egypt during the winter there had been a huge massing of British troops, which was increased in January by the divisions from Cape Helles. The command, divided between the General Commanding the Mediterranean Expeditionary Force, the General Commanding in Egypt, and the General Commanding the Levant base, reached a pitch of subtle differentiation which it required the soul of a mediæval schoolman to understand. Early in March Sir John Maxwell returned to England, and Sir Archibald Murray was left in undivided charge.

By that time the troops had begun to move—one division going to Mesopotamia, and the original Anzac Corps and some of the old 8th Corps to the Western front. There still remained a large force, part of which was in process of training, and during the first months of the year there was a certain activity on the Eastern and Western borders.

We left the fighting on the Tripoli frontier at the end of January, when General Wallace's forces had broken the main strength of the so-called Senussi and driven them westwards. Major-General W. E. Peyton, who had commanded the 2nd Mounted Division at Suvla, now succeeded General Wallace, and throughout February General Lukin's force was quelling the last remnants of resistance, and pushing close up to the frontier line. On 26th February

Feb. 26. Lukin defeated the enemy at Agagia, near Barrani, fifty miles east of the border. His column was mainly composed of South African infantry and mounted troops, and the Dorset Yeomanry in the pursuit lost heavily in officers from the Bedouin fire tactics. Gaafer, the Germanized Turk in command, and his staff were captured by the Yeomanry charge. Colonel Souter, commanding the Dorsets, has vividly described the last stage : " The attack was made in two lines, the horses galloping steadily, and well in hand. Three Maxims were brought into action against us ; but the men were splendidly led by their squadron and troop leaders, and their behaviour was admirable. About fifty yards from the position I gave the order to charge, and with one yell the Dorsets hurled themselves upon the enemy, who immediately broke. In the middle of the enemy's lines my horse was

killed under me, and by a curious chance its dying
strides brought me to the ground within a few yards
of the Senussi general, Gaafer Pasha."

On 14th March Lukin occupied Sollum, the
Egyptian port on the frontier, which had *March* 14.
been evacuated three months before.
Sollum lies on the flat shore of a bay, and behind it
the escarpment of the Libyan plateau rises steeply

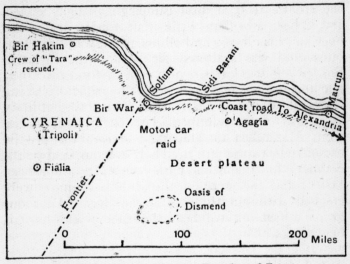

Operations on the Western Frontier of Egypt.

to a height of 700 feet. Lukin took the escarpment
from behind, by way of the Halfia Pass, and as soon
as the plateau was won the town was his. Meantime a detachment of the Duke of Westminster's
armoured cars performed brilliant service in hamper-
ing the enemy's retreat. Airplane reconnaissance
on the morning of the 14th showed that the enemy

headquarters at Bir War, six miles west of Sollum, were empty, and, making a detour of thirty miles, the cars started in pursuit. They headed off the fleeing convoy in the south, and, after a fight which stretched for seven miles, collected over fifty dead, some forty prisoners, three field guns, nine machine guns, besides shells and 300,000 rounds of ammunition.

With the capture of Sollum and the clearing of the frontier the Senussi campaign virtually ended. It had been a brilliant little affair, for the enemy lost over half his officers and all his artillery and machine guns, and was scattered far beyond the Egyptian border. It was carried out, too, in trying weather, hailstorms and great cold being diversified with long spells of scorching heat. Water there was little of, and most of the supply had to be brought by sea from Alexandria to Matruh, and sent forward by camel train to the front. There was no food in the country, for the usual barley crops had not been raised, and the steps of the British columns were clogged with famishing Arab families. After our humane fashion, we beat the enemy and fed his belongings.*

---

* Sir John Maxwell's dispatch sums up the results of the campaign: "The effect of this success has been to remove the anxiety which was at one time felt as to the possibility of hostile outbreaks in Egypt itself, where agitation was known to be rife. The attitude of the people in Alexandria, and more especially of the very large Bedouin population of the Behera province, has completely changed, and any prestige which we have lost through the evacuation of Sollum has been more than recovered. Moreover, through his failure as a temporal leader, Sayed Ahmed has lost much of the influence which was attached to him as a spiritual head."

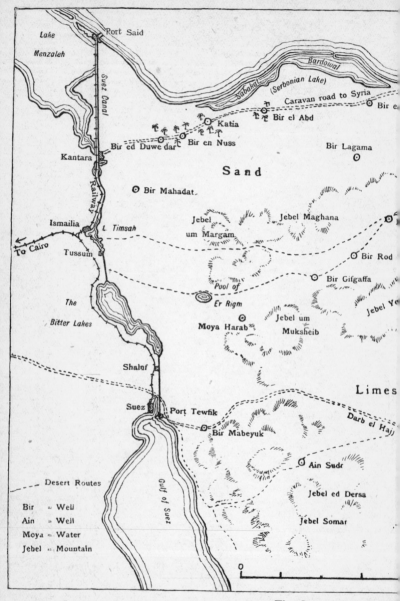

Lake Menzaleh

Port Said

Suez Canal

Bardowal

Sabahat (Serbonian Lake)

Caravan road to Syria

Bir e

Bir el Abd

Katia

Bir ed Duwe dar

Bir en Nuss

Bir Lagama

Kantara

Railway

Bir Mahadat

S a n d

Jebel um Margam

Jebel Maghana

Ismailia

L. Timsah

To Cairo

Tussum

Bir Rod

Bir Gifgaffa

Pool of

Er Rigm

Jebel Ye

The Bitter Lakes

Moya Harab

Jebel um Muksheib

Shaluf

L i m e s

Suez

Port Tewfik

Darb el Hajj

Bir Mabeyuk

Gulf of Suez

Ain Sud

Desert Routes

Jebel ed Dersa

Bir = Well
Ain = Well
Moya = Water
Jebel = Mountain

Jebel Somar

The Suez Canal and the

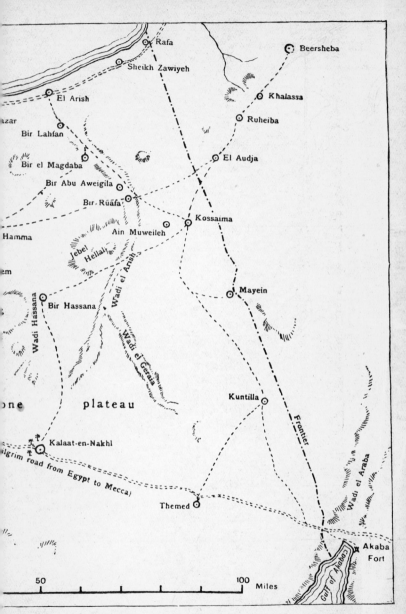

Desert Routes to Egypt.

One striking incident deserves to be remembered. As has been recorded elsewhere, the *Tara*, an armed patrol boat, which in happier days had plied on the Dublin-Holyhead route, was torpedoed the previous November in the Mediterranean. Three of her boats reached the African coast, and the ninety-two men were taken prisoners by the Senussi. They were moved into the interior, and suffered every kind of indignity and privation. After the capture of Sollum information came that the remnant of the crews of the *Tara* and the *Moorina* was at Bir Hakim, about seventy miles distant. A force of nine armoured cars, twenty-six other cars, and ten motor ambulances set off on the morning of 17th March to attempt their rescue. By an amazing combination of boldness and good fortune they found the prisoners March 17. and brought them safely back, having performed a journey of over three hundred miles. It was an enterprise which in normal times would have been considered to belong rather to the realms of wild romance than to the sober chances of war.*

The scene now changes to the eastern frontier of Egypt, where, in the Sinai desert, Turkish forces from the Beersheba base continued their spasmodic operations. As we have seen, there were three main routes across the desert to the canal—the coast route by El Arish to Kantara, the central route from El Audja to Ismailia, and the southern route from Akaba to Suez. British parties had been pushed east as far as the oasis of Katia,

* For this exploit the Duke of Westminster received the Distinguished Service Order. He was recommended for the Victoria Cross.

on the northern route, about thirty miles from the canal, and on 13th April an Australian column *April 13.* raided Jifjaffa—on the central route, some sixty miles from the canal—and broke up an enemy detachment which was boring there for water. In this expedition the Australian Light Horse covered 160 miles of soft sand in three and a half days, and did forty-six miles on the day of the fight.

On Easter Sunday, 23rd April, we were less fortunate. Early in the morning a heavy mist *April 23.* cloaked the desert, and under its cover the Turks effected a surprise attack on Katia village. The place was held by the Gloucestershire, Warwickshire, and Worcestershire Yeomanry, and the superior numbers of the enemy, which included a battalion composed of Austrians and Germans, compelled them to fall back, fighting a rearguard action. Reinforcements arrived, and the advance was checked, but not before we had lost heavily in dead and prisoners. Presently the enemy withdrew, having himself suffered many casualties, and our aircraft successfully bombed his retreat. On the same day a bold attack was made much farther west at the post of Duweidar, only fifteen miles from the canal. The place was held by one company of the 4th Royal Scots Fusiliers, a Territorial battalion from Ayrshire. The odds were at first about six to one, but the gallant few held their ground till they were reinforced by two other companies of the battalion. The Turks were beaten off with a loss of seventy dead and thirty prisoners, and a squadron of the Australian Light Horse harassed their retirement. During April and May the Turkish posts in the Sinai desert were repeatedly assailed by our aircraft, and buildings, water and petrol tanks, and boring plant de- *May* 18. stroyed. On 18th May El Arish was bombarded from the sea by British monitors, with

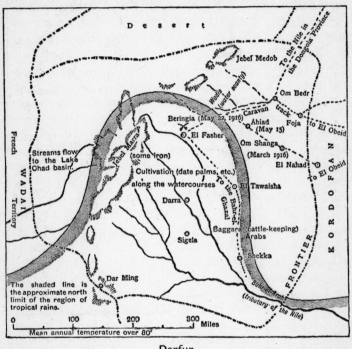

Darfur.

sea-planes to direct their fire, when the fort was demolished and the Turkish camp and aerodrome heavily damaged.

Meantime in the southern part of the Libyan desert British columns prevented any massing of disaffected tribesmen. Darfur, the most westerly

of the Sudan protected states, whose capital, El
Fasher, is some five hundred miles south-west of
Khartum, had since the beginning of the year given

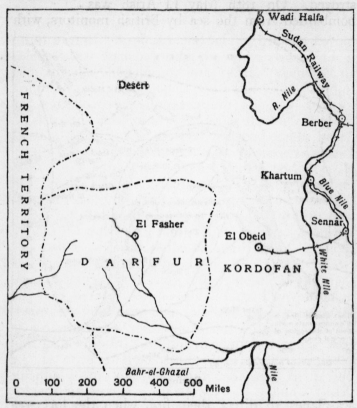

Sketch Map showing the Relation of Darfur to the
Upper Nile Region.

ground for anxiety. Its Sultan, Ali Dinar, had
grown truculent, and early in February took to
raiding on the Kordofan frontier.

Accordingly, the Sirdar of the Egyptian army, Sir R. Wingate, concentrated in March a force at El Nahad on that border. The force was conveyed by the Sudan railway to El Obeid, and marched to its concentration point. At the end of March it moved forward to Om Shanga, on the caravan route to El Fasher, where an advanced base was formed. In Sudanese warfare any considerable advance has to be made by successive stages, each point occupied forming a depot where supplies are collected for the next onward move. Early in May the oasis of Abiad, about half-way between Om Shanga and El Fasher, was occupied, and from this point on 15th May a mixed force of all arms, *May* 15. under Colonel Kelly, marched on El Fasher. On the 22nd the Sultan, with a force of 2,600 riflemen, was utterly defeated at the village of Beringia, twelve miles north of the *May* 22. capital. The British casualties were five killed and twenty-three wounded, and the enemy's loss not less than one thousand. El Fasher was occupied, large quantities of military stores were captured, and the inhabitants were speedily and peacefully disarmed. Ali Dinar, with a small following, fled westwards to seek sanctuary among the Fur tribesmen of the Jebel Marra hills. A satisfactory feature of the operations was that this campaign in a difficult desert country was carried to a successful conclusion entirely by the soldiers of the Egyptian army under their British leaders, without the support of any white troops.

CHAPTER C.

SPRING ON THE RUSSIAN FRONT.

The Critical Weeks in April—German and Russian Dispositions—
Occupation of Uscieszko Bridgehead—Activity of Ewarts's
Army—The Advance south of Lake Narotch—The Eight
Russian Attacks—Artillery withdrawn—The German Counter-
offensive—The Battle of 28th April—Position in Transcau-
casia—Yudenitch's Strategy—The Advance on Trebizond—
Importance of the City—Fall of Trebizond, and Position
thereafter.

IVANOV'S Christmas attack on Czernovitz—
which, though it failed in its immediate purpose, undoubtedly forestalled an advance by
von Mackensen towards Kiev, and dislocated Germany's Balkan plans—was followed by three months
of normal trench fighting. It was generally believed that the spring would see a great effort by
von Hindenburg to take Dvinsk and Riga. There
were two weeks in April when the western entrance
to the Gulf of Riga was free from ice, while the
northern inlet was still barred to Russia. It was
anticipated that during that time, when the Russian
navy could not protect the Russian flank, an attack
would be made to force the coast road. But a spring
offensive in that region laboured under special
difficulties, owing to the melting of the snow and
the brimming marshes and rivers, and there were
other observers who believed that von Hindenburg,

if he struck at all, would choose an area due east of Vilna, where the many lakes were divided by high and dry ridges.

The allocation of German troops, so far as it could be ascertained, gave support to the latter view. In the north von Hindenburg commanded all the forces from the sea to the river Pripet. This command, with the exception of one Austrian corps, was wholly German. It contained two groups—a small one on the right wing, under Prince Leopold of Bavaria, including a detachment around Pinsk of three infantry and two cavalry divisions, and to the north von Woyrsch's 9th Army. All the rest was under von Hindenburg's direct authority, and consisted from left to right of von Buelow's army of Riga, von Scholtz's 8th Army against Dvinsk, von Eichhorn's 10th Army from Vidzy to Smorgon, and, on the right, the 12th Army, now under von Fabeck, who had been brought from the Western front. The Russian main commands were the Army of the North, now under General Kuropatkin, which stretched from the Gulf of Riga to Vidzy ; the Army of the Centre, under Ewarts, from Vidzy to south of the river Pripet ; and the Army of the South, under Ivanov, from the Pripet to the Bukovina. On the front facing Kuropatkin it was believed that the Germans had no more than 300,000 bayonets ; while opposite Ewarts they had by April concentrated not less than 700,000. South of the Pripet were the Austrian armies, under the Archduke Frederick—from left to right the 4th Army, under the Archduke Joseph Ferdinand ; the 3rd Army, under Puhallo ; the 2nd Army, under Boehm-Ermolli ; the composite army, under Bothmer ; and

the army under von Pflanzer-Baltin. These forces
were almost purely Austrian, though Bothmer had
with him a few German divisions. Opposite them
lay Ivanov's four armies—from north to south the
8th, under Brussilov; the 11th, under Sakharov;
the 7th, under Scherbachev; and the 9th, under
Lechitsky.

In the northern and southern groups there was
little special activity to record during the late winter
and the early spring. Every week there were raids
and counter-raids, and efforts on both sides to seize
knuckles of firm ground and so improve their positions. In the northern sector, between Riga and
March 22. Dvinsk, on 22nd March, the Russians
carried a portion of the German front,
taking a village and a wood east of Augustinhof.
In the southern sector there was some desperate
fighting round the bridgehead of Uscieszko, which
Scherbachev had approached on the first day
of January, but had failed to take. The place
was a natural stronghold, situated on high ground
between the Dniester and its tributary the Zurin.
The precipitous slopes, clothed with undergrowth,
had been converted into a maze of trenches
and galleries, and had been surrounded with immense wire entanglements. During February the
Russians laid siege to this fortress, which from
its position dominated a large part of their front.
There is still considerable doubt as to what hap-
Feb. 10. pened. On 10th February the Russians,
having sapped below the Austrian wire,
made a fierce bayonet attack on the place, and
seem to have carried it, and even to have sent a
detachment across the Dniester. But it was either

not captured as a whole or was subsequently lost, for on 20th March there was a heavy action, *March* 20. in which the Austrians, on their own admission, were driven pell-mell across the river, and the bridgehead of Uscieszko passed definitely into Russian hands.

The main battle of these months was fought by Ewarts's right centre, in the neighbourhood of Lake Narotch, against von Hindenburg's right centre, the army of von Eichhorn. Ewarts's command consisted of the 1st, 2nd, 10th, 4th, and 3rd Armies, and of these the 2nd, under General Smirnov, extended from half-way between Vidzy and Postavy, past Smorgon, to a point a little south of the river Vilya. It was the largest of all the Russian armies, numbering no less than eleven corps. We are concerned now with the left wing, between Lakes Narotch and Vishnevsky, which was made up of three corps in line, the 5th, 35th, and 36th, with the 3rd Siberians in reserve—the whole under the charge of General Baluyev. The Russian offensive, which began on 18th March, inaugurated a series of *March* 18– battles which lasted till the middle of *April* 14. April. It is not yet possible to say with certainty that this movement frustrated and diverted the expected attack of von Hindenburg on Riga during the dangerous fortnight when the gulf was partially ice-free. It may be that that movement had been already given up owing to the condition of the ground in the Dvina valley. But it is permissible to believe that in any case Ewarts's offensive would have changed the purpose of the German High Command. The pass between Lakes Narotch and Vishnevsky is the direct road to Vilna and

Kovno. Von Hindenburg could not risk a breach of his front at a point of such strategic importance A blow there he must summon all his strength to parry.

The German front in the East, as we have seen, was not the continuous line of fortifications which was found on the West. In places it was only a trench deep, and in some of the marshy regions there were no trenches at all, the ground being held by patrols from both sides, which were constantly engaged in small duels. But in the vital parts there were fortifications on the Western scale, and this was the case in the corridor between Lakes Narotch and Vishnevsky. The chief feature of the place is a big bog about half-way between the lakes, which in March was wholly impassable except by the rare causeways. North of it stretched a line of low sandy slopes to the edge of Lake Narotch, with, behind them to the west, further pockets of bog. The German first line lay along and behind the crown of the slopes, well placed so as to provide enfilading fire against any attack, and protected by five or six lines of wire entanglements. Three hundred yards behind lay their second line, curving back in the north to rest on a small marsh. Between that marsh and the lake was a dry strip, containing the farm of Augustovo and a church tower with a German machine gun on the top.

General Baluyev's plan was to attack with the 5th Corps on the right against the main position on the slopes. A division of the 35th Corps was directed to advance in the centre immediately to the north of the Great Marsh, while on the south of the marsh the two divisions of the 36th Corps were to move up a grassy slope similar to the terrain of the 5th Corps. A very considerable concentration of field and heavy guns was provided before the action, with a fair supply of shells, though there was some lack of high explosives for the heavy guns. Before the first attack on 18th March there was a two days' artillery preparation, to which the Germans made little reply. The supply of ammunition for the field guns was calculated for ten days, and each separate attack was preceded by a bombardment of from twelve to forty hours' duration.

In all eight attacks were made—on 18th March, on the nights of the 21st, 22nd, 25th, 27th, and 31st, on 7th April, and on 14th April. The ground was chiefly won at night, and the last two daylight attacks accomplished little. By 15th April the 5th Corps had carried the first and second German lines opposite, and the low hills behind them which the enemy had used as an observation post—a distance of over a mile. The two Russian divisions employed were the 7th and 10th, and they all but annihilated the 75th German division, which lost over 1,200 prisoners and many slain. The enemy resisted chiefly with machine guns, of which he had eight per battalion, as against the Russian two. The 35th Corps in the centre had a more difficult task. They carried the German first line, but found the wire intact before the second, and, in spite of splendid courage, were unable to break through. One regiment of the corps swore to carry the position before it ; it failed, but when another regiment succeeded later it found four hundred dead of the first still in the German wires. In all, the 35th Corps advanced about half a mile. South of the

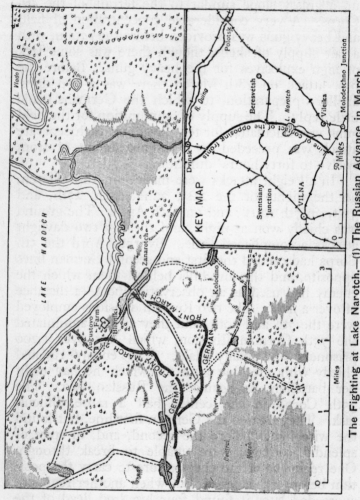

The Fighting at Lake Narotch.—(1) The Russian Advance in March.

KEY MAP

Great Marsh the 36th Corps was held fast. It carried part of the German first line, but could not hold it, and at the close of the action it had won nothing but a wooded cemetery on the first slope, which it held as an outpost.

So far the attack had been moderately successful, mainly because there had been sufficient artillery preparation to enable the superb Russian infantry to get to grips with the enemy. General Ewarts had performed the task he had set himself, and had diverted von Hindenburg from an attack on Riga during the critical April weeks. It had been a costly exploit, for he had lost not less than twelve thousand men ; but the troops were in good spirits. They had seen their guns dominate those of the enemy, and that was so novel an experience that their hopes ran high. The depleted divisions were filled up from the depots, and, if the wastage of guns and ammunition could be made good, the position was secure.

Unfortunately, ground won by artillery was destined to be lost by its absence. The Russian Staff regarded the operations as concluded, and resolved to move the reserves of guns elsewhere. The total supply was still quite inadequate for the whole front, and the fashion was followed of concentrating in turn at different points. Accordingly the whole of the heavy artillery reserve was removed with the exception of two batteries, and these were left with a scanty supply of shells. Moreover, the aeroplanes used for " spotting " were packed for removal, and the captive balloons were taken down. The Germans soon perceived what had happened from their air reconnaissance. All the 26th of April

they were bringing their guns and ammunition stores
April 27. forward, and on the 27th they set to
work to find the ranges of the Russian
front and reserve trenches and their scanty field
batteries.

The Russian front on the 27th was held by the
two divisions of the 36th Corps south of the Great
Marsh. Across the Marsh ran a line of outposts,
partly from the 25th Division of the 36th Corps
and partly from the 7th Division of the 5th Corps.
From the Marsh to Lake Narotch lay the 5th Corps,
the 7th Division on the left and the 10th on the
right. The 3rd Siberian Corps was in reserve to
the 36th Corps, and the 35th Corps to the 5th Corps.

The storm fell entirely on the line of the 5th
Corps. At 4.45 on the morning of 28th April 120
April 28. heavy guns opened against it, principally on its left flank. Thence the bombardment spread along the whole front, chiefly
high explosives; and since there could be no Russian
reply, both field and heavy guns were pushed
up close to the front line. Before 11 a.m. all
telephone communication was cut between the eight
battalions of the four regiments in line and their
reserves. The Smolensk regiment on the Russian
left centre, which had lost more than half its
strength in the earlier advance, suffered the most.
The half-dried marshes which patched the front
did not allow of proper entrenching; often the
only defences were parapets of sandbags, and there
were no protected approaches from the rear.
Long before noon all the breastworks had been
obliterated, and the enemy had his field guns firing
at close range in his own first line.

About 11 a.m. the German infantry began to advance in skirmishing order. The flank of the Smolensk regiment was turned, and what was left of it was compelled to fall back. This opened an alley-way into the Russian position, and the five German divisions of attack poured through. Practically

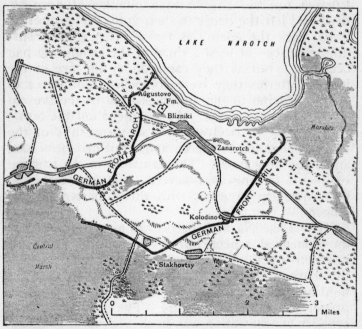

The Fighting at Lake Narotch.—(2) The German Counter-attack in April.

unopposed, they advanced for a mile and a half, passing their old first-line trenches which the Russians had won a month before, and pushing on beyond the slopes where had lain the original Russian line.

At this point the two reserve regiments of the

5th Corps came into action. Marching north, they struck at the flank of the German frontal advance. It was now about three o'clock in the afternoon, and the Germans had covered between two and a half and three miles of ground, during which their artillery fire had been suspended. At the sight of the Russian reserves the German infantry at once retired and left the battle to their guns. The reserves drove back the enemy as far as his original front-line trenches—at least a third of the ground he had occupied ; but as they came under the fire of the heavy batteries they were compelled themselves to retreat, leaving to the Germans most of the ground already advanced over. As the night fell the battle died away. In twelve hours all the results of the Russian advance in March and April had been lost, and something more. The casualties in the Russian regiments in line were severe—from two-thirds to three-quarters in each, with three-quarters of the officers.

The Lake Narotch battle was a mere episode in its strategical aspect, but it was one of the most instructive actions in the campaign. It revealed in the sharpest relief the old lesson that before superior fighting quality can have its effect the way must be prepared by an adequate fire. The original Russian artillery concentration was small, judged by Western standards ; but even an approach to equality in heavy guns was sufficient for the incomparable Russian infantry. To withdraw the batteries was an invitation to the enemy to advance to an easy conquest. What he gained he gained wholly by his guns. In the words of an eye-witness : " The German infantry did not advance to an attack, but

to an occupation, and retired wherever it met with
any opposition, as if the enemy himself had determined to economize his infantry from the outset,
and to depend entirely on the successes of his heavy
guns. The heavy guns stopped firing only when
the infantry advanced, and on the appearance of
Russian reserves the infantry retired of itself to the
nearest cover, and the heavy guns opened again."
Regiments which were half composed of young recruits needed especially the protection of artillery;
yet for six hours the Russians stood a devastating fire,
to which they could make no reply, and only fell back
when they were outflanked and reduced to a handful.
It was a clear proof of Russian *moral*, and of the
inexorable need for an adequate artillery machine.
As the fates willed it, the battle of Lake Narotch
was destined to be the last which Russia fought
" with the bare breasts of her soldiers."

The fall of Erzerum on 16th February left General Yudenitch with an intricate problem. His forces
were not large, and the main line of the
Turkish retreat—down the Kara Su or *Feb.* 16.
Western Euphrates towards Erzinghian—was through
difficult mountain country, with positions everywhere capable of a stout defence. He was compelled to advance on a broad front, and while his
centre moved west from Erzerum it was essential
that his left wing should advance from Mush and
Bitlis towards Diarbekr, while his right wing should
sweep the country between Erzerum and the Black
Sea. He was aware that Enver would strain every
nerve to redeem the Turkish defeat. He knew that
troops were being hurried eastwards as fast as the

wretched communications would allow, while rumour
had it that the Aleppo corps was coming north, and
that divisions were being sent from Mesopotamia.
It would be a week or two before the first Turkish
reinforcements could arrive, and the winter weather
put a brake upon his own and the enemy's speed.
He therefore devoted himself to perfecting his own
communications, and to disposing his forces in such
a way that they would hold all the routes by which
an outflanking movement might be possible. His
left wing moved slowly on Diarbekr. His left centre
advanced down the Western Euphrates. His right
centre followed the highroad from Erzerum to Trebizond, towards the town of Baiburt. A small connecting column took the hill road between Erzerum
and the port of Rizeh, and occupied the town of
Ispir, in the glen of the Upper Chorok. His right
wing was directed against Trebizond.

Trebizond was the most famous of the cities of
Northern Anatolia. Originally a Greek colony from
Sinope, it was the last stage in the march of Xeno-
phon's Ten Thousand. When Julius Cæsar con-
quered the King of Pontus he made it a Roman
colony. From its harbour Arrian started on his
famous voyage, and on Arrian's advice Hadrian
raised it to a great city. Throughout the Middle
Ages it was the trade centre through which the
merchandise of Persia, India, and China flowed to
the markets of Europe. After the coming of the
Turks it remained a forlorn remnant of the Eastern
Empire till eight years after the fall of Constantinople,
when the last emperor submitted to Mohammed the
Conqueror.

The importance of the place to Russia did not lie

in its usefulness to the enemy. Since she had won
the control of the Black Sea, Trebizond had been
of little value to the Turks as a base for sea-borne
supplies. But it would be of immense value to any
Russian advance, not only as the best harbour on

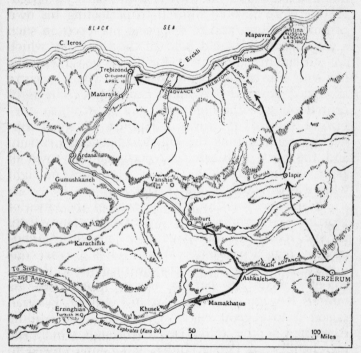

Russian Operations in Armenia after the Fall of Erzerum.

that coast, but as the radius from which ran all the
chief roads in that part of Asia Minor. Its capture
would give to the right flank a much-needed security,
and would afford a new base, thereby shortening the
line of communications, and relieving Batum and

the Kars railway of the heavy strain which they had
hitherto borne. Yudenitch's strategy was to win
Trebizond by an advance on all his front, which
would pin the enemy to his positions, while the
operative force on his right would attempt to reach
its goal by means of the sea-coast. His main forces
would, therefore, be ready for the enemy reserves
when they should arrive, and would distract any
part of them from going to the relief of the corps
which held Trebizond. In a sense, therefore, the
Trebizond campaign was an isolated operation. Almost up to the date of its fall Yudenitch was engaged
with the new Turkish divisions on the roads to
Erzinghian and Baiburt and Diarbekr. It was the
day after Enver's main counter-offensive had deci-
sively failed that the Russians entered the ancient
city.

It would appear, though the evidence is by no
means clear, that a certain part of the attacking force
reached the coast by the road from Erzerum to
Rizeh, and a certain part from Batum. But in
winter these hill roads were so perilous that the
larger portion of the army of assault had to be brought
by sea. On 4th March, under cover of
March 4. the fire of warships, Russian troops were
landed on the shore at Atina, sixty miles east of
Trebizond. It met with little resistance, and next
evening had occupied Mapavra, nine miles along the
coast to the south-west. On the 8th the
March 8. enemy was thrown back behind the river
Kalopotamos, thirty-five miles from Trebizond.
Then came a pause, and in twenty days, owing to
the difficulty of the shore road, only five miles were
covered. On 6th April the Russians reached the

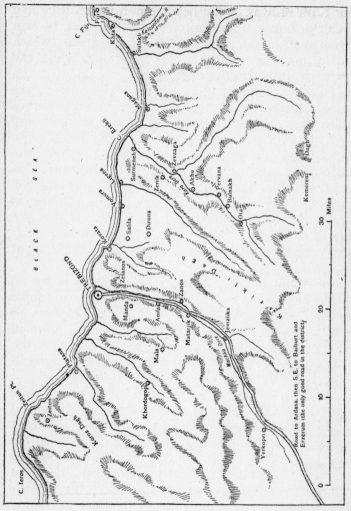

The Trebizond District.

main line of the Trebizond defence, the stream called
April 6.   the Kara Dere, which, issuing from
a gorge among precipitous hills, flows
through some ten miles of easier country and enters
the sea through a marsh just east of Cape Erekli.
The Turks were easily driven from the right bank,
but on the left shore, on a ridge 2,000 feet high,
they had prepared a strong position which could
not be turned by any flank attack to north or south.

The frontal assault on the Kara Dere position
lasted for nine days. On 15th April the crest was
April 15.   carried, and the enemy fled in precipi-
tate retreat towards the city. Several
little streams crossed the intervening ground, and
just east of Trebizond was a highish ridge ; but the
defence was in no condition to tarry anywhere.
Next day the Russians were only twelve miles from
the walls, and on the morning of 18th April, after
April 18.   a further landing had been made west
of the city, Trebizond was in their
hands. The garrison—what was left of 50,000 men
—fled southwards in the direction of Baiburt.

The whole Trebizond operation was skilfully
conceived, and carried out with the same precision
as had marked the advance on Erzerum. The steady
pressure of Yudenitch's central army virtually isolated the city, and the assaulting force, assisted from
the sea, could pursue its course without fear of
surprise or sudden enemy reinforcements. The
capture of Trebizond gave Russia a flanking point
in that front—Trebizond–Erzinghian–Diarbekr—
which she must win before she could carry the
campaign into the true Turkish stronghold. Till
that line was won she was fighting in the chaos of

highland which was, so to speak, the wire entanglement of the main position. Once it was reached the second stage would begin, and she would be striking at the granary of Turkey, the great Anatolian plain, whose loss, more even than that of Constantinople, would mean the downfall of the Osmanli.

CHAPTER CI.

THE POLITICAL SITUATION.

Increasing Optimism in Britain—Its Causes—Less Criticism of the
Government—The Wittenberg Scandals—Staff Work for
Peace—The Budget of April 4, 1916—The Chancellor of the
Exchequer's Forecast—British Financial Position compared
with Germany's—Dr. Helfferich's Speech—Changes in Ger-
man Naval Commands—Retirement of von Tirpitz—Its
Consequences—The Submarine Campaign—Sinking of the
Sussex—President Wilson's Note—Germany accepts Amer-
ican Demands—The German Chancellor's Speeches—Sir
Edward Grey's Reply—Situation in France—Death of Gen-
eral Gallieni—Situation in Russia—M. Sturmer becomes
Premier—The Re-opening of the Duma—The Military Service
Question in Britain—Difficulties with the Derby Recruits—
Introduction of Universal Service—The Irish Rebellion—Its
Causes.

THE early months of 1916 saw a more optimistic
temper abroad in the West than had been
known since the preceding spring. Even the
fall of Kut failed to shake this composure—perhaps
because the disasters of the second half of 1915 had
driven most men to write off from the national
assets the various divergent operations in the East.
The desperation of Germany's blind offensives, her
foolish boasting—so loud that it suggested an uneasy
mind—her summons to her opponents to " look at
the map " and admit her victory, seemed to argue
some loss of grip on the situation. Public cheerfulness was increased by the superb French stand

during the First Battle of Verdun. Here was a case of Germany using all her peculiar strength on one narrow section and failing to force it. Her losses, even in the eyes of the most sceptical, were far greater than those of the defence. If the mighty machine which had blown up the Russian front on the Donajetz a year before could do no better than this, it looked as if its days were numbered. The Allies were now on a level with their enemy in *matériel*, and they had the greater total number of men. They believed that the fighting quality of their infantry was better, and it appeared that they had the saner strategical plan.

Part of the restored confidence—in Britain, at any rate—was due to a better feeling towards the much-criticised civil Government. The Cabinet had taken certain steps, long overdue, towards making the nation a true partner in the war. Policy, so far as it concerned the blockade, the war in the air, and the conduct of the Navy, had been debated frankly in Parliament, and criticism, since it was given a fair outlet, lost its danger and gained in practical value. The passing of the new Military Service Act had satisfied the national conscience, though it was clear that its imperfections would have to be remedied by a more comprehensive measure. The worst difficulties with Labour seemed to be over, and, broadly speaking, the mind of the nation was occupied with certain definite points of administrative reform rather than with a general feeling of satiety towards its governors. Critics, to be sure, remained who pounced upon the foibles of politicians and pled for a " clean sweep." Their devotion to some strong, simple saviour of his country made them

dredge deep in political and non-political life to find
their ideal. But such an attitude was in reality a
form of mysticism, analogous to the old quest for
a panacea. It was a mood of imaginative rhetoric
rather than common sense. In the name of practical
politics they sought something which was notably
unpractical. For the man of destiny is the gift of
God, and is not to be found by painful seeking.
When he comes it is silently and without advertisement, and his own people commonly know him not.

We have spoken of degrees in the national confidence, but these were trivial mutations against a
solid background of resolution. At no moment was
there ever the faintest weakening on the purpose
of the war, or any despair of the issue. As the
months passed the German aims in all their egotism
and arrogance became clear to every unit among the
Allies, and their utter intolerableness was, if anything, more obvious in their floundering peace talk
than in the rodomontade with which the war began.
In April an incident occurred which revolted the
inmost soul of the British people as nothing had
done since the early atrocities in Belgium. Three
British R.A.M.C. officers returned as exchanged
prisoners, and told the story of what had happened
at the Wittenberg camp. The place, on the report
of American representatives, had been a scandal
from the beginning. In December 1914 typhus
broke out among the 15,000 British, French, and
Russian prisoners there. At that time food and
clothing were bad and inadequate, and the men
were so shamefully crowded that personal cleanliness was impossible. As soon as the disease appeared every German officer fled, including the

doctors, and did not return for six months. The principal medical officer, one Aschenbach, who was in charge of the medical arrangements, did, indeed, return for a brief visit, clad in a mask and rubber gloves and every device to safeguard his worthless life. For two months the disease raged unchecked, and the camp guards contented themselves with shouting their directions across the barbed wire, and sending in food by overhead trollies. In February six British R.A.M.C. officers were sent from Halle to Wittenberg. Three of them died of typhus, but by their efforts the disease was ultimately stamped out in May 1915. The story, which reposed on unshakable evidence, convicted a number of German officers of the last extreme of cruelty and cowardice, and the German Government as a brazen accessory. Wittenberg came to rank with Louvain as a watchword for relentless war upon an infamy which poisoned the world.

So far as the fighting services were concerned, the nation at large looked with composure on the administration of the Admiralty and the War Office, and with perfect confidence on the admirals at sea and the generals in the field. It recognized that staff work had at last been rated at its proper value, and the stalwart figure of Sir William Robertson was a guarantee that never again should empiricism rule our general strategy. But it was also becoming widely felt that staff work was necessary too for civilian administration, and was especially needful for those intricate problems which would face the country at the conclusion of peace. One section in Britain seemed to hold the schoolboy view that all that was required was to give Germany a thorough

beating, shake hands, and live happily with her ever
afterwards. That was not the view of those most
familiar with German methods, and it was certainly
not the view of our allies of France and Russia.
They knew that Germany would never be so dangerous as in the period of apparent quiescence produced by her defeat, and that much that was gained
by war might be lost to the Allies in the first twelve
months after peace. It was known that she had
made far-reaching plans, after her patient fashion,
to meet the financial, economic, and political difficulties that would confront her, and it was very
certain that Britain, absorbed in departmental activities, had no scheme to counter these. Lord Haldane raised the question in the House of Lords,
and the Prime Minister promised that a " Peace
Book " on the analogy of the " War Book " of a
General Staff would be prepared. But no adequate
machinery was provided for its preparation, and if
the matter were to be left to the odd men and the
scanty leisure of the various departments the result
would be farcical. There was a real national anxiety
that our unreadiness for war should not be matched
by a like unreadiness for peace. A great impulse in
the direction of forethought and organization was
given by the visit of Mr. Hughes, the Prime Minister of the Australian Commonwealth and the most
prominent leader of Labour in the Empire. In a
series of brilliant speeches he warned his country-
men to take heed that what was won by the valour
of the fleets and armies did not slip from slack
civilian hands. Britain was weary of the kind of
thinking which is done only under the goad of an
unlooked-for necessity.

The introduction of new Budgets in Britain and Germany, and a number of financial statements issued in both countries, make some review desirable of the economic position of the belligerents at this stage of the war.

The Budget, which was introduced by the British Chancellor of the Exchequer on 4th April, was mainly an increase in existing taxes—a series of fresh cuts from the old joints. *April 4.* The expenditure for the year 1915–16 had been 1,559 millions, 31 millions less than the estimate ; the revenue was 337 millions, 32 millions in excess of the estimate. This left a deficit of 1,222 millions, which had been made good for the present by the various war loans, the sale of Exchequer Bonds and Treasury Bills, and the Anglo-French American Loan. For the coming year Mr. McKenna estimated the total expenditure at 1,825 millions, the total revenue at 502 millions, leaving a deficit to be met by borrowing of 1,323 millions. The new taxes included an impost on tickets of admission to various amusements, and taxes on matches and mineral waters ; the rate of income tax for earned incomes was increased from 2s. 1⅕d.–3s. 6d. to 2s. 3d.–5s., and for unearned from 2s. 9⅗d.–3s. 6d. to 3s.–5s. ; the duties on sugar were raised ½d. per pound, on cocoa 4½d. per pound, and on coffee and chicory 3d. per pound ; and the excess profits tax was increased from 50 per cent. to 60 per cent. This enlarged taxation was boldly but not very scientifically conceived, since it laid far too great a share of the extra burden on the professional and middle classes. There was justice in the complaint that more of the revenue might have been raised by indirect taxation.

But a time of war allows small leisure for fiscal reform, and statesmen not unnaturally tend to follow what for the moment is the line of least resistance.

The Chancellor of the Exchequer permitted himself a forecast of the situation at the end of 1916–17. Our permanent revenue, leaving out the temporary yield of the excess profits tax, would then be 423 millions, our total indebtedness 3,440 millions, which, deducting the 800 millions advanced to the Allies and Dominions, left a net debt of 2,640 millions. Allowing for a sinking fund, this meant an annual debt charge of 145 millions. These enormous sums dazzled the eyes of the ordinary man, and left him giddy. It was impossible to base any reasoned view of the financial position on figures which so far transcended all former experience and calculation. But it was none the less true that, in comparison with former crises, and taking into account the total wealth and earning capacity of the nation, the colossal expenditure was well within our means. We were conducting our war finance on sound principles. While Germany proposed to raise at the outside 24 millions by special taxation, we had obtained from the same source, in the first twenty months of war, over 146 millions, and in 1916–17 we were raising over 300 millions. Our system of credit had stood the unparalleled strain, and our banking methods were vindicated beyond question in the eyes of the most querulous critic. The balance against us in foreign trade remained our chief difficulty, but we had done much in the past year to adjust it. One remarkable phenomenon was the revival of our export trade, in spite of the fact that our internal industries were being carried

on with less than half of their normal man-power.
The year 1916 promised to show an increase over
1915 in exports of some 100 millions, which would
make it only some 40 or 50 millions short of the
total for the last complete year of peace. With
regard to our industries, all were flourishing, with
the exception of the cotton, building, and printing
trades. Wages had risen enormously, and so had
the cost of living. The situation was unique, and
the return to normal conditions would no doubt
present an awkward problem ; but, on the other
hand, the impetus given to certain vital matters,
such as agriculture, might continue beneficently after
peace. The economic position of Britain, when it
was remembered to how large an extent she bore
also the burdens of her Allies, was in many ways
not the least of the surprises of the war.

The student who turned to Germany found a
very different state of affairs. Her pre-war organization had made her financial problem simple, but
nothing could make the simplicity sound. She
gambled from the beginning on a huge indemnity,
and therefore she met her expenditure almost
wholly by loans. When the prospect of an indemnity grew dim, she continued the practice ; for
you cannot manufacture new revenue when there
is little taxable production. Her four ingeniously
manipulated loans had raised a large sum on paper,
but she had provided scarcely any additional annual
revenue to meet the enormous debt charge. She
had increased her paper circulation by over 700
millions, while Britain had only found it necessary
to increase hers by 100 millions. She was import-
ing from neutrals, but she had few exports with which

to pay for imports. The decline in the value of the
mark in neutral markets—an average depreciation of
29 per cent.—showed that her industrial output was
shrinking, as more and more men were taken for
the field. The German Minister of Finance, Dr.
Helfferich, made a speech in the Reichstag on 16th
March 16. March in which he vainly endeavoured
to justify German methods. For a man
of his undoubted ability and financial acumen it
was a singular confession of weakness. He took
credit that Germany had not imitated the British
practice of new taxation, but had followed " the
principles of orderly Imperial housekeeping," whatever these might be. But in the next breath he pled
for new taxes, since " we cannot demand or accept
milliards from a people which for the fourth time,
in ardent patriotism and confidence, offers its sav-
ings to the Empire, unless we assure the due payment of interest." On this it might have been
observed that the amount of new taxation proposed
did not come within measurable distance of paying
that interest. He criticised the British fashion of
short-term debts, which he estimated at nearly 750
millions. In this sum he included Exchequer Bonds,
which had a five-year currency, as well as the American Loan. But Germany's own short-term debt at
the end of February exceeded 800 millions. Moreover, the British system of continuous loans by bill
or bond was a sound one ; it represented a real sub-
scription of existing funds ; whereas the big German
long-term loan was largely a creation of artificial
bank credits. Finally, he boasted that Germany was
only spending half the sum that Britain spent daily
on the war. In 1916 our daily expenditure was

close on 5 millions, that of France about 2½ millions,
that of Russia just over 3 millions, and that of Italy
something under 1 million. But he omitted to
mention the fact that the British figures included
separation allowances and loans to the Allies, which
the German did not, and these items between them
came to little less than 1½ millions per day. Germany had to carry Austria, Bulgaria, and Turkey
on her shoulders, and it was probable that her daily
outlay, direct and indirect, was equal to that of
Britain.

Germany's economic position in the first half
of 1916 was beyond doubt exceedingly grave. She
had staked everything on illusory indemnities, to
which Dr. Helfferich no longer referred ; at the best
he now talked of a " financially favourable peace."
Her colonies had gone, her foreign investments, her
overseas commerce, her merchant shipping. She
had by now exhausted most of the benefit in the
way of raw material won from the territories she
had occupied. Even a draw, which would be for
her a kind of victory, would leave her bankrupt.
Her one hope lay in neutrals who might, for consideration received, nurse her back to solvency. Of
these the chief was the United States, and her relations with America during this period furnished not
the least instructive chapter in her campaign.

In the early part of March there were remarkable
changes at the German Marinamt. Grand Admiral
von Tirpitz resigned on the plea of ill-health, and
was succeeded by his former subordinate, Admiral
von Capelle. The news caused a sensation not only
throughout the rest of Europe, but in Germany it-

self. To the ordinary German von Tirpitz was the author and conductor of that submarine campaign which atoned in the popular mind for the inertia of the High Seas Fleet, and the exponent of that ruthlessness in maritime warfare which must some day shatter the naval pride of Britain. The reason for his fall was the character of the man. He was obstinate and short-sighted, and a hopeless colleague for a *politique* like the Imperial Chancellor. He was a confirmed intriguer, and, like some distinguished sailors elsewhere, had at his bidding an obedient *claque* of journalists. As the situation with America grew more difficult and delicate it was clearly impossible to have so reckless and headstrong an administrator at the head of the most controversial department in the service. The fall of von Tirpitz was a triumph for the more cautious von Bethmann-Hollweg.

It is probable that it was intended after his going to move more slowly with the submarine campaign, or at any rate to avoid a glaring advertisement of its truculence. But, as has happened before in history, while the Minister went his policy remained. The importance of submarine ruthlessness was so deeply set in the popular mind that the Government dared not slacken in their efforts. It was officially announced that the practice of sinking armed merchantmen would be continued. Two Dutch liners, the *Tubantia* and the *Palembang*, were torpedoed without warning. Finally, on 24th March came one

March 24. of the most flagrant outrages in the history of the war—the sinking by a submarine of the Channel steamer *Sussex*. A number of American citizens were among the victims,

and Washington asked Berlin for explanations. The
German Government replied by casting doubt upon
the origin of the disaster—a doubt which America
was soon in a position by indisputable evidence to
dispel.

On 19th April President Wilson made a speech
in Congress which trenchantly indicted the whole
German policy of submarine warfare. *April* 19.
He returned to the thesis laid down in
the first *Lusitania* Note, and since then overlaid by
special pleas, that the submarine was not an admis-
sible weapon for commerce destruction. It was
" grossly evident that warfare of such a sort, if
warfare it be, cannot be carried on without the most
palpable violation of the dictates alike of right and
humanity. . . . The use of submarines for the destruction of an enemy's commerce is of a necessity,
because of the very character of the vessels employed and the very methods of attack which their
employment as of course involves, incompatible
with the principles of humanity, the long-estab-
lished and incontrovertible rights of neutrals, and
the sacred immunities of non-combatants." He
ended by declaring that he considered it his duty
to inform Germany that " unless the Imperial German Government should now immediately declare
and effect an abandonment of its present methods
of warfare against passenger and freight vessels, the
Government can have no choice but to sever diplomatic relations with the Government of the German
Empire altogether." The night before a Note *
in these terms had been sent by Mr. Lansing to
Berlin.

* See Appendix III.

Here was at last the true ultimatum, which admitted of no misinterpreting. The Tirpitz policy of ruthlessness must be relinquished in theory and practice, or America would join the belligerent Allies. The German reply, published on 4th May, was of the familiar type—a plea in con-

May 4.   fession and avoidance. It claimed that Germany had exercised a " far-reaching restraint " on her submarine warfare, solely in the interests of neutrals. It declared that this warfare could not be dispensed with, since it had been undertaken " in self-defence against the illegal conduct of Britain while fighting a bitter struggle for national existence." But it announced a concession. The German naval force was to " receive the following orders for submarine warfare in accordance with the general principle of visit, search, and destruction of merchant vessels recognized by international law. Such vessels, both *within and without the area declared as a naval war zone*, shall not be sunk without warning, and without saving human life, unless the ship attempt to escape and offer resistance." In return for this favour Germany expected that America " will now also consider all impediments removed which may have lain in the way of neutral co-operation towards the restoration of the freedom of the seas," and " will now demand and insist that the British Government shall forthwith observe the rules of international law universally recognized before the war," in the matter of interference with sea-borne commerce.

In the connection in which it was delivered the reply could only be construed as a specific abandonment of the policy of " ruthlessness." It was so

ınterpreted by the United States. In his reply of
8th May, Mr. Wilson accepted the " Imperial Government's abandonment of a $\quad$ *May 8.*
policy which had so seriously menaced the good
relations of the two countries," and added that he
relied upon its " scrupulous execution." As for
Germany's attempt to acquire something in return
for her concession the President did not mince
matters. " The Government of the United States
notifies the Imperial Government that it cannot for
a moment entertain, much less discuss, the suggestion that respect by the German naval authorities
for the right of citizens of the United States upon
the high seas should in any way, or in the slightest
degree, be made contingent upon the conduct of
any other government as affecting the rights of
neutrals and non-combatants. The responsibility
in such matters is single not joint, absolute not
relative." *

A diplomatic correspondence is to be read in the
light of its attendant circumstances. Germany's
reply and America's counter-reply, made in a time
of great international strain, and in precise lan-
guage, constituted something very different from
the looser discussions of the past year. The belief
seemed to be justified that the American President
had spoken his last word, and that, if his conditions
were not fulfilled, a breach between the two Powers
would follow without further *pourparlers*. That
Germany should be willing to relinquish a policy
so loudly proclaimed and so popular with the nation
at large, argued that the influence of the Imperial

* The same principle had been laid down in the American
reply to the German Note of July 8, 1915.

Chancellor and the *politiques* was for the moment predominant, and that he and his friends were beginning to envisage the future with a certain sobriety.

But when we turn to the speeches of von Bethmann-Hollweg during these months, we shall not find any abatement of intransigence or any just appraisement of the situation. He upbraided the Allies almost with tears for refusing to recognize when they were beaten. He implored them to look at the map ; as if the extent of occupied territory constituted a decision. The more far-flung the lines of an army the greater its ultimate destruction if its strength fails. He repeated the fairy tale about Germany having entered upon war solely for the protection of her unity and freedom. All she sought, he said, was a Germany so strong that no one in the future would be tempted to seek to destroy her. And then he preached his own doctrine of nationalities. Did any one suppose that Germany would ever surrender to the rule of reactionary Russia the peoples she had liberated " between the Baltic Sea and the Volhynian swamps " ? As for Belgium, there could be no *status quo ante*. " Germany cannot again give over to Latinization the long-oppressed Flemish race." Well might Dr. Liebknecht, the Socialist deputy, ejaculate, " Hypocrisy ! " The British Prime Minister had declared that the first condition of peace was the complete and final destruction of the military power of Prussia. But that, said von Bethmann-Hollweg, is the same thing as our unity and freedom. The confession was significant. It was precisely because Germany defined that unity and freedom in terms of Prussian militarism that peace could only come with the latter's destruction.

Some weeks later Sir Edward Grey, in an interview with an American journalist, sketched a very different kind of freedom. " What we and our Allies are fighting for is a free Europe. We want a Europe free, not only from the domination of one nationality by another, but free from hectoring diplomacy and the peril of war ; free from the constant rattling of the sword in the scabbard, from perpetual talk of shining armour and War Lords. . . . What Prussia proposes is Prussian supremacy. She proposes a Europe modelled and ruled by Prussia. She is to dispose of the liberties of her neighbours and of us all. We say that life on those terms is intolerable. . . . Herr von Bethmann-Hollweg affirms that Great Britain wants to destroy ' united and free Germany.' We never were smitten with any such madness. We should be glad to see the German people free, as we ourselves want to be free, and as we want the other nationalities of Europe and of the world to be free. It belongs to the rudiments of political science, it is abundantly taught by history, that you cannot enslave a people and make a success of the job—that you cannot kill a people's soul by foreign despotism and brutality. We aspire to embark upon no such course of folly and futility towards another nation. We believe that the German people, when once the dreams of world empire cherished by pan-Germanism are brought to nought, will insist upon the control of its Government ; and in this lies the hope of secure freedom and national independence in Europe. . . . The Prussian authorities have apparently but one

idea of peace—an iron peace imposed upon other
nations by German supremacy. They do not understand that free men and free nations will rather die
than submit to that ambition, and that there can be
no end to war till it is defeated and renounced."

In France during the first part of 1916 there was
no political incident of note to chronicle. General
Gallieni was compelled by ill-health to resign the
Ministry of War, and was succeeded by General
Roques, who had commanded the 1st Army in the
Vosges, and had once led the 12th Corps at a critical
moment of the Marne battle. On 27th May Gallieni
May 27. died, and was mourned by his country as
Britain mourned for Lord Roberts. He
was pre-eminently the veteran soldier of France,
whose career made a continuous link between her
deepest humiliation and her greatest glory. He
had fought in the war of 1870, and as the maker of
French West Africa, Tonkin, and Madagascar had
won high honour during the decades before 1914.
When the great struggle came his health kept him
back from the actual battle-front ; but as Governor
of Paris in that hectic first week of September he
had done much to make possible the victory of the
Marne, and his grave and single-hearted courage had
been an inspiration to his people.

In Russia the spring saw two important Cabinet
changes. General Polivanov, the Minister of War,
was transferred to another post, and was succeeded
by General Schouvaiev. M. Goremykin, the Premier,
resigned on the ground of ill-health, and his place
was filled by a comparatively unknown man, M.

Boris Sturmer. The Duma was reopened by the Emperor on 22nd February after its long prorogation, and the occasion was re- *Feb.* 22. markable for a review of the whole situation in foreign affairs by M. Sazonov, and eloquent expressions of the national resolution by the President, M. Rodzianko, and the new Prime Minister. In these speeches an appeal was made to the different schools of politics to let disputable questions of internal reform sleep for the moment, and close their ranks against the common enemy. The spokesman of the Progressive *bloc* responded in the same spirit, and the unanimity of the people at large found an echo among their representatives. It was of special significance that most of the speeches referred to Poland, now bearing the brunt of the German invasion. Germany had done her best to win the Poles to her allegiance by loud-mouthed talk of Polish unity, and by founding in Warsaw a Polish university. But she took away with one hand what she gave with the other ; and while she proclaimed herself a supporter of Polish nationalism, she plundered the land recklessly, and used the remnants of the population as pawns in her barbaric game. The Poles had suffered from both sides in the exigencies of war ; but it was to their eternal credit that they showed few signs of accepting the German bribe. The story of Posen rang too newly in their ears. Their nationalism, purified in the furnace, saw its best hope in the triumph of Russia.

The coming into operation in Britain of the Military Service Act on February 10, 1916, did not end the recruiting difficulties. The work of granting exemptions lay with the local tribunals, and they

Feb. 10. showed a wide latitude in the interpreta-
tion of their duties. In some rural districts the able-bodied sons of farmers suddenly
appeared as shepherds and cowmen, demanding
and receiving exemption. The War Office were
compelled to press for a revision of the list of reserved occupations, and new instructions had to be
issued to the tribunals. There was trouble, too,
with that typical British product, the conscientious
objector. Logically, his position was impossible.
He claimed the rights and declined the most urgent
duty of citizenship, and chose in effect to declare
himself an outlaw from the commonweal. Repug-
nance to military service was to be expected from
many ; but in order to provide a respectable cloak
for such shirking, the obscure side-chapels of religion and politics suddenly found their votaries many
times multiplied. It was no easy task to riddle out
from such claimants the *bonâ fide* objectors and the
charlatans ; but the work was performed on the
whole with tact and fairness. Many of those who
declined the combatant *rôle* were willing enough to
serve with the Red Cross or the Army Service Corps,
and a non-combatant battalion was formed for railway work in France. It was confidently hoped that
fresh air and manual labour might have a salutary
effect on invalidish consciences.

But the main trouble arose from the position of
the married men, who had registered in the Derby
scheme under the impression that no married men
would be called up so long as any single men remained unattested. In the rush and confusion of
that campaign, which had something of the old

electioneering business about it, wild promises had
been made by canvassers which now recoiled on the
Government's head. Lord Derby was justified in
claiming that his pledge to the married men had
been strictly fulfilled—the Military Service Act had
been passed to bring in the single men ; and the
married men who had attested had done so with
full knowledge that they would be called up. But
it was difficult for a married man to see hordes of
the single creeping into reserved occupations, while
he, owing to his patriotism, was being put to a
serious economic loss. The discontent became so
grave that the calling up of the married groups was
postponed, and the Cabinet was forced to find some
way out of the difficulty. There was the further fact
that even the Military Service Act would scarcely
provide the numbers wanted to raise our field force
to the desired level, and to keep it there. The
military authorities furnished a note of their requirements, and declined to depart from it.

There was obviously no way of getting rid of
the practical injustice caused by the various ten-
tatives of the past months except an impartial conscription of all men of military age, whether married
or single. But the Cabinet was slow to come to
this decision. They agreed upon a scheme of " contingent compulsion," which meant that if after a
certain period sufficient men were not recruited by
ordinary enlistment, Parliament would be asked for
compulsory powers. They also proposed to prolong
the service of time-expired men till the end of the
war, to bring all youths under the Military Service
Act as soon as they reached the age of eighteen,
and to transfer men enlisted for territorial battalions

to any unit where they might be needed. At a two days' secret session of the House of Commons these projects were submitted, and confidential information was given to members as to the exact military requirements of the nation. But when, on 22nd

April 22. April, leave to introduce the new Bill was asked for, the scheme was promptly rejected. The Labour members themselves disowned it as unjust and feeble, and demanded, now that the necessity had arisen, the straight course of " equal

May 3. sacrifice." On 3rd May the Prime Minister introduced a Bill to extend, as from 24th June, the provisions of the Military Service Act to all unattested married men. From that date every male British subject ordinarily resident in Great Britain, and between the ages of eighteen and forty-one, was to be deemed duly enlisted in the regular army for the duration of the war. The third reading of the Bill was carried by a majority of 250 to 35,

May 25. and it received the Royal assent on 25th May. In a message issued on that day the King expressed to his people his recognition of the patriotism and self-sacrifice which had raised already by voluntary enlistment no less than 5,041,000 men—" an effort far surpassing that of any other nation in similar circumstances recorded in history, and one which will be a lasting source of pride to future generations."

Voluntary enlistment had, indeed, done marvels, and it was well that the world should have seen so shining a proof of the British temper. But its work was done, and, unless endless hardship was to be caused, it must be replaced by a different system. The long controversy was over, conscription was the law of the land, and the whole of British manhood was at the disposal of the State. Moreover, the revolution was whole-hearted, and met with only the slenderest opposition. Such a change, it is probable, could not have been wrought by any sweeping or heroic measures in the early days of the war. It needed time for opinion to ripen and the necessities of the case to force themselves upon the public mind. But it is very certain that the country was ready for the step long before the Cabinet had screwed up its courage. In this matter in nerve and seriousness the leaders lagged far behind their followers. The people of Britain surrendered what some chose to call their " birthright " of voluntaryism not because the Government demanded the sacrifice, but because they forced it on the Government. Had the rulers been a little closer to the nation many heart-breaking delays would have been saved, and much needless waste in money and men.

In a work like the present, which is a chronicle of military and naval operations, domestic politics are only touched on in so far as they have a bearing on the campaign. But it is necessary to devote a short space to one episode, the roots of which lay deep in old political controversies—an adventure which, as it happened, ended in a fiasco, but which in its inception was definitely linked to the main struggle. Fruitless volumes might be written in an endeavour to trace the full historical origin of the Irish rebellion of Easter week, 1916. So far five hundred years of experiments had failed to make Ireland an integral part of Britain. There had been opportunities—golden opportunities some of them—

but they had been missed. Till half a century ago
Ireland had been penalized; since then she had
been partly scolded and partly coddled; but the
treatment had always been differential. No opportunity had been given for the land to grow up into
that equal and like-minded partnership which means
unity as well as union. As a consequence Britain
had grown weary of the subject, and had almost
relinquished the attempt in despair. Sane men had
reached the conclusion that any course would be
better than to leave Ireland to be angled for by
British political parties and made the gambling
counter in a worthless game. If an incorporating
union had failed, there might remain the chance of
a looser federal tie, under which the Irish people
could attain that national maturity which had hitherto
been denied them. But while it is hard to unite, it
is often not less difficult to disentangle, and with the
first talk of a separatist policy it became clear that
Ireland was not, strictly speaking, a unit at all. If
three-fourths of the land were ready to renounce
the incorporating union, the strong and serious
Scoto-Irish stock of the North were not less resolved
to cling to it.

The handling of the problem by the British
Government between the years 1910 and the outbreak of war will probably rank high among the
political ineptitudes of history. The Home Rule
scheme was introduced at a time when it must inevitably have been suspected of an origin in party
exigencies rather than in sober statecraft. The
Arms Act had been repealed, and the majority of
the Ulster population put themselves in a state of
preparedness to resist the proposals by war. Now,

if a sober and law-abiding people decide that a certain policy is so subversive of their principles and so fatal to their future that it must be met by armed revolution, it is usual for a democratic Government to call a halt and find some other way. But if the Government in its turn concludes that such resistance is factious and unreasonable and must be crushed, then it is its business promptly to arrest the ringleaders and crush the movement. Mr. Asquith's Government did neither. It allowed Ulster to raise and discipline a highly efficient army, and it went on with its Home Rule Bill. The Nationalists very naturally claimed the same right to arm and drill their people, and the National Volunteers came into being. The result was that in July 1914 Ireland was split up into two armed camps, and it seemed that not even the dissolution of the Government and the disappearance of the Bill could have averted civil strife.

As we have seen, the outbreak of the war with Germany called a truce between the combatants—a truce most honourably observed by the respective leaders. Sir Edward Carson and Mr. Redmond flung themselves into the work of recruiting, and Ireland's well-wishers hoped that the partnership of North and South in the field might bring about that sense of a common nationality without which Home Rule would be a forlorn experiment. Germany had counted much on Irish disloyalty and disunion. Her merchants had supplied arms on the most moderate terms to Ulstermen and Nationalists alike, and when, at the end of July 1914, a riot broke out in Dublin and the King's Own Scottish Borderers came into conflict with the mob, one of her principal

agents was reported to have sent to his chief the
telegram—

" Nun kann's losgehen "—" *Now we can go ahead.*"

As matters shaped themselves, her anticipation was
falsified. But as the months passed it became apparent that there were certain smouldering ashes in
Ireland which, judiciously fanned, might kindle into
a blaze. Treason was preached openly by word and
pen, and little notice was taken of it by the authorities. Recruiting was obstructed with impunity to the
obstructors. German money was spent freely, and
a nucleus of disaffection was found in the organization called Sinn Fein, which owed no allegiance to
any of the recognized Irish parties.

Sinn Fein—which means " Ourselves " — was
a body founded some sixteen years before by a
section of extreme Nationalists, who had lost faith
in the Irish Parliamentary party. It advocated pas-
sive resistance to all British interference, a boycott
of British goods, and—with a wiser inspiration—the
development of Irish crafts and industries and a
distinctive Irish literature. For long it was a harm-
less academic movement, much frowned on by the
politicians, and drawing its strength chiefly from
the enthusiasts of Irish art and poetry. In a loose
and incoherent way it stood for the same idea as a
man like Sir Horace Plunkett, who urged his country-
men to find salvation in their own efforts rather than
in the caprices of the Parliamentary game. But
after the outbreak of war it took to itself sinister
allies. The remnants of the Larkinite Citizen Army
joined with it in founding the Irish Volunteers,
whose aims were avowedly anti-British and repub-

lican; and, assisted by German gold, they proceeded
to arm and train their followers as a revolutionary
force. The Irish Government, in spite of repeated
warnings, did little or nothing to check the movement. Mr. Birrell had consistently adopted the
principle that till Home Rule arrived no rule was
the best substitute, and his Under-Secretary, Sir
Matthew Nathan, seems to have shared these enlightened views.

Sir Roger Casement, formerly a British consular
officer, who had done good service at various tropical
stations, had before the war identified himself with
the extreme Nationalist party, and presently departed
for Germany, where he hotly espoused the German
cause. He was given the task of going round the
prisoners' camps in the attempt to form an Irish
Brigade, but to the eternal glory of the Irish soldier
his overtures met for the most part with scorn and
derision. Ultimately Germany seems to have grown
tired of her ally, and desired him to make good his
promises of raising an Irish revolt. It is difficult to
believe that she can have had much confidence in
the success of the adventure, but she hoped that
sufficient din would be raised to attract a number
of British troops to Ireland, and she was prepared
to support the gambler's throw with a bombardment by her battle-cruiser squadron at some point
on the East Anglian coast.

Late on the evening of 20th April a German
vessel, disguised as a Dutch trader and laden with
arms, together with a German submarine, *April 20.*
arrived off the Kerry coast, not far from
Tralee. The vessel was stopped by a British patrol
boat and ordered to follow to Queenstown harbour.

On the way she hoisted the German flag and sank herself, her crew being taken prisoners. Meantime Sir Roger Casement and two companions were put ashore from the submarine in a collapsible boat. The local Sinn Feiners failed to meet them, and Casement was arrested early on Good Friday morn-

April 21. ing, 21st April, and taken to England.*
The capture of their leader upset the plans of the rebels in Dublin. On the Saturday the Easter manœuvres of the Sinn Fein Volunteers were hastily cancelled ; but so much incriminating evidence was abroad that they decided that the boldest

April 24. game was the safest. On Easter Monday, while a half-hearted attack was made on the Castle, armed bands seized St. Stephen's Green, the Post Office, the Law Courts, and part of Sackville Street. Troops were hastily brought in from the Curragh, a gunboat on the Liffey shelled the rebel headquarters, a cordon of soldiers was stretched round the centre of the city, and martial

April 26. law was proclaimed. On Wednesday a Territorial brigade, the 178th, consisting of the 5th, 6th, 7th, and 8th Battalions of the Sherwood Foresters, arrived from England, and next day Sir John Maxwell, who had returned from the command in Egypt, was given plenary power to deal with the situation. Bit by bit the rebels were driven out of their strongholds, and by Saturday they were surrendering in batches. By Monday, 1st May, it

May 1. was announced that the revolt in Dublin was crushed, and the outbreaks in Enniscorthy, Athenry, Clonmel, and other country

* He was ultimately tried for high treason and condemned to death, and was hanged on 3rd August.

districts were dying down. Fifteen of the leaders were tried by court-martial and shot, and a number of others condemned to varying terms of imprisonment. The military casualties were 521 of all ranks, including seventeen officers killed. There were nearly 800 civilian casualties—many of them insurgents—including at least 180 dead.

Amid so many greater matters it is needless to dwell on this tragic and sordid episode. From the start it was what Horace Walpole called the most futile of things, a " rebellion on the defensive." Wearers of the British uniform, some of them returning wounded from the front, were shot down in cold blood, and there were, unhappily, instances of childish, light-hearted cruelty, not unknown in Irish history, in this tawdry Commune. Not thus was the conduct of the Wild Geese who fought in Clare's Brigade, or the Jacobites who followed the Chevalier to Culloden. Sympathy and respect must be denied to men who, however natural their estrangement from Britain, were fighting in alliance with a Power which had proclaimed herself the enemy of all liberty and all nationality. But it is plain that the rising did contain in its ranks a number of febrile and perverted idealists, and it was the blame of Britain that such idealism was not turned to noble uses. Ireland had been given no chance of seeing in the war her own national cause. The splendid doings of her battalions were hidden from the knowledge of the ordinary man, and she had no opportunity of thereby gaining that enthusiasm and sense of partnership without which no cause will commend itself to an emotional and imaginative people. The corner-boy who sniped from Liberty

Hall was of the same stock as the men who forced
the Gallipoli landing. The consequence was that,
since honest idealism was not awakened, the path
was clear for the visionary and the quack.

The true Ireland was not to be found in the
vapouring brigandage of the Sinn Feiners, but in
the many thousands, drawn from every corner of
the land, who were true to their salt and fought in
the British lines with a gallantry and resolution
unsurpassed in the campaign. Forty-eight hours
after the Dublin rising began the German troops
opposite Irish battalions exhibited notices announ-
cing that the English were shooting down their
wives and brothers, and were answered with
" Rule, Britannia! " A company of the Munster
Fusiliers crossed the No Man's Land that night, cut
the enemy's wire, and brought off the placard in
triumph. It was Ireland's answer not only to Germany, but to those traitors who would defile her
honour at home.

CHAPTER CII.

THE BRITISH LINE IN THE WEST.

German Disposition opposite British Front—Haig's Telegram to Joffre—British relieve French 10th Army—Arrival of Russian Contingent—British Losses in Period of Quiescence—Britain's Military Effort—Training of the New Troops—An Address to Officers—February Fighting in Ypres Salient—The Loss of The Bluff—Recapture of The Bluff—The Fight at St. Eloi—The Holding of the Craters—Gas Attacks at Loos and Messines—May Fighting on Vimy Ridge—The Canadians' Fight at Ypres in June—Death of von Moltke.

WHEN the Imperial Crown Prince unleashed his attack on Verdun one part of his purpose, as we have seen, was to induce a British counter-offensive. Hence the German lines were not thinned in the north. The plan on page 100 will show the dispositions in the early months of 1916. Opposite the Belgians and French on the Yser were the Naval Corps and two and a half Landwehr and Ersatz divisions. Opposite the British—when they had relieved the French 10th Army—was the Fourth Army of the Duke of Wurtemberg, the Seventh Army of the Bavarian Crown Prince, and the right wing of the Second Army of von Below. In all, excluding the cavalry, there were forty German divisions in line or in local reserve. With the exception of one Landwehr brigade, the troops facing the British were all good Active or Reserve formations,

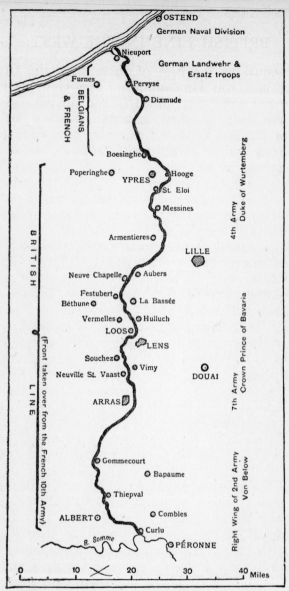

The British Line from Belgium to the Somme in
the first half of 1916.

quite equal to the best of those with the Crown Prince and von Hindenburg. The German High Command were determined to run no risks on the northern side of their gigantic Western salient. Except for the Verdun area, their men were more numerous and of better quality opposite the British front than in any other part of their far-flung defence.

Verdun soon became a maelstrom which sucked in all their free strategic reserves, and demanded the complete attention of the German Staff. Hence any great movement in the north was impossible, even if one had ever been contemplated. The war all but stood still, while the world watched the most heroic and skilful defence that history has known. In March Sir Douglas Haig telegraphed to General Joffre : " While deploring the loss of gallant Frenchmen in the great battle still raging, the British army desires to assure you of its admiration of the heroic performance of the French army around Verdun, where Germany has chosen to break her strength in vain against the unconquerable soldiers of France." General Joffre replied : " The French army thanks the British army for its expression of hearty goodwill, which it has been kind enough to address to us while the great battle of Verdun is still in progress. In its fierce struggle the French army is confident that it will obtain results from which all the Allies will reap an advantage. It remembers also that its recent call on the comradeship of the British army met with an immediate and complete response."

Verdun was France's exclusive business, and her generals chose to hold the line there with their own troops, and to ask for no reinforcements from the

British front. But help was given in another way.
General Joffre's concluding words refer to the change
in the northern dispositions which was completed
during March. The British armies took over the
whole front from Ypres to the Somme, and the
French 10th Army, which had held the line from
Loos to a point south of Arras, was released for
service elsewhere. This was not the only contribution made by the Allies during that long struggle.

April 20. On 20th April a contingent of Russian
troops, some 8,000 strong, landed at
Marseilles. They were brought across Siberia, and
then by sea from Dalny, by way of the Suez Canal.
Their number could represent no great accession to
the French field force, but their presence was a proof
of the new unification of command among all the
Allies which was needed to give effect to their unity
of purpose. General Joffre welcomed the new-
comers in a felicitous Order of the Day :—

" Our faithful ally, Russia, whose armies are already fighting so valiantly against Germany, Austria, and Turkey, has
wished to give further proof of her friendship for France and
even more signal proof of her devotion to the common cause.

" Russian soldiers, selected from among the bravest and led
by the best-known officers, are coming to fight in our ranks.

" You will welcome them as brothers. You will show
them how warm is the feeling you have for those who have
left their country to fight at our side.

" On behalf of the French army I welcome the officers,
non-commissioned officers, and men who have landed in
France. I bow before their colours, upon which will soon be
inscribed the glorious names of common victories."

To the outside critic it appeared that during the
first half of 1916 the British army was stagnant in the
West. It was a shallow judgment. That it took no

part in the Verdun battles was not its own desire, but a wise decision approved by the French Generalissimo. Its duty was the hard one of waiting—long months of desultory trench fighting with no concerted movement, no great offensive purpose, to quicken the spirit. It was a costly duty. Frequently the daily toll was over 1,000; and if we take only an average daily loss of 500, that gives a total in six months of 90,000 men. From it all there came, apparently, no military result of any consequence. The British army was neither attacking nor seriously on the defence, and it is likely that those indeterminate weeks were for officers and men among the hardest to bear in the whole campaign.

Nevertheless this time of apparent stagnation was in a very real sense a blessing, for it enabled Britain to complete her field army, and to perfect its training. Before midsummer the total of the British levy was over 5,000,000. The nation is so prone to self-criticism that few realized the stupendous and unparalleled character of the British military effort. There had been nothing like it in the history of any nation. With the possible exception of France, she had mobilized for the direct and indirect purposes of war a larger proportion of her population than any belligerent country. Moreover, while engaged in also supplying her Allies, she had furnished this vast levy with its necessary equipment. She had jettisoned all her previous theories and calculations, and in a society which had not for a hundred years been called upon to make a great effort against an enemy, a society highly differentiated and industrialized, a society which lived by sea-borne commerce, and so could not concentrate like certain other lands exclusively on military preparation, she had provided an army on the largest scale, and provided it out of next to nothing. She had to improvise officers and staff, auxiliary services, munitionment—everything. She had to do this in the face of an enemy already fully prepared. She had to do it, above all, at a time when war had become a desperately technical and scientific business, and improvisation was most difficult. It is possible to assemble speedily hosts of spearmen and pikemen, but it would seem beyond human capacity to improvise men to use the bayonet and machine gun, the bomb and the rifle. But Britain had done it, and had done it for the most part by voluntary enlistment.

It was easy for critics to point out defects in her organization. Mr. Churchill, in a speech in the House of Commons in May, argued with some force that there was an undue proportion of ration strength to fighting strength ; that half the total ration strength of the army was still at home ; that of the half abroad, half fought and half did not fight ; that of the half that fought, about three-quarters were infantry in the trenches, on whom fell almost all the loss; that of every six men recruited at one end, only one infantry rifle appeared over the parapets at the other ; and that some 2,000,000 soldiers had never been under fire. Undoubtedly there was room for "combing-out"; for the *embusqué* existed in the British as in other armies, and the staff at home had grown to a preposterous size. But in modern war, with its intricate organization, it was clear that an army must have a far greater proportion of men behind the line than in any former campaign. The apparatus was so vast that the operative point must seem small in contrast to the mechanism which produced it.

" During the period under review," wrote Sir Douglas Haig in his first dispatch, " the forces under my command have been considerably augmented by the arrival of new formations from home, and the transfer of others released from service in the Near East." To produce that homogeneity which is necessary in a field army, much thought had to be given to field training. " During the periods of relief," Sir Douglas wrote, " all formations, and especially the newly-created ones, are instructed and practised in all classes of the present and other phases of warfare. A large number of schools also exist for the instruction of individuals, especially in the use and theory of the less familiar weapons, such as bombs and grenades. There are schools for young staff officers and regimental officers, for candidates for commissions, etc. In short, every effort is made to take advantage of the closer contact with actual warfare, and to put the finishing touches, often after actual experience in the trenches, to the training received at home." The British armies in the field for the first half of 1916 were one great training school.

With what judgment and enthusiasm this training was pursued may be learned from some notes of an address given to a school for young officers by one of the most brilliant, and one of the youngest, of British generals :—

" I would begin by impressing on you the great importance of your work. You must realize that, however good and skilful the disposition may be, battles must be won by *fighting ;* the heroism, skill, and firmness of the most junior officers will have the most far-reaching results. You are responsible for the successful leading of your men in battle ; you are responsible for their safety, as far as this can be ensured, while gaining success in battle ; you are responsible for their health, for their comfort, for their good behaviour and discipline. Finally, and not least, you are responsible for maintaining the honour of England, for doing all you can to ensure the security of England, and of our women and our children after us.

" To bear all these responsibilities successfully you must acquire, first, KNOWLEDGE. You must know what to do and how to do it, in order to lead your men with success and honour, and protect them from destruction or loss, which will be suffered if you are ignorant of your work and of your profession. . . . Secondly, you must acquire CHARACTER—that is, resolution, self-confidence, self-sacrifice—in order to inspire your men by your example, sustain their courage in danger by your example and their endurance in hardship by your example.

" Now as regards the first—KNOWLEDGE—remember two things. . . . (1) Knowledge is not a Heaven-sent gift ; it is the outcome of study, hard work, and thought. (2) It is an absolute necessity to you as an officer. It is the foundation of your own character, for without it you cannot gain self-confidence. You must know your job. If you do not you can have no confidence in yourself, and the men can, and will, have no confidence in you either. Knowledge is therefore the first great essential for your capacity to command your men.

" As regards the second requirement of an officer—CHARACTER. . . . The character of the officer is the foundation of the discipline of his men. Men can only be commanded successfully by *men*. No troops ever possessed a discipline that was worth a damn—that could stand the great disintegrating strain of battle—who were commanded by weak, slow, irresolute ' Old Women.' ' Old Women ' are not confined to persons who wear petticoats, nor to persons over seventy years of age. I have met ' Old Women ' in trousers, and of any age between twenty and fifty. . . . Don't be an ' Old Woman ' whatever else you may be.

" The creation of discipline and the maintenance of discipline are among your most important duties. Your orders, and the orders given by your N.C.O.'s, must always be obeyed without hesitation, with energy and with cheerfulness. Never pass any lapse from duty, however trivial, without taking notice of it. Drop hard on to slackness, disobedience, slovenliness. Never stand any rot or nonsense. Insist on great cleanliness, on great alertness, quickness, and cheerfulness.

" I don't want you to go away, however, with the idea that the men must be treated like dogs—very far from it. You don't want to curse or damn every time you notice things wrong. Sometimes a word of encouragement, or a patient listening to an explanation, or a smile when pointing out the fault, will go a long way. Remember that though we are officers and the men are privates, still *we are all comrades* in the great dangers and the great struggle ; make the men feel that you realize this comradeship *and love it.*

" But you cannot be too particular in insisting on a smart, alert, cheerful appearance, and on the prompt and willing accordance of all honours and salutes. It is only that company or that battalion which shows attention to all this which really does possess discipline. Without discipline, no body of men will stand an hour of real danger. . . . These matters of appearance and respect to officers are not eyewash. They are the outward and visible sign of the inward and spiritual grace, as the parson says !

" The company or the battalion is the best looking-glass of its officers. In the company and the battalion you see the image of the officers—you see yourselves. When you note a company on the march—slack-looking, miserable, dirty, slow, and almost sulky in coming to attention, with half a dozen stragglers creeping on behind, and the officers and N.C.O.'s taking no notice—you can tell at once that these are bad officers, and that no discipline and no energy exist there. On the contrary, when you see a company marching well closed-up—men with heads erect (even though covered with the mud of the trenches), and quick and energetic in their movements as they come to the salute—these show good officers and a well-disciplined company. . . . When you take your men into action, either in ordinary trench warfare or in a big attack, all this discipline will repay you and your men themselves a thousandfold.

" Keep up your own energy and that of your men, and maintain the offensive spirit most carefully. . . . To do this, don't overlook the fact that one of your chief duties is to be always thinking. You have got brains; don't forget to use them. That is what you are an officer for. . . . *You must always be thinking.* How can you make the trench (or your position wherever it is) more secure, or more comfortable for the men ? Or how can you attack the enemy ? Or inflict some blow or loss on him ? Thus you will keep up the spirit of energy and of the offensive which is of such immense importance. . . . All energy is born of thought; therefore remember that to think is one of your great duties.

" Try and carry out these principles, and put the know-ledge you have acquired here into execution when you return to your battalion. Do not overlook the fact that—though you must possess (and show that you possess) decision and resolution in order to instil discipline into your men—merely to insist on obedience, smartness, and compliance with all orders is not sufficient. Do not forget that the men are your comrades; and do not overlook the fact that the British soldier has a great soul, and can and does appreciate what courage, honour, patriotism, and self-sacrifice mean. . . . Talk to your men often on these great qualities, both in lectures and to individuals personally. You will always find a ready response, which will one day stand you in good stead; and, what is more important still, will stand England and the Empire in good stead."

Apart from the steady normal bombardment, the main activities on the British front were mining, and the enterprises which Sir Douglas Haig has called " cutting-out parties." Both had been going on all winter, but in the new year they became a formula and a habit. Their chief use was to keep the spirit of the offensive alive in our men, to harass the enemy, and to provide information as to the exact German dispositions. Everywhere from Ypres to the Somme such raids were attempted, and on the whole we, who were the initiators of the adventures, kept the lead in them. But the Germans retaliated with various raids which, after their fashion, were more elaborately organized than ours. Some mobile batteries, which our men knew as the " travelling circus," toured along their front, and at different places opened a fierce bombardment, under cover of which their infantry raided our front line, and carried off prisoners. It was remarked that these attempts were specially common south of Arras. Places like Gommecourt, La Boisselle, and Carnoy were frequently selected, as if the enemy had grown suspicious of that section of front which had never yet been the *terrain* of any great attack.

The most serious fighting in the first half of the year took place in and around the Ypres salient. There was no Third Battle of Ypres, as many expected ; but there was a long-drawn struggle for certain points, which in the total wastage produced the results of a great action. In that ill-omened salient, as we have seen, the Germans held all the higher and better ground, and especially all the points which gave direct observation for artillery. Our trenches were for the most part in the waterlogged flats, and when we reached dry ground, as a rule we were commanded from elevations in front and flank. Further, all our communications were at the mercy of the enemy's shell fire.

The trouble began on 8th February, when the German guns opened a heavy bombardment, which endured for several days. On the 12th, *Feb. 8–12.* early in the morning, an infantry attack was delivered at the extreme left of our line, near the point of junction with the French on the canal. The German bombers took a section of our trenches, but our counter-attack immediately drove them out. For the rest of the day the bombardment continued, and in the evening a second attempt was made to rush the British left—this time without any success.

Feb. 13. Next day the centre of interest moved to the other side of the salient. At Hooge the Germans had sapped out, and linked up their sap-heads into a connected line 150 yards from our front. On the 13th their guns obliterated our front trenches. On the 14th, in the *Feb.* 14. afternoon, the whole section was under an intense bombardment, a series of mines were exploded, and infantry attacks were launched against our positions at Hooge and at the north and south ends of Sanctuary Wood. They failed utterly, being checked by our rifle and machine-gun fire long before they reached their objective.

Farther south they had better fortune. On the north bank of the Ypres-Comines Canal is a ridge, 30 to 40 feet high, which owes its existence largely to the excavations for the canal. It is part of that horseshoe of shallow upland which separates the Ypres basin from the vale of the Lys, and connects in the south with the ridge of Messines. This particular hillock was covered with trees and was held by both sides, and to that eastern part of it over which our line passed we gave the name of The Bluff. The bombardment on the afternoon of the 14th all but obliterated our trenches there, and the infantry rush which followed captured them and their continuation to the north—in all, about 600 yards. It was an awkward piece of ground to lose, and the Division under Major-General Pilcher counter-attacked at once, winning back two of the lost trenches. But the Germans had dug themselves in securely, and brought up batteries which

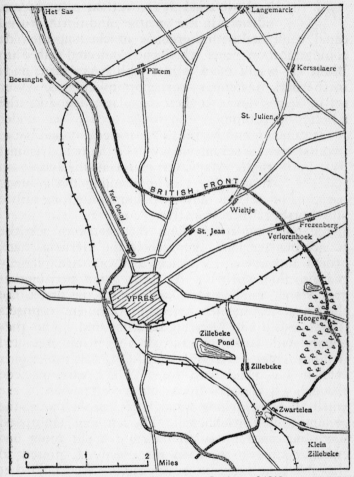

The Ypres Salient in the Spring of 1916.

deluged all the area of danger. On the night of the
Feb. 15. 15th we tried to recover the place by an
advance in the open ground north of the
canal, combined with a grenade attack along the old
communication trench which had connected with The
Bluff. It was a black night, with heavy rain, and
in the dark quagmires our effort miscarried. We
set ourselves down to shell the place, and wait for
a better opportunity.

It came on 2nd March, after the enemy had been
in possession for seventeen days. To the 3rd Division,
March 2. under Major-General Haldane, was entrusted the task of winning the ground
back. For several days we bombarded steadily,
and bursts of fire from trench mortars and occasional bombing attacks kept the enemy in a state
of nervous tension. Apparently the Germans had
orders themselves to attack, but our fire pinned
them to their shelters. At 4.29 on the morning of
2nd March, our infantry, wearing for the first time
their new steel helmets, effected a complete surprise.
They rushed the German trenches and found the
enemy with bayonets unfixed, and many of them
without rifles or equipment. The British right
carried The Bluff with ease. The centre pushed
through the German front, and took the third line,
which they held long enough to enable the main
ground to be consolidated. The left was held up at
first, but since those on its right could bring an
enfilading fire to bear on the enemy, it presently
was able to advance to its objective. We found the
German trenches full of dead as the result of our
bombardment. Five officers and 250 men were
captured, and one party of fifty who took refuge in

a crater at the east end of The Bluff were collected at our leisure. We had won back all the lost ground, as well as a considerable part of the German line. Counter-attacks in the afternoon achieved nothing. One German detachment, advancing to the charge, hurled their bombs beyond the British trenches, and held up their hands to surrender.

At the end of the month the British again attacked. The Ypres salient now represented a shallow semicircle, beginning in the north at Boesinghe, on the Ypres-Dixmude Canal, and ending in the south at St. Eloi. At the latter point a small German salient had encroached on our line, to the depth of about 100 yards on a front of 600. It was resolved to get rid of this, and straighten our front, the place being roughly defined by the crossroads south of the village of St. Eloi, where the Messines and Warneton roads branch off. The first step was the exploding, on 27th March, of six large mines within the salient, a shock so colossal that it *March 27.* was felt in villages far behind the battle ground. Our men saw a sheet of flame with dark things whirling in it, and then a monstrous canopy of dust. Half a minute later the infantry—the Northumberland Fusiliers and the Royal Fusiliers from the 3rd Division—were racing across the open to the German trenches. The enemy wire was intact, and so were the parapets; but the Fusiliers were through them before the defence had time to collect its wits. Inside the salient there was nothing but death and destruction; but machine guns were busy on the flanks, and the left of the attack did not reach its objective, so that a way was left for the Germans to occupy one of the mine craters. The next few

days were spent in repelling counter-attacks and
endeavouring to oust the enemy from the crater
which he held. This was successfully accomplished
on 3rd April, and we thus gained the whole of our
original objective—the German first and second
lines on a front of 600 yards. We had
April 3. captured five officers and 195 men on
27th March, and five officers and eighty men on
3rd April.

Then followed some weeks of confused and
difficult fighting. The 3rd Division was relieved
by the 2nd Canadian Division, under Major-General
Turner, V.C., whose task was to consolidate the
ground won. But little of the work had been done ;
little could be done owing to the weariness of the
troops which had made the attack, and the water-
logged soil now churned into glutinous mire by the
shelling and the mine explosions. The communication trenches had all been obliterated, and the
German second line beyond the crater, which we
nominally held, had never been properly converted,
and was in any case practically destroyed by our
own artillery fire. There was a very general doubt
as to where exactly was the British front line, and
where was the German.

In such conditions it was not difficult for the
enemy to push us out of his old second line. The
Canadians—especially the 6th Brigade—were now
holding isolated craters with no good communications between them. The near side of each crater
was under direct enemy observation and constant
fire, so that supplies and reliefs could only come up
at night, and it was all but impossible to evacuate
the wounded. At any one moment it was difficult

to say what craters were held, and this uncertainty led to mistakes in sending up reliefs and considerable losses. Meantime an incessant bombardment went on, and some of the craters were reduced to mere mud holes in No Man's Land, incapable of being held by either side. The Canadians occupied a demolished and much inferior position against greatly superior artillery, with few chances of communication, and no cover for approach except the darkness of the night.

The tactical history of those intricate days is still impossible to write, but the general result was that we found the gains of March 27th and 3rd April untenable, and gradually loosened our hold on them. The story is best summarized in the words of the Commander-in-Chief. " On the morning of 6th April," Sir Douglas Haig wrote, *April* 6. " the enemy attacked with one battalion supported by another ; he penetrated our new lines, and gained the two westernmost craters. It is difficult to follow in detail the fighting of the next three weeks, which consisted in repeated attacks by both sides on more or less isolated mine craters, the trench lines having been destroyed by shell fire. Great efforts were made to maintain communication with the garrison of these advanced posts, and with considerable success. But there were periods of uncertainty, and some misconception as to the state of affairs arose. On the 11th it was reported to me that we had recaptured all that remained of *April* 11. the position won by us on the 27th March and 3rd April. This report, probably due to old craters having been mistaken for new ones, was subsequently found to be incorrect. The new craters, being ex-

posed to the enemy's view, and to the full weight of
his artillery fire, have proved untenable, and at the
present hour our troops are occupying trenches in
the general line which were held by them before
the 27th."

April saw one other notable attack in the Ypres
salient. On the 19th, when the Germans delivered one
April 19. of their fiercest assaults on the St. Eloi
craters, they attacked also farther north at
Wieltje and on the Ypres-Langemarck road. At the
latter place they captured a considerable length of
trenches across the road, which made our front sag
dangerously at a very vital point. Two days later, on
April 21. the night of Good Friday, 21st April, the
Shropshire Light Infantry won back the
ground, with the support of the French guns on
their left. It was a fine exploit, performed under
appalling conditions, for the darkness was one sheet
of rain, and the soil was like porridge. The old
shell holes were full of water, and a man who stum-
bled in was in danger of drowning. One of the
columns of the attack—solely owing to the nature of
the ground—took several hours to cover 200 yards.

The end of April saw a great activity in gas
attacks, as if the enemy sought to commemorate
fittingly his introduction of the weapon a year before. At 5.10 a.m. on the 27th, after a heavy bombard-
April 27. ment the day before, gas was released
toward the chalk pit salient north-east
of Loos, while a barrage of lachrymatory shells was
directed to our support and reserve lines. Two
hours later came a second emission of gas, followed
by a furious bombardment of our first trenches.
The front was held by Irish troops, and when the

infantry attack came they awaited it with complete composure, mowing it down with machine-gun and rifle fire. Two small portions of our line were penetrated, but the assailants were promptly expelled with severe losses. Two days later the attack was repeated at Hulluch ; but this time it was a wild fiasco. The wind veered, and the gas was driven back over the German lines, bleaching and colouring all the hinterland to the *April* 29. depth of nearly two miles. The enemy fled back, and was caught by our barrage. That same day, 29th April, there was another gas attack in the Wulverghem area, west of Messines. It had the usual attendants of a preliminary bombardment and a simultaneous barrage, and following upon it no less than eight infantry attacks were launched. Two of them had a fleeting success, but one was almost immediately repelled, and the other was shattered by a counter-attack forty minutes later. The German aim seems to have been the destruction of mine shafts, and in this purpose they signally failed.

In the middle of May the Vimy ridge, which had been quiet for some months, became again the centre of interest. On the 15th, at 8.30 p.m., we blew up several mines on the ridge, and the craters were for some days hotly con- *May* 15. tested. A battalion of the Lancashire Fusiliers occupied the German first line on a front of 250 yards, and for some days held the position under a storm of shell. Early on the morning of 21st May the fire rose to hurricane pitch, and that evening the German infantry attacked the north *May* 21. end of the ridge and carried our first line on a front of 1,500 yards. Our trenches were completely wiped out, and it was calculated that the enemy had concentrated one hundred batteries on this small section.

May 25. The fighting died down about 25th May. Meanwhile at Loos and the Hohenzollern Redoubt there had been considerable mining on both sides, with results on the whole to the British advantage.

In June these scattered activities drew to a head in one section, as if to anticipate the great Allied offensive now looming in the near future. The place was once again the Ypres salient, that section of it from Hooge to the Ypres-Comines railway. It was held at the moment by the Canadians—the 3rd Division, under Major-General Mercer. South of Hooge lay the collection of broken tree trunks called Sanctuary Wood ; then the flat watery fields around Zwartelen, where the Household Cavalry made their famous dismounted charge at the First Battle of Ypres ; then just north of the Ypres-Menin railway the mound which was famous as Hill 60. Behind, between the British front and Ypres, was the hamlet of Zillebeke, with its melancholy pond. The area of the attack was nearly two miles in width, and being the apex of a salient, the Germans were able to concentrate their fire from three sides. The chief guns used were the 5.9-inch, but almost every other kind of piece was also in action.

At 9 o'clock on the morning of the 2nd a bombardment was loosed on the British front trenches,

June 2. and a barrage was placed over the whole hinterland. General Mercer, the divisional commander, and General Williams, commanding the 7th Brigade, were at the moment making a tour of the firing-line, and waited there to see it through. The fire grew hotter with each minute, and to those who witnessed it from behind it seemed more intense than any previous bombardment of the war. At midday the infantry attack was delivered by some ten battalions, an immense concentration for so narrow a front. The Germans

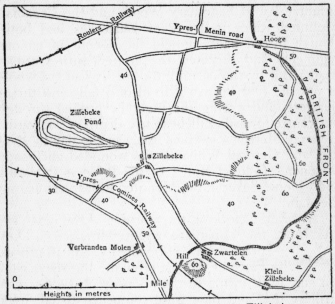

The Ypres Salient.—The Front about Zillebeke.

advanced with full kit and in regular formation, believing that the guns had done the work for them. They were speedily undeceived. Dazed and broken men rose out of the shattered trenches and disputed their advance with desperate gallantry. Of one battalion it is recorded that " few of the men who remained had any rifles left that were fit for use if their owners had been fit to use them. But when they saw the enemy close at hand they climbed from the trenches to meet them; and, some blind and deaf and staggering, they charged magnificently and pitifully to their death with no weapons but broken rifle butts, bits of entrenching tools, and in some cases their fists." Princess Patricia's Light Infantry lay in Sanctuary Wood, and the Canadian Mounted Rifles in front of Zillebeke; and both, though forced back, upheld the honour of famous regiments and carpeted the ground with German dead. But by the evening the enemy had the whole of our old first line on a front of a mile and three-quarters, and during the night he pushed through our centre towards Zillebeke to a depth of 700 yards. General Mercer was killed early in the day by shell fire, and General Williams was wounded and made prisoner. Colonel Buller of the Princess Patricia's and Colonel Baker of the Mounted Rifles were among the slain.

At seven o'clock on the morning of the next day, 3rd June, the Canadians counter-attacked. They pressed on most gallantly, and won back much of the lost ground. But they could *June 3.* not stay in it, owing to the intensity of the German artillery fire, and they were compelled to fall back from most of that shell-swept area, which became a kind of extended No Man's Land. For two days the battle was stationary, and then at midday on 6th June the German guns opened again, concentrating on the front south and *June 6.* north of the shattered village of Hooge. North of that place they exploded a series of mines between three and four in the afternoon, and presently their infantry had penetrated our first-line trenches. This meant that the extreme point of the Ypres salient had been flattened in, that our front now ran behind what had once been Hooge village, and that the enemy had advanced as far as the Bellewaarde brook.

The reason of the German effort was difficult to grasp. Their advance meant that their front descended from the higher ground to the marshy hollows. There can have been no serious intention of breaking through, and the threat would not divert us from any plans elsewhere. For a week the battle declined to an intermittent bombardment, for infantry raids were impossible owing to the downpour of rain. Then at 1.30 on the morning of 13th June a fresh Canadian division—the 1st, under Major-General Currie—attacked on a front of 500 yards, extending from the south end of Sanctuary Wood to a point 1,000 yards north *June* 13. of Hill 60. They found that the enemy had not gone far in consolidating his gains, and they found, too, that our previous bombardments had done great execution. They occupied all his advanced line, and regained their original front trenches in the most important part of the section, inflicting heavy losses on the enemy, and taking 123 prisoners. Such gains in the marshes of the salient were of little serious value, but they were a proof that the enemy could not take positions there in which he could abide.

On 18th June General von Moltke died, at the age of sixty-eight. As Chief of the German Staff at the opening of the war he had been responsible for taking from its pigeon- *June* 18. hole the famous plan which Germany had been working at for so many years. That plan failed utterly at the Marne and Ypres, and Moltke was succeeded by the younger and abler von Falkenhayn, to whom fell the difficult task of revising the whole German scheme and organizing his country for that war of endurance of which she had never dreamed. The death of this bearer of a famous name and exponent of traditional German strategy had at the moment a dramatic significance. It marked the end of the long second stage of the war in the West, the stage in which Germany had held her lines by virtue of a superior machine, and had vainly endeavoured to break the Allied strength. For, while the Canadians were struggling at Ypres for a few hundred yards of swamp, and the tide of assault at Verdun was breaking on the bastion of the French defence, in Picardy the Allied guns were massing, and great armies were making ready for an implacable offensive.

CHAPTER CIII.

THE BATTLE OF JUTLAND.

Preliminaries.

FROM the opening of the war the British navy
had been sustained by the hope that some day
and somewhere they would meet the German
High Sea Fleet in a battle in open sea. It had been
their hope since the hot August day when the great
battleships disappeared from the eyes of watchers
on the English shores. It had comforted them in
the long months of waiting amid the winds and
snows of the northern waters. Since the beginning

of the year 1916 this hope had become a confident
belief. There was no special ground for it, except
the general one that as the case of Germany became
more desperate she would be forced to use every
asset in the struggle. As the onslaught on Verdun
grew more costly and fruitless, and as the armies of
Russia began to stir with the approach of summer,
it seemed that the hour for the gambler's throw
might soon arrive.

The long vigil was trying to the nerve and temper
of every sailor, and in especial to the Battle Cruiser
Fleet, which represented the first line of British sea
strength. It was the business of the battle cruisers
to make periodical sweeps through the North Sea,
and to be first upon the scene should the enemy
appear. They were the advance guard, the *corps de
choc* of the Grand Fleet; they were the hounds
which must close with the quarry and hold it till
the hunters of the Battle Fleet arrived. Hence the
task of their commander was one of peculiar anxiety
and strain. At any moment the chance might come,
so he must be sleeplessly watchful. He would have
to make sudden and grave decisions, for it was certain that the longed-for opportunity would have to
be forced before it matured. To bring the enemy
to action risks must be run, and the strength of a
fleet is a more brittle and less replaceable thing than
the strength of an army. New levies can be called
for on land, and tolerable infantry turned out in a
few months; but it takes six years to make a junior
naval officer, it takes two years to build a cruiser,
and three years to replace a battleship. The German
hope was by attrition or some happy accident to
wear down the superior British strength to an

equality with their own. A rash act on the part of a British admiral might fulfil that hope ; but, on the other hand, without boldness, even rashness, Britain could not get to grips with her evasive foe.

So far Sir David Beatty and the Battle Cruisers had not been fortunate. We must not regard the North Sea at the time as an area where only British and neutral flags were flown. From the shelter of the mine-strewn waters around Heligoland the German warships made occasional excursions, for they could not rot for ever in harbour. Germany's battle cruisers had more than once raided the English coasts. Her battleships had made stately progresses in short circles in the vicinity of the Jutland and Schleswig shores. But so far Sir David Beatty had been unlucky. At the Battle of the Bight of Heligoland on August 28, 1914, his great ships had encountered nothing more serious than enemy cruisers. At the time of the raid on Hartlepool in December of the same year he had just failed, owing to fog, to intercept the raiders. In the Battle of the Dogger Bank on January 24, 1915, an accident to his flagship had prevented him destroying the whole German fleet of battle cruisers. It was clear that the Germans, if caught in one of their hurried sorties, would not fight unless they had a very clear advantage. Hence, if the battle was to be joined at all, it looked as if the first stage, at all events, must be fought by Britain against long odds.

On Tuesday afternoon, 30th May, the bulk of the British Grand Fleet left its bases on one of its customary sweeps. It sailed in two divisions. To the north was the Battle Fleet under Sir John Jellicoe—the Battle

Tuesday, May 30.

Squadrons ; one Battle Cruiser Squadron, the 3rd, under Rear-Admiral the Honourable Horace Hood ; the 1st Cruiser Squadron, under Rear-Admiral Sir Robert Arbuthnot, Bart. ; the 2nd Cruiser Squadron, under Rear-Admiral Heath ; the 4th Light Cruiser Squadron, under Commodore Le Mesurier ; and the 4th, 11th, and 12th Destroyer Flotillas. Farther south moved the Battle Cruiser Fleet, under Sir David Beatty—the 1st and 2nd Battle Cruiser Squadrons, under Rear-Admiral Brock and Rear-Admiral Pakenham ; the 5th Battle Squadron, four vessels of the *Queen Elizabeth* class, under Rear-Admiral Evan-Thomas; the 1st, 2nd, and 3rd Light Cruiser Squadrons, and the 1st, 9th, 10th, and 13th Destroyer Flotillas. It will be noticed that the two divisions of the Grand Fleet were not sharply defined by battleships and battle cruisers, for Sir John Jellicoe had with him one squadron of battle cruisers, and Sir David Beatty had one squadron of the largest battleships.

On the morning of the last day of May the German High Sea Fleet also put to sea, and sailed north *Wednesday,* a hundred miles or so from the Jutland *May 31.* coast. First went Admiral von Hipper's Battle Cruisers, five in number, with the usual complement of cruisers and destroyers. Following them came the Battle Fleet, under Admiral von Scheer. With a few exceptions, all the capital ships of the German navy were present in this expedition. What the purpose of von Scheer was we can only guess. Warned of the British sailing, he may have hoped to engage and destroy a portion of the British fleet before the remainder came to its aid. He may have contemplated a raid upon some

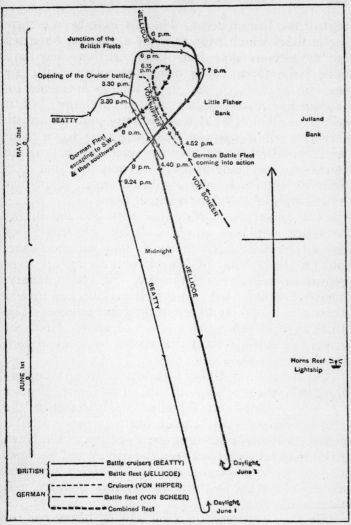

Battle of Jutland.—Track Chart.

part of the British coast. He may have been escorting cruisers which were to make a dash for open sea and act as commerce destroyers. Or there may have been some far-reaching design associated with the sea war against Russia. It is idle to speculate on the precise reason which brought him out, but it seems probable that it was no mere practice cruise. German public opinion was beginning to demand some proof of naval activity since the submarine campaign had languished. It may be that von Scheer's enterprise was a gamble forced upon him by the state of popular feeling at home.

The last week of May had been hot and bright on shore, with low winds and clear heavens; but on the North Sea there lay a light summer haze, and on the last day of May loose gray clouds were beginning to overspread the sky. Sir David Beatty, having completed his sweep to the south, had turned north about midday to rejoin Sir John Jellicoe. The sea was dead calm, like a sheet of glass. His light cruiser squadrons formed a screen in front of him from east to west.

At 2.20 p.m. *Galatea* (Commodore Alexander-Sinclair), the flagship of the 1st Light Cruiser Squadron, signalled enemy vessels to the

2.20 *p.m.* east. Sir David Beatty at once altered course to south-south-east, the direction of the Horn Reef, in order to get between the enemy and his base.

2.25 *p.m.* Five minutes later *Galatea* signalled again that the enemy was in force, and no mere handful of light cruisers. At 2.35 the

2.35 *p.m.* watchers on *Lion* saw a heavy pall of smoke to the eastward, and the course was accordingly altered to that direction, and presently

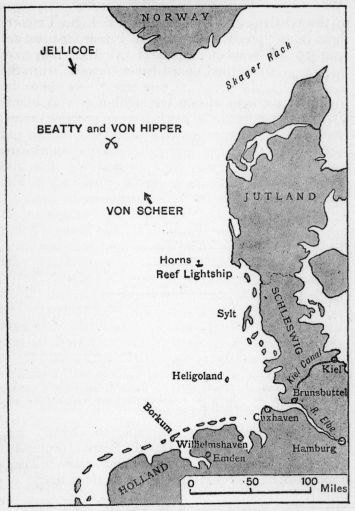

NORWAY

JELLICOE

Skager Rack

BEATTY and VON HIPPER

VON SCHEER

JUTLAND

Horns
Reef Lightship

Sylt

SCHLESWIG

Kiel Canal

Kiel

Heligoland

Brunsbuttel

Borkum

Cuxhaven

R. Elbe

Wilhelmshaven

Hamburg

Emden

HOLLAND

0   50   100
                    Miles

Battle of Jutland.—Sketch showing the general situation at the opening of the action between the Battle Cruiser Fleets.

to the north-east. The 1st and 3rd Light Cruiser Squadrons spread in a screen before the battle cruisers. A seaplane was sent up from *Engadine* (once the Cunard Liner *Campania*) at 3.8,

3.30 p.m. and at 3.30 its first report was received. Flying at a height of 900 feet, within two miles of

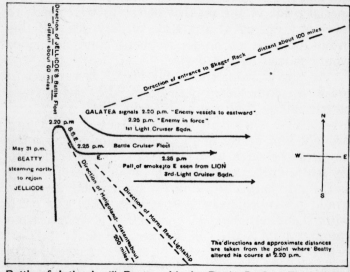

Battle of Jutland.—(1) Beatty with the Battle Cruiser Fleet sights the enemy, and alters his course to cut the hostile fleet off from its base and bring it to action.

hostile light cruisers, it was able to identify the enemy. Sir David Beatty promptly

3.31 p.m. formed line of battle, and a minute later came in sight of von Hipper's five battle cruisers.

The First Stage—3.48 p.m. to 5 p.m.

Of all human contests, a naval battle makes the greatest demands upon the resolution and gallantry of the men and the skill and coolness of the commanders. In a land fight the general may be thirty miles behind the line of battle, but the admiral is in the thick of it. He takes the same risk as the ordinary sailor, and, as often as not, his flagship leads the fleet. For three hundred years it had been the special pride of Britain that her ships were ready to meet any enemy at any time on any sea. If this proud boast were no longer hers, then her glory would indeed have departed.

At 3.30 that afternoon Sir David Beatty had to make a momentous decision. The enemy was clearly falling back upon his main Battle Fleet, and every mile the British admiral moved forward brought him nearer to an unequal combat. For the moment the odds were in his favour, since he had six battle cruisers against von Hipper's five, as well as the 5th Battle Squadron, but presently the odds would be enormously against him. He was faced with the alternative of conducting a half-hearted running fight with von Hipper, to be broken off before the German Battle Fleet was reached, or of engaging closely and hanging on even after the junction with von Scheer had been made. In such a fight the atmospheric conditions would compel him to close the range and so lose the advantage of his heavier guns, and his own battle cruisers were less stoutly protected than those of the enemy, which had the armour of a first-class battleship. Sir David Beatty was never for a moment in doubt. He chose the course which was not only heroic, but right on every ground of strategy. Twice already by a narrow margin Beatty had missed bringing the German capital ships to action. He was resolved

that now he would forgo no chance which the fates
might send.

Von Hipper was steering east-south-east in the
direction of his base. Beatty changed his course to
conform, and the fleets were now some 23,000 yards
apart. The 2nd Light Cruiser Squadron took
station ahead with the destroyers of the 9th and
13th Flotillas ; then came the 1st Battle Cruiser
Squadron, led by *Lion ;* then the 2nd ; and then
Evan-Thomas, with the 5th Battle Squadron. Beatty
formed his ships on a line of bearing to clear the
smoke—that is, each ship took station on a compass
bearing from the flagship, of which they were diag-
onally astern. At 3.48 the action began,
3.48 *p.m.* both sides opening fire at the same
moment. The range was 18,500 yards, the direction was generally south-south-east, and both fleets
were moving at full speed, an average perhaps of
twenty-five knots. The wind was from the south-
east, the visibility for the British was good, and
the sun was behind them. They had ten capital
ships to the German five. The omens seemed
propitious for victory.

In all battles there is a large element of sheer
luck and naked caprice. In the first stage, when
Beatty had the odds in his favour, he was destined
to suffer his chief losses. A fortunate shot struck
Indefatigable (Captain Sowerby) in a vital place, and
she immediately blew up. The German gunnery at
the start was uncommonly good ; it was only later,
when things went ill with them, that their shooting
became wild. Meantime the 5th Battle
4.15 *p.m.* Squadron had come into action at a
range of 20,000 yards, and engaged the rear enemy

ships. From 4.15 onward for half an hour the duel between the battle cruisers was intense, and the enemy fire gradually grew less rapid as ours increased. At 4.18 the German

4.18 p.m.

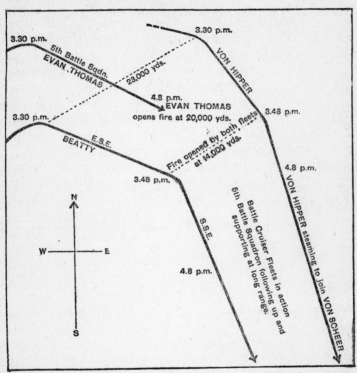

Battle of Jutland.—(2) Opening of the Action between the Battle Cruiser Fleets.

battle cruiser third in the line was seen to be on fire. Presently *Queen Mary* (Captain Prowse) was hit, and blew up. She had been at the Battle of the Bight of Heligoland; she was perhaps the best gunnery ship in the fleet; and her loss left Beatty with only four battle cruisers. Happily she did not go down before her superb marksmanship had taken heavy toll of the enemy. The haze was now settling on the waters, and all that we could see of the foe was a blurred outline. The sea was full of submarines, but by singular good fortune the British ships passed through them without mishap.

Meantime, as the great vessels raced southwards, the lighter craft were fighting a battle of their own. Eight destroyers of the 13th Flotilla—*Nestor*, *Nomad*, *Nicator*, *Narborough*, *Pelican*, *Petard*, *Obdurate*, and *Nerissa*, together with *Moorsom* and *Morris* of the 10th, and *Turbulent* and *Termagant* of the 9th, moved out at 4.15 for a torpedo attack, at the same time as the enemy destroyers came forward for the same purpose. The British flotilla at once came into action at close quarters with fifteen destroyers and a light cruiser of the enemy, and beat them back with the loss of two destroyers. This combat had made some of them drop astern, so a full torpedo attack was impossible. *Nestor*, *Nomad*, and *Nicator*, under Commander the Honourable E. B. S. Bingham, fired two torpedoes at the German battle cruisers, and were sorely battered themselves by the German secondary armament. They clung to their task till the turning movement came which we shall presently record, and the result of it was to bring them within close range of many enemy battleships. Both *Nestor* * and *Nomad* were badly hit, and only *Nicator* regained the flotilla. Some of

* *Nestor* was sunk, and Commander Bingham was saved and taken to Germany as a prisoner of war. He received the Victoria Cross.

the others fired their torpedoes, and apparently the
rear German ship was struck. The gallantry of these
smaller craft cannot be overpraised. That subsidiary battle, fought under the canopy of the duel
of the greater ships, was one of the most heroic
episodes of the action.

We have seen that the 2nd Light Cruiser Squadron was scouting ahead of the battle cruisers. At
4.38 *Southampton* (Commodore Good-
enough) reported the German battle fleet   4.38 *p.m.*
ahead. Instantly Beatty recalled the destroyers, and
at 4.42 von Scheer was sighted to the
south-east. Beatty put his helm to the   4.42 *p.m.*
starboard and swung round to a northerly course.
From the pursuer he had now become the pursued,
and his aim was to lead the combined enemy fleets
towards Sir John Jellicoe. The 5th Battle Squadron,
led by Evan-Thomas in *Barham*, now hard at it with
von Hipper, was ordered to follow suit. Meanwhile
Southampton and the 2nd Light Cruiser Squadron
continued forward to observe, and did not turn till
within 13,000 yards of von Scheer's battleships, and
under their fire. At five o'clock Beatty's
battle cruisers were steering north, *Fear-*   5 *p.m.*
less and the 1st Destroyer Flotilla leading, the 1st
and 3rd Light Cruiser Squadrons on his starboard
bow, and the 2nd Light Cruiser Squadron on his
port quarter. Behind him came Evan-Thomas, attended by *Champion* and the destroyers of the 13th
Flotilla.

The Second Stage—5 p.m. to 6.50 p.m.

It is not difficult to guess what was in the mind
of von Scheer and von Hipper. They had had the

good fortune to destroy two of Beatty's battle cruisers, and now that their whole fleet was together they hoped to destroy more. It seems clear that the weather conditions that afternoon made Zeppelins useless, and accordingly they knew nothing of Jellicoe's presence in the north. They believed they had caught Beatty cruising on his own account, and that the gods had delivered him into their hands. From 4.45 till 6 o'clock to the mind of the German admirals the battle resolved itself into a British flight and a German pursuit.

The case presented itself otherwise to Sir David Beatty, who knew that the British Battle Fleet was some fifty miles off, and that it was his business to coax the Germans towards it. He was fighting now against heavy odds, eight capital ships as against at least nineteen, but he had certain real advantages. He had the speed of the enemy, and this enabled him to overlap their line and to get his battle cruisers on their bow. In the race southwards he had driven his ships at full speed, and consequently his squadron had been in two divisions, for Evan-Thomas's battleships had not the pace of the battle cruisers. But when he headed north he reduced his pace, and there was no longer a tactical division of forces. The eight British ships were now one fighting unit.

It was Beatty's intention to nurse his pursuers into the arms of Jellicoe. For this his superior speed gave him a vital weapon. Once the northerly course had been entered upon the enemy could not change direction, except in a very gradual curve, without exposing himself to enfilading fire from the British battle cruisers at the head of the line. He was, as the French say, *accroché*, and though in a

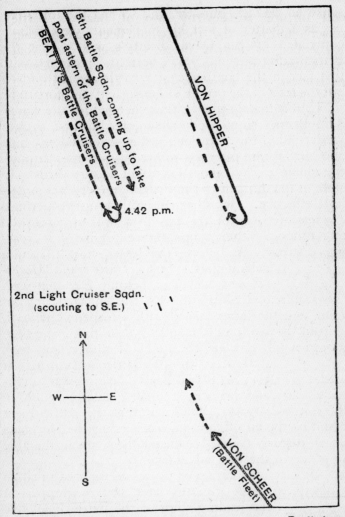

5th Battle Sqdn. coming up to take post astern of the Battle Cruisers

BEATTY'S Battle Cruisers

VON HIPPER

4.42 p.m.

2nd Light Cruiser Sqdn.
(scouting to S.E.)

N

W — E

S

VON SCHEER
(Battle Fleet)

Battle of Jutland.—(3) German Battle Fleet comes up : Beatty turns northward to draw the enemy on to Jellicoe's Battle Fleet.

sense he was the pursuer, and so had the initiative,
yet as a matter of fact his movements were mainly
controlled by Sir David Beatty's will. That the
British admiral should have seen and reckoned with
this fact in the confusion of a battle against odds is
not the least of the proofs of his sagacity and fortitude.

Unfortunately the weather changed for the worse.
The British ships were silhouetted against a clear
western sky, but the enemy was shrouded in mist,
and only at rare intervals showed dim shapes through
the gloom. The range was about 14,000 yards. In
spite of the difficulties the British gunnery was singularly effective. One German battle cruiser—perhaps
Lutzow—fell out of the line in a broken condition,
and others of their ships showed signs of increasing distress. As before, the lesser craft played a
gallant part. At 5.5 *Onslow* and *Moresby*, who had been helping *Engadine* with
the seaplane, took station on the engaged bow of
Lion, and the latter struck with a torpedo the sixth
ship in the German line and set it on fire. She then
passed south to clear the range of smoke, and took
station on the 5th Battle Squadron. At
5.33 Sir David Beatty's course was north-
north-east, and he was gradually hauling round to
the north-eastward. He knew that the Battle Fleet
could not be far off, and he was heading the Germans
on an easterly course, so that Jellicoe should be able
to strike to the best advantage.

At 5.50 on his port bow he sighted British
cruisers, and six minutes later had a glimpse of
the leading ships of the Battle Fleet five
miles to the north. He at once changed
course to east and increased speed, bringing the

5.5 *p.m.*

5.33 *p.m.*

5.50 *p.m.*

range down to 12,000 yards. He was forcing the enemy to a course on which the British Battle Fleet might overwhelm them.

We must now turn to the doings of the Battle Fleet itself. When Sir John Jellicoe was informed that the enemy had been sighted he was distant from Beatty between fifty and sixty miles. He at once proceeded at full speed on a course south-east by south to join the battle cruisers. The engine rooms made heroic efforts, and the whole fleet maintained a speed in excess of the trial speeds of some of the older vessels. The Commander-in-Chief's own tribute deserves quotation : " It must never be forgotten that the prelude to action is the work of the engine-room department, and that during action the officers and men of that department perform their most important duties without the incentive which a knowledge of the course of the action gives to those on deck. The qualities of discipline and endurance are taxed to the utmost under these conditions, and they were, as always, most fully maintained throughout the operations now reviewed. Several ships attained speeds that had never before been reached, thus showing very clearly their high state of steaming efficiency." It was no easy task to effect a junction at the proper moment, since there was an inevitable difference in estimating the rendezvous by " reckoning." Moreover, the hazy weather made it hard to recognize which ships were enemy and which were British when the moment of meeting came.

The 3rd Battle Cruiser Squadron, under Rear-Admiral Hood, led the Battle Fleet. At
5.30 Hood observed flashes of gun-fire 5.30 *p.m.*
and heard the sound of guns to the south-west-

ward. He sent *Chester* (Captain Lawson) to in-
5.45 *p.m.* vestigate, and at 5.45 this ship engaged
three or four enemy light cruisers. For
twenty minutes the fight continued against heavy

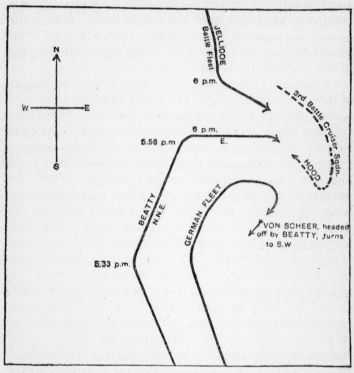

Battle of Jutland.—(4) The junction of the British fleets. Beatty
heads off von Scheer, who turns and retires south-westward
before the combined fleets.

odds, and here occurred one of the most conspicuous
instances of gallantry in the battle. Boy (1st Class)
John Travers Cornwell was mortally wounded early

in the fight, and all the crew of the gun where he was stationed lay dead or dying around him. He nevertheless remained alone at his post, waiting orders, and exposed to constant fire. He was only sixteen and a half, and he did not live to receive the reward of his courage.* " I recommend his case for special recognition," wrote Sir David Beatty, " in justice to his memory, and as an acknowledgment of the high example set by him."

Chester rejoined the 3rd Battle Cruiser Squadron at 6.5. Hood was too far to the east, so he turned north-westward, and five 6.5 *p.m.* minutes later sighted Beatty. He received orders to take station ahead, and at 6.20 he led the line, " bringing his squadron into action ahead in a most inspiring manner, worthy 6.20 *p.m.* of his great naval ancestors." He was now only 8,000 yards from the enemy, and under a desperate fire. His flagship, *Invincible*, was sunk. " I saw one of her picket boats," wrote an observer, " go hundreds of feet up into the air, spinning like a leaf in an eddy of wind, followed by a huge lick of flame as high as her masts. A great belch of smoke, and then it was all over." With her perished an admiral who in faithfulness and courage must rank with the heroic figures of British naval history. This was at the head of the British line. Meantime the 1st and 2nd Cruiser Squadrons accompanying the Battle Fleet had also come into action. *Defence* and *Warrior* had sunk an enemy light cruiser about six o'clock. *Canterbury*, which was in company with the 6 *p.m.* 3rd Battle Cruiser Squadron, had engaged enemy

* The Victoria Cross was conferred on him posthumously.

light cruisers and destroyers which were attacking
the destroyers *Shark*, *Acasta*, and *Christopher*—an
engagement in which *Shark* was sunk. A survivor
of *Shark* has described the scene : " Right ahead of
us and close at hand we saw two columns of German destroyers. We were racing along at the time,
and our skipper took us at full speed right towards
the enemy lines. There was a column of their small
craft on each side of us, and as soon as we got
abreast of them we attacked at close range, and
managed to torpedo a couple of enemy destroyers,
one on each beam. All the time we were getting it
hot—guns were popping at us from all quarters, and
we were firing back as hard as we could go, as well
as using our torpedo tubes. Of course a fight under
these conditions could not last long for us. We had
been engaged about ten minutes when two torpedoes
hit fairly, one on each side of our ship, and ripped
three holes in her, so that she sank almost at once."

6.16 p.m. At 6.16 the 1st Cruiser Squadron,
driving in the enemy light cruisers,
had got into a position between the German and
British Battle Fleets, since Sir Robert Arbuthnot
was not aware of the enemy's approach, owing to
the mist, until he was in close proximity to them.
Defence was sunk, *Warrior* passed to the rear disabled, and *Black Prince* received damage which led
later to her destruction. The last act of the
Admiral before his death was to signal a cheerful
apology to his squadron.

Meantime Beatty's lighter craft had also been
6.5 p.m. hotly engaged. At 6.5 *Onslow* sighted
an enemy light cruiser 6,000 yards off,
which was trying to attack *Lion* with torpedoes, and

at once closed and engaged at a range from 4,000 to
2,000 yards. She then closed with the German battle
cruisers, but after firing one torpedo she was struck
amidships by a heavy shell. Undefeated, she fired
her remaining three torpedoes at the enemy Battle
Fleet. She was then taken in tow by *Defender*, who
was herself damaged, and in spite of constant shelling the two gallant destroyers managed to retire in
safety. " I consider the performances of these two
destroyers," wrote Sir David Beatty, " to be gallant
in the extreme, and I am recommending Lieutenant-
Commander J. C. Tovey, of *Onslow*, and Lieutenant-
Commander L. R. Palmer, of *Defender*, for special
recognition." Again, the 3rd Light Cruiser Squadron, under Rear-Admiral Napier, which was well
ahead of the enemy on Beatty's starboard bow,
attacked with torpedoes at 6.25, *Falmouth* and
Yarmouth especially distinguishing themselves. One German battle cruiser was   6.25 *p.m.*
observed to be hit and fall out of the line.

From 5.45 to 6.50, while the two British fleets
were coming into line, the situation was highly
delicate, and the fighting was necessarily intricate
and confused. The position at 6.50 was, shortly, as
follows : Beatty had turned the German
van, and his course from 6.50 onward   6.50 *p.m.*
was south-east, gradually moving towards south.
The 1st and 2nd Battle Cruiser Squadrons led ; then
the 3rd Battle Cruiser Squadron ; then followed the
divisions of the Battle Fleet—first the 2nd Battle
Squadron, under Vice-Admiral Sir Thomas Jerram ;
then the 4th, under Vice-Admiral Sir Doveton
Sturdee, containing Sir John Jellicoe's flagship,
Iron Duke ; and finally the 1st, under Vice-Admiral

Sir Cecil Burney. In the weather conditions it was impossible to work the fleet by independent divisions, so the formation adopted was a single line.

Evan-Thomas's 5th Battle Squadron, which had up to now been with Beatty, intended to form ahead of the Battle Fleet, but the nature of the deployment compelled it to form astern. *Warspite* had her steering-gear damaged, and drifted towards the enemy's line under a furious cannonade. For a little she involuntarily interposed herself between *Warrior* and the enemy's fire. Matters were presently put right ; but it is a curious proof of the caprices of fortune in battle that while a single shot at the beginning of the action sank *Indefatigable*, this intense bombardment did *Warspite* little harm. Only one gun turret was hit, and her engines were uninjured.

At 6.50, then, the two British fleets were united, the German line was headed off on the east, and Beatty and Jellicoe were working their way between the enemy and his home ports. "The grandest sight I have ever seen," wrote an eye-witness, "was the sight of our battle line—miles of it fading into mist—taking up their positions like clockwork, and then belching forth great sheets of fire and clouds of smoke." The enemy was now greatly outnumbered, and the skill of the British admirals had won a complete strategic success. But the fog was deepening, and the night was falling. It looked as if daylight might be wanting to give the British a chance of winning a decisive victory.

The Third Stage—6.50 *p.m.* to 9 *p.m.*

The third stage of the battle—roughly, two hours
long—was an intermittent duel between the main

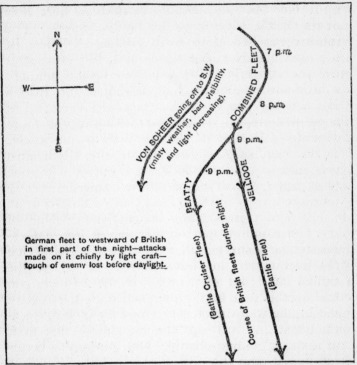

Battle of Jutland.—(5) **Von Scheer** in full retreat—Jellicoe driving
him away to the south-westward and interposing between him
and his naval bases.

fleets. Admiral von Scheer had no wish to linger,
and he moved southwards at his best speed, with the
British line shepherding him on the east. We have
seen the nature of the British dispositions at this

moment. The whole fleet now formed one fighting unit, but it will be clearer if we take the work of the battle cruisers and the battleships separately.

Beatty had succeeded in crumpling up the head of the German line, and its battleships were now targets for the majority of his battle cruisers. The visibility was becoming greatly reduced. The mist no longer merely veiled the targets, but often shut them out altogether. This not only made gunnery extraordinarily difficult, but prevented the British from keeping proper contact with the enemy. At the same time, such light as there was was more favourable to Beatty and Jellicoe than to von Scheer. The German ships showed up at intervals against the sunset, as did Cradock's cruisers off Coronel, and gave the British gunners their chance.

Of the effects of the gunnery an extract from an officer's letter gives some conception: " One of our 12-inch-gun ships put her salvos into a German ship so accurately that the enemy vessel heeled right over under the heavy blows. Of course the German went out of action. If the 12-inch gun could do this to a ship, how much more destructive must be the well-directed fire from 15-inch or 13.5-inch guns. . . . It was the big calibre that told, and it was a gunner's battle. Our gunnery is better at all points than that of the enemy."

From seven o'clock onward Beatty was steering south, and gradually bearing round to south-west and west, in order to get into touch with the enemy. At 7.14 he sighted them at a range of 15,000 yards — two battle cruisers and two battleships of the *Koenig* class. The sun had now fallen behind the

7 *p.m.*

7.14 *p.m.*

western clouds, and at 7.17 Beatty increased speed
to twenty-two knots, and re-engaged.
The enemy showed signs of great dis-   *7.17 p.m.*
tress, one ship being on fire and one dropping astern.
The destroyers at the head of the line emitted
volumes of smoke, which covered the ships behind
with a pall, and enabled them at 7.45 to
turn away and pass out of Beatty's sight.   *7.45 p.m.*

At 7.58 the 1st and 3rd Light Cruiser Squadrons
were ordered to sweep westwards and
locate the head of the enemy's line,   *7.58 p.m.*
and at 8.20 Beatty altered course to west to support. He located three battle cruisers
or battleships, and engaged them at   *8.20 p.m.*
10,000 yards range. *Lion* repeatedly hit the leading ship, which turned away in flames with a heavy
list to port, while *Princess Royal* set fire to one
battleship, and the third ship, under the attack of
New Zealand and *Indomitable*, hauled out of the line
heeling over and on fire. Once more the mist descended and enveloped the enemy, which passed
out of sight to the west. Then came a strange
shock which sent a quiver through every British
ship as if a mine or a shoal had been struck. Some
great enemy vessel had blown up somewhere in the
mist to the westward.

To turn to the Battle Fleet, which had become
engaged at 6.17 p.m., during deployment, with
battleships of the *Kaiser* class. It first took course
south-east by east ; but as it endeavoured
to close it bore round to westward.   *6.17 p.m.*
The aim of von Scheer now was escape and
nothing but escape, and every device was used to
screen his ships from British sight. Owing partly

to the smoke palls and the clouds emitted by the destroyers, but mainly to the mist, it was never possible to see more than four or five enemy ships at a time. The ranges were, roughly, from 9,000 to 12,000 yards, and the action began with the British Battle Fleet on the enemy's bow. Under the British attack the enemy constantly turned away, and this had the effect of bringing Jellicoe to a position of less advantage on the enemy's quarter. At the same time it put the British fleet between von Scheer and his base.

In the short periods, however, during which the Germans were visible, they received a heavy fire and were constantly hit. Some were observed to haul out of line, and at least one was seen to sink. The German return fire at this stage was feeble, and the damage caused to our battleships was trifling. Von Scheer relied for defence chiefly on torpedo attacks, which were favoured by the weather and the British position. A following fleet can make small use of torpedoes, as the enemy is moving away from it ; while the enemy, on the other hand, has the advantage in this weapon, since his targets are moving towards him. Many German torpedoes were fired, but the only battleship hit was *Marlborough*, which was, happily, able to remain in line and continue the action.

The 1st Battle Squadron, under Sir Cecil Burney, came into action at 6.17 with the 3rd German Battle Squadron at a range of 11,000 yards ; but as the fight continued the range decreased to 9,000 yards. This squadron received most of the enemy's return fire, but it administered severe punishment. Take the case of *Marlborough* (Captain George P. Ross).

At 6.17 she began by firing seven salvos at a ship of the *Kaiser* class ; she then engaged a cruiser and a battleship ; at 6.54 she was hit by a torpedo ; at 7.3 she reopened the action ; and at 7.12 fired fourteen salvos at a ship of the *Koenig* class, hitting her repeatedly till she turned out of line. *Colossus*, of the same squadron, was hit, but only slightly damaged, and several other ships were frequently straddled by the enemy's fire.

The 4th Battle Squadron, in the centre, was engaged with ships of the *Koenig* and the *Kaiser* class,* as well as with battle cruisers and light cruisers. Sir John Jellicoe's flagship, *Iron Duke*, engaged one of the *Koenig* class at 6.30 at a range of 12,000 yards, quickly straddled it, and hit it repeatedly from the second salvo on- *6.30 p.m.* wards till it turned away. The 2nd Battle Squadron in the van, under Sir Thomas Jerram, was in action with German battleships from 6.30 to 7.20, and engaged also a damaged battle cruiser.

In the van of the Battle Fleet, acting as a link between Jellicoe and Beatty, went Rear-Admiral Heath's 2nd Cruiser Squadron, which had now received *Duke of Edinburgh* from the 1st Cruiser Squadron. There also was the 4th Light Cruiser Squadron, under Commodore Le Mesurier, which attacked enemy destroyers at 7.20 p.m., and again at 8.18, in support of the 11th Destroyer Flotilla. In the second attack it came under the fire of the enemy battle fleet at between 6,500 and 8,000 yards. *Calliope*, the flagship, was several times

* The *Koenig* class before the action comprised *Grosser Kurfürst, Kronprinz Markgraf ;* the *Kaiser* class, *Friedrich der Grosse, Prinzregent Luitpold, Koenig Albert, Kaiserin.*

hit, but without serious damage. The light cruisers

8.40 *p.m.* attacked the enemy with torpedoes, and at 8.40 an explosion was observed on board a ship of the *Kaiser* class. In these actions four enemy destroyers were sunk by our gun-fire.

By nine o'clock the enemy had completely disappeared, and darkness was falling fast. He had

9 *p.m.* been veering round to a westerly course, and the whole British fleet lay between him and his home ports. It was a strategic situation which, but for the fog and the coming of night, would have meant his complete destruction. Sir John Jellicoe had now to make a difficult decision. It was impossible for the British fleet to close in the darkness in a sea swarming with torpedo craft and submarines, and accordingly he was compelled to make dispositions for the night, which would ensure the safety of his ships and provide for a renewal of the action at dawn. In his own words : " I manœuvred to remain between the enemy and his base, placing our flotillas in a position in which they would afford protection to the fleet from destroyer attack, and at the same time be favourably situated for attacking the enemy's heavier ships." About the same time Sir David Beatty, to the south and westward, had made the same decision on his own account. He informed Sir John Jellicoe of his position and the bearing of the enemy, and turned to the course of the Battle Fleet.

The Fourth Stage—Night of May 31st–*June* 1st.

The night battle was waged on the British side entirely by the lighter craft. It will be remembered

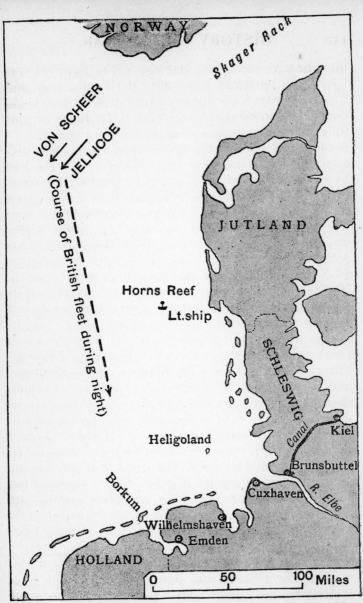

Battle of Jutland.—General situation about sunset, May 31. Von Scheer driven off to S.W.—Jellicoe interposing between him and his naval bases.

that Beatty had with him the 1st, 2nd, and 3rd
Light Cruiser Squadrons, and the 1st, 9th, 10th, and
13th Destroyer Flotillas. The 1st and 3rd Light
Cruiser Squadrons were continuously in touch with
the battle cruisers, and usually ahead of them. There
they protected the head of the British line from
torpedo attack. The 2nd Light Cruiser Squadron
was at the rear of the battle line, and at 9 p.m. it
repelled a destroyer attack upon Evan-Thomas's

10.20 *p.m.* battleships. At 10.20 *Southampton* and
Dublin were in action with five enemy
cruisers, and lost many men during the fifteen
minutes' fight. At half-past eleven *Birmingham*

11.30 *p.m.* sighted several heavy ships steering south.
These were some of the enemy battle-
ships slipping past the British stern in the fog and
darkness.

In the rear of the line were also *Fearless* and
the 1st Destroyer Flotilla, which during the night
observed a battleship of the *Kaiser* class utterly alone,
and steaming at full speed. This solitary ship
seems to have been attacked by destroyers farther
astern, for presently from that direction came the
noise of a heavy explosion. The 13th Flotilla, under
Captain James Farie in *Champion*, was also astern
of the Battle Fleet. At half-past twelve on the

June 1, morning of 1st June a large vessel crossed
12.30 *a.m.* its rear, opening a heavy fire as she
passed on *Petard* and *Turbulent.* At
3.30 *Champion* was engaged with four enemy de-

3.30 *a.m.* stroyers, and an hour before *Moresby*
had fired a torpedo with success at four
ships of the *Deutschland* class.

Beatty's destroyers having been in action since

four o'clock in the afternoon, the principal attacks
were made by the 4th, 11th, and 12th Flotillas,
which accompanied Jellicoe, and which had had less
continuous fighting. *Castor* (Commodore Hawkesley), in the 11th Flotilla, sank an enemy destroyer
at point-blank range. The 12th Flotilla (Captain
Anselan J. B. Stirling) attacked a squadron of six
large vessels, including some of the *Kaiser* class.
The third ship in the line was torpedoed and blew
up, and twenty minutes later the fourth ship in
the line was also hit. *Onslaught*, of this flotilla, was
severely damaged ; but Sub-Lieutenant Kemmis
and Midshipman Arnot, the only officers not disabled, took the ship out of action, and brought her
safely home.

The heaviest fighting fell to the lot of the 4th
Flotilla, under Captain Wintour. Two torpedoes
were observed to take effect ; but *Tipperary* was
sunk, with the greater part of her crew. Captain
Wintour was killed early in the action, when Lieutenant Kemp took command. Two rafts were got
away from the sinking vessel, and a number of survivors from them were afterwards picked up ; but
the young lieutenant went down with his ship.
The British destroyers, of all the vessels engaged in
the battle, won perhaps the greatest glory. " They
surpassed," wrote Sir John Jellicoe, " the very
highest expectations that I had formed of them."

An officer on one of the flotillas has described
that uneasy darkness : " We couldn't tell what was
happening. Every now and then out of the silence
would come *bang*, *bang*, *boom*, as hard as it could
go for ten minutes on end. The flash of the guns
lit up the whole sky for miles and miles, and the

noise was far more penetrating than by day. Then you would see a great burst of flame from some poor devil, as the searchlight switched on and off, and then perfect silence once more." The searchlights at times made the sea as white as marble, on which the destroyers moved " black," wrote an eye-witness, " as cockroaches on a floor."

At earliest dawn on 1st June the British fleet, which was lying south and west of the Horn Reef, turned northwards to collect its light craft, and to search for the enemy. But the enemy was not to be found. Partly he had slipped in single ships astern of our fleet during the night ; partly he was then engaged in moving homewards like a flight of wild duck that has been scattered by shot. He was greatly helped by the weather, which at dawn on 1st June was thicker than the night before, the visibility being less than four miles. About four o'clock a Zeppelin passed over the British

4 *a.m.* fleet, and no doubt by wireless signalled to any remaining German units where lay the safe

11 *a.m.* passage. All morning till eleven o'clock Sir John Jellicoe waited on the battle-field, watching the lines of approach to German ports, and attending the advent of the enemy. But no enemy came. " I was reluctantly compelled to

1.15 *p.m.* the conclusion," wrote Sir John, " that the High Sea Fleet had returned into port." Till 1.15 p.m. the British fleet swept the seas, picking up survivors from some of our lost

June 2, destroyers. After that hour waiting
9.30 *p.m.* was useless, so the fleet sailed for its bases, which were reached next day, Friday, 2nd June. There it fuelled and replenished

with ammunition, and at 9.30 that evening was
ready for further action.

Results.

The German fleet, being close to its bases, was
able to publish at once its own version of the battle.
A resounding success was a political necessity for
Germany, and it is likely that she would have claimed
a victory if any remnant of her fleets had reached
harbour. As it was, she was overjoyed at having
escaped annihilation, and the magnitude of her
jubilation may be taken as the measure of her fears.
It is of the nature of a naval action that it gives
ample scope for fiction. There are no spectators.
Victory and defeat are not followed, as in a land
battle, by a gain or loss of ground. A well-disciplined country with a strict censorship can frame
any tale it pleases, and stick to it for months without
fear of detection at home. Moreover, she needed
some fillip for her new loan. Accordingly Germany
claimed at once a decisive success. According to
her Press the death-blow had been given to Britain's
command of the sea. The Kaiser soared into the
realms of poetry. " The gigantic fleet of Albion, ruler
of the seas, which, since Trafalgar, for a hundred
years has imposed on the whole world a bond of
sea tyranny, and has surrounded itself with a nimbus
of invincibleness, came into the field. That gigantic
Armada approached, and our fleet engaged it. The
British fleet was beaten. The first great hammer
blow was struck, and the nimbus of British world
supremacy disappeared." Germany announced trivial losses—one old battleship, *Pommern ;* three small

cruisers, *Wiesbaden*, *Elbing*, and *Frauenlob ;* and five destroyers. A little later she admitted the loss of a battle cruiser, *Lutzow*, and the light cruiser *Rostock*, which at first she had kept secret "for political reasons." *

It is a striking tribute to the prestige of the British navy that the German fairy tale was received with incredulity in all Allied and in most neutral countries. In a small mountain village in the Apennines, the inhabitants of which, owing to economic difficulties, had small enthusiasm for the war, the news arrived that the British navy had been beaten. "That is a lie," was the unanimous decision of the village; "nothing on earth can defeat the British navy." But false news, once it has started, may be dangerous; and in some quarters in America, even among friends of the Allies, there was at first a disposition to accept the German version. The ordinary man is apt to judge of a battle, whether on land or sea, by the crude test of losses. The British Admiralty announced its losses at once with a candour which may have been undiplomatic, but which revealed a proud confidence in the invulnerability of the navy and the steadfastness of the British people. These losses were : One first-class battle cruiser, *Queen Mary ;* two lesser battle cruisers, *Indefatigable* and *Invincible ;* three armoured cruisers, *Defence*, *Black Prince*, and *Warrior ;* and eight destroyers, *Tipperary*, *Ardent*, *Fortune*, *Shark*, *Sparrowhawk*, *Nestor*, *Nomad*, and *Turbulent*. More vital than the ships was the loss of some thousands of gallant men, including some of the most

* The German official account of the action, published during June, was a tissue of careful falsifications.

distinguished of the younger admirals and captains.*

Even if Germany's version of her losses had been true, it is scarcely necessary to say that they were heavier than Britain's in proportion to her total strength at sea. But her version was not true ; it was not half the truth. The port of Wilhelmshaven was closed to the world, that no man might verify the actual casualties. It is probable that the *Pommern* whose loss was admitted was not the old *Pommern* of that name, which had been sunk by Commander Max Horton in the previous July, but a new first-class battleship. It is not yet possible to estimate the total German losses, owing to the conditions of low visibility during the day battle and the approach of darkness before the action was completed. Sir John Jellicoe, basing his calculation upon the results of careful inquiries, issued a list that in his opinion gave the minimum as to numbers. According to

* The class and displacement of the lost ships were as follows :—

							Tons.
1. *Queen Mary*	Battle cruiser	.	.	.	.	27,000
2. *Indefatigable*	,,	,,	.	.	.	18,750
3. *Invincible*	,,	,,	.	.	.	17,250
4. *Defence*	Armoured cruiser	.	.	.	.	14,600
5. *Black Prince*	,,	,,	.	.	.	13,550
6. *Warrior*	,,	,,	.	.	.	13,550
7. *Tipperary*	Destroyer	.	.	.	.	1,430
8. *Ardent*	,,	.	.	.	.	935
9. *Fortune*	,,	.	.	.	.	935
10. *Shark*	,,	.	.	.	.	935
11. *Sparrowhawk*	,,	.	.	.	.	935
12. *Nestor*	,,	.	.	.	.	1,000
13. *Nomad*	,,	.	.	.	.	1,000
14. *Turbulent*	,,	.	.	.	.	1,430

Total . . 113,300

this list Germany lost two battleships of the largest
class and one of the *Deutschland* type, one battle
cruiser, five light cruisers, one of which may have
been a battleship, six destroyers, and one submarine.
These were certain and observed losses. In addition, one first-class battleship and one battle cruiser *
and three destroyers were seen to be so severely
hit that in all likelihood they went down before
reaching harbour. It should further be remembered
that many of the ships which escaped were so seriously damaged by gun-fire and torpedo attack that
they would not be available for many months. The
German fleet returned to the Elbe bases lacking
some of its finest ships, and with most of the remainder temporarily out of action.†

It was only the ignorant who imagined that the
loss of a few ships could mean a weakening of British
naval prestige. A fleet, if it is to be better than
scrap iron, must be risked gallantly when occasion
offers. The real test of success is the fulfilment of
a strategic intention. What was Germany's aim ?
Her major purpose was to destroy the British com-

---

* Probably *Seydlitz* (24,610 tons).

† Taking the German losses at Sir John Jellicoe's lowest
estimate we get :—

	Tons.
2 *Dreadnoughts*	47,900
1 *Deutschland*	13,200
1 Battle Cruiser, *Lutzow*	28,000
5 Light Cruisers (*Rostock* class)	24,500
6 T.B.D.'s	4,800
1 Submarine	800
Total,	119,200

This, it will be observed, shows an *absolute* loss higher than
the British by some 6,000 tons.

mand of the ocean. In that she never came near succeeding. From the moment of von Scheer's return to port the British fleet held the sea. The blockade which Germany thought to break was drawn tighter than ever. Her secondary aim was so to weaken the British fleet that it should be more nearly on an equality with her own. Again she completely failed, and the margin of British superiority was in no way impaired. Lastly, she hoped to isolate and destroy a British division. That, too, failed. The British Battle Cruiser Fleet remained a living and effective force, while the German Battle Cruiser Fleet was only a shadow. The result of the battle of 31st May was that Britain was more confirmed than ever in her mastery of the waters. Its effect on the campaign at large was at once apparent. Russia was established in her control of the Eastern Baltic, and the grandiose German scheme for aiding her Eastern campaign by sea perished in the smoke of the Jutland battle.

One word must be said upon British tactics and strategy. From a tactical point of view the battle appears as an example of a tactical division of a fleet, undertaken in order to coax a laggard enemy to battle. Such a plan has, of course, its own risks ; but without risks no admiral or general has ever won success. Criticism and discussion inevitably follow all naval actions, unless, as in the case of Nelson's three battles, they are so obviously conclusive that argument is futile. But if the Battle of Jutland had not the dramatic close of Trafalgar or the Nile, yet in a true sense it was decisive. It defeated, utterly defeated, the German plan. If it was not—as with two hours more daylight it would have been—a

complete destruction of Germany's sea power, it
was a complete demonstration of Britain's crushing
superiority. Sir David Beatty faced great odds and
great difficulties in the spirit of Hawke and Nelson.
" He once more showed," wrote the Commander-
in-Chief, " his fine qualities of gallant leadership,
firm determination, and correct strategical insight.
He appreciated the situation at once on sighting
his enemy's lighter forces, then his battle cruisers,
and finally his battle fleet. I can fully sympathize
with his feelings when the evening mist and failing
light robbed the Fleet of that complete victory for
which he had manœuvred, and for which the vessels
in company with him had striven so hard." It is a
tradition of the British Admiralty that it praises
sparingly, and only praises when the merit of an
achievement is beyond question. The well-chosen
words in which it approved Sir John Jellicoe's
leadership were more impressive than the rhetoric of
the chiefs of parvenu navies. " The results of the
action prove that the officers and men of the Grand
Fleet have known both how to study the new problems with which they are confronted, and how to
turn their knowledge to account. The expectations
of the country were high ; they have been well
fulfilled. My Lords desire to convey to you their
full approval of your proceedings in this action."

Not less conspicuous than the leadership was the
amazing fighting quality of the British sailors. It was
more than a century since Britain had had the opportunity of a first-class naval action, and it may confidently be said that not even at Trafalgar did the
spirit of her seamen shine more brightly. The
story of the fighting of a battleship like *Marlborough*,

a cruiser like *Southampton*, and destroyers like *Tipperary*, *Onslow*, and *Defender*, will become part of our national epic. It is no case for the flowers of rhetoric. Such a spirit is best praised, not in the literary epithets of the historian, but in the simple and heartfelt tribute of the man who guided it. " The conduct of officers and men," wrote Sir John Jellicoe, " throughout the day and night actions was entirely beyond praise. No words of mine can do them justice. On all sides it is reported to me that the glorious traditions of the past were most worthily upheld, whether in heavy ships, cruisers, light cruisers, or destroyers—the same admirable spirit prevailed. Officers and men were cool and determined, with a cheeriness that would have carried them through anything. The heroism of the wounded was the admiration of all. I cannot adequately express the pride with which the spirit of the Fleet filled me."

Following close upon the greatest naval fight of history came the news of a sea tragedy which cost Britain the life of her foremost soldier. It had been arranged that Lord Kitchener should undertake a mission to Russia to consult with the Russian commanders as to the coming Allied offensive, and to arrange certain details of policy concerning the supply of munitions. The party consisted, among others, of Sir Frederick Donaldson of the Ministry of Munitions ; General Ellershaw ; Colonel Fitzgerald, Lord Kitchener's military secretary ; and Mr. H. J. O'Beirne of the Foreign Office, who was regarded as the ablest of our younger diplomats. On Monday evening they embarked in the armoured cruiser

Hampshire (Captain Herbert Savill), which had
returned three days before from the Battle of Jutland. About 8 p.m. that evening the ship sank in
wild weather off the western coast of the Orkneys,
either from striking a floating mine or one of the
knife-edged under-water reefs of those parts. Four
boats left the vessel, but all were overturned. One
or two survivors were washed ashore on the in-
hospitable coast ; but of Lord Kitchener and his
colleagues no word was ever heard again.

The news of his death filled the whole Empire
with profound sorrow, and the shock was felt no less
by our Allies, who saw in him one of the great pro-
tagonists of their cause. The British army went into
mourning, and all classes of the community were
affected with a grief which had scarcely been paralleled since the death of Queen Victoria. Labour
leader, trade-union delegate, and the patron of the
conscientious objector were as heartfelt in their
regret as his professional colleagues or the army
which he had created. He died on the eve of the
main Allied offensive, and did not live to see the
consummation of his labours. But in a sense his
work was finished, for more than any other man he
had the credit of building up that vast British force
which was destined to be the determining factor in
the war.

At the hour of his death he was beyond doubt
the most dominant personality in the Empire, and
the greatest of Britain's public servants. His popular
prestige was immense, for he had that air of mystery
about him and that taciturnity which the ordinary
man loves to associate with a great soldier. His
splendid presence, his iron face, his silence, his

amazing record, raised him out of the ranks of mere notabilities to the select circle of those who even in their lifetime became heroes of romance. He was a lonely figure, with no talent for the facile acquaintanceships of the modern world ; but few men have inspired a more ardent affection among those who were admitted to the privilege of his friendship. Popular repute is apt to be melodramatic and to simplify unduly. Lord Kitchener was by no means the man of granite and iron whom the public fancy envisaged. He was a stern taskmaster, inflexibly just, and unfailingly loyal, but he had a deep inner fount of kindliness. He did not cultivate the gift of expression ; but now and then, as after the Vereeniging Peace Conference, he showed something like a genius for the fitting word. He had humour, too, of a kind which the world little realized —that sense of the comedy of situation which keeps a man's perspective true.

To his abilities it is likely that history will do ample justice. He had behind him mighty positive achievements—the conquest of the Sudan, the completion of the South African campaign, a singularly successful administrative career in Egypt, and, above all, the organization of Britain for her greatest war. But in his own day the popular judgment was as wide of the mark as to the exact quality of his genius as to the nature of his personality. The capture of Omdurman and the eulogies of a famous war correspondent had established him as the complete administrator, the master of details, the business man *in excelsis*. But it is probable that the true bent of his mind was not towards detail. He was not the perfect administrator, for he did not understand the art of delegating duties to others. He tended always to draw all work into his own capable hands. He was fond of short cuts and summary methods, and there were occasions when the result was confusion. His true genius lay in his foresight and imagination. That is why he was so brilliant an Oriental administrator, for he could read the native mind. That is why, in August 1914, when most people expected a short campaign, he declared that the war would last for three years, and made his plans accordingly. There were some in the British army, and there were some in the Allied forces, who ranked above him as scientific soldiers, learned in the latest military art. There were some who could have handled better than he a force in the field. There were those, too, who equally well could have organized the business side of an army. But there was no man living who saw the main issues so simply and clearly. He had the *flair* for the essentials, though he might err over details. He had the vision which is possible only to the rare few whose souls are of the spacious and simple cast and are undistracted by the tumult of petty absorptions. It is the most priceless gift which a leader can show, for " where there is no vision the people perish."

He had also a singular personality, which dominated without effort those who came into touch with it. No man of our time enjoyed a completer public confidence, and he had won it without any of the arts of the demagogue. A kind of daimonic force radiated from him and affected millions who had never seen him. Without being a politician, he had the greatest of the politician's gifts—the power of creating a tradition which, so to speak, multiplied his personality indefinitely, and made the humblest and remotest recognize in him their leader. In the dark days of August 1914 it is not too much to say that he was the one man to whom the nation turned, and without the magic of his name Britain's stupendous military effort could not have been made.

Of the many noble tributes to his memory one of the finest came from a journal published in the French trenches. To France the man who in his youth had fought in her ranks against Germany had become almost a figure of legend, and the manner of his death took captive her imagination. The great soldier of England lay at rest beneath those waves which England had ruled so long.

> " Sous l'if ou le cyprès ne cherchez pas la place
>   Où du dernier sommeil dort le grand Kitchener ;
>   Les noms qui sont gravés sur le marbre s'effacent ;
>   Mais il a pour tombeau l'immensité des mers.
>   Passagers ici-bas, nos pauvres mains sont prêtes
>   Avec des fleurs d'un jour à couronner son front,
>   Mais c'est la grande voix de la grande tempête
>   Qui, dans l'éternité, répétera son nom." *

* The following is a free translation :—

> " Cypress nor yew shall weave for him their shade ;
>   Cypress nor yew shall shield his quiet sleep ;
>   Marble must crack, and graven names must fade—
>   He for his tomb hath won the changeless deep.
>   We mortal pilgrims bring our transient gift,
>   Fast-fading flowers, as garlands for his fame ;
>   But 'tis the tempest and the thunderous drift
>   That to eternity shall sound his name."

CHAPTER CIV.

THE AUSTRIAN ATTACK IN THE TRENTINO.

Italy's true Achievement—The Nature of her Front—Political
Difficulties—Value of her Intervention—The Attack on
Gorizia, October–December 1915—The Winter Campaign in
the Mountains—Activity on Isonzo in March 1916—Capture
of Col di Lana—Fight for Adamello Ridges—Austrian Dispositions—The Austrian Offensive—Its Reasons—Italian
Position in Southern Trentino—Its Weakness—Italian Dispositions—Beginning of Bombardment—Italian Centre falls
back—Withdrawal South of the Posina—The Fight for the
Buole Pass—The Fight for Pasubio—The Struggle for the
Posina Ridges—Position on Sette Communi Plateau—Arsiero
and Asiago given up—Austria within Four Miles of Val Sugana—Cadorna gets his New Army—The Offensive checked
—Results of the Attack—Its Value for Italy—Beginning of
Brussilov's Advance in Galicia.

THE achievement of Italy during the first year
of war was too little appreciated by the world
at large, and even her Allies were in some
doubt as to its precise character. Her difficulties
from the start had been very great. She began with
a frontier so drawn at every point as to give the
advantage to the enemy. Her main thrust could
only be eastwards across the Isonzo; but, alone of
the Allies, she had her flank and her communications directly threatened should she pursue her
natural line of offensive. Hence she was compelled
to fight hard and continuously on two fronts—to
press against the Isonzo barrier, and at the same

time to win safety in Carnia, the Dolomites, and the Trentino. Napoleon in 1798 and Massena in 1805 did not dare to cross the Isonzo till Joubert in one case and Ney in the other had forestalled the danger of an enemy flank attack from the hills. Italy's battle-front was, therefore, not less than five hundred miles from the Stelvio in the north to the sea at Montfalcone. Moreover, they were five hundred of the most difficult miles in Europe. Beyond the Isonzo lay that strange plateau of the Carso, which had long been selected for the Austrian defence. There trenches and shelters were hewn out of the solid rock, since ordinary field entrenchments were impossible in a land where there was no soil. The enemy had to be ousted from his hold before any advance could be made, and the campaign became in the strictest sense an attack upon a fortress. North of the Carso was the town of Gorizia, a formidable entrenched camp defended by 200,000 troops, and, with its flanking positions, showing a width of over sixty miles. North and west of the Isonzo was the long horseshoe of the mountain front. Every pass was, to begin with, in Austria's hands, and to win security the enemy had to be pressed back over the watershed. Moreover, on Italy's left flank the ominous salient of the Trentino ran down into the Lombard plain, and offered a choice of a hundred starting-points for an Austrian assault upon the Italian rear. In strategical anxieties and tactical difficulties the Italian battleground was one of the worst in the whole *terrain* of the campaign.

These military drawbacks found a counterpart in the condition of Italian politics. The great

majority of the nation was whole-heartedly for the
Allied cause ; but so far war had only been declared against Austria-Hungary, and Germany was
nominally not yet an enemy. The immense pur-
chase which Germany had won by her control of
Italian commerce and finance made a breach with
her unacceptable to many classes. This partial
avoidance of the main issue led to some fumbling
in Italian policy, and to the intrigues which always
attend indecision. Moreover, it prevented the army
from being what it was elsewhere, the whole nation
in arms. During the long and desperate winter
struggle the troops which, under Cadorna, held
their own so gallantly among Alpine snows and the
floods of the Isonzo, did not yet represent the true
sum of Italy's fighting strength.

If we realize the Italian difficulties, we shall do
justice to the magnitude of the achievement. Her
intervention was an invaluable contribution to the
Allied strategical purpose. She had drawn against
her thirty-eight Austrian divisions, and these included some of the best troops of the Dual Mon-
archy, such as the 14th Army Corps of Tirol. She
had drawn them to a front where they were more
or less segregated from the rest of the Austrian
forces, for the Italian *secteur* was not an extension
of the main Eastern front. Hence the Austrian
Staff were placed in the position that they could not,
after the German manner, move rapidly reinforcements to different parts of their line. Owing to the
divergent nationalities under their command, they
were unable to treat their armies as a homogeneous
whole which could be moved solely according to
military considerations. The existence of the Italian

front, therefore, hampered that mobility on which the Central Powers, holding the interior lines, chiefly relied.

During the winter there was a steady pressure along the whole line, even in regions where the weather seemed to compel inaction. October and November saw considerable activity in the Gorizia

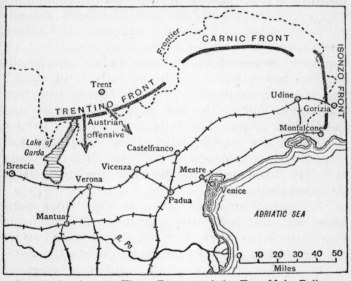

Sketch showing the Three Fronts and the Two Main Railway Lines of Communication for the Isonzo Front.

region, which led Western observers to predict the speedy fall of that fortress. On 21st October, after an artillery preparation of *Oct. 21, 1915.* fifty hours, the third main assault since the declaration of war was made on the Isonzo position. The fighting was fierce along the rim of the Doberdo plateau and towards San Martino, and some trenches were captured on the Podgora height. In three days 3,000 prisoners were taken. At the same time, in the Trentino, the troops descending from Monte Altissimo cut the Austrian communications by the direct road from Riva to Rovereto. The bombardment on the Isonzo continued for a fortnight, and great damage was done to Gorizia itself. Further trenches were gained on the Podgora height, and on 20th November the village of Oslavia, north-west of Gorizia, was carried, and on the Carso ground was won on the north slopes of Monte San Michele and southwest of San Martino. Till the end of the month the struggle went on ; but the enemy was now reinforced, and in the first days of December the battle died away. The Italians had won a narrow strip along the western edge of the Carso, and had improved their position at Podgora ; but they were still far from bursting through the formidable Austrian defences.*

Nov. 20.

For the main achievement of the winter campaign we must look to the great hills. It is probable that history has never seen such mountain warfare as was now waged from the Stelvio round the skirts of the Trentino, among the limestone crags of Cadore and Carnia, and down the dark gorges of the Upper Isonzo. During the summer and early autumn the main passes had been won by Italy. The great Austrian lateral railway through the Pusterthal was under the fire of the guns behind Cristallo. Far up into the glaciers, and on the icy ridges, were Italian observation posts directing the

* See the Italian semi-official survey printed as Appendix VI.

guns behind the cliffs, and the heavy guns themselves were often emplaced at heights usually reached
only by the mountaineer. There were batteries at
an elevation of 9,000 feet, of which each gun weighed
eleven tons, the carriage five tons, and the platform
thirty tons. Many of the engineering and transport feats almost surpass belief ; for not only did men
and guns reach unheard-of eyries, but they were
able to maintain themselves there during the winter
storms. It was difficult enough in the summer,
when the Alpini in their *scarpetti da gatta*, or string-
soled shoes, climbed the smooth white precipices
of Tofano and Cristallo ; but in winter, when ice
coated the rocks, and among the high peaks of the
Western Trentino avalanches hung poised on every
cliff, it became the sternest trial of human endurance. Every one who has mountaineered in the
Alps in winter is aware that extraordinary climbs
may be made, given fair weather conditions ; but
he knows too that the day must be picked, and that
Nature may not easily be defied. But the work of
Italy's mountain defenders went on by day and
night, and stayed not for the wildest weather. Food
and ammunition must be brought up to the high
posts at whatever cost.

Much was done by the *filorie*, or aerial cables, on
which a load of half a ton could travel, in the same
way as in Norway the hay crop is sent down from
the high *saeter* meadows to the deep-cut valleys.
But no mechanical device could seriously lessen the
constant difficulties and dangers. It must be remembered, too, that in the mountains the Italian
Alpini found no mean antagonists. Whoever knows
the hardy people of Tirol will not underrate their

hillcraft and courage. There were desperate encounters in that icy wilderness of which the tale has
not yet been told, and when the snow melted grim
sights were to be seen. On Monte Nero one morning the Italian line saw suddenly a new army on
the hillside standing in a strange attitude. They
were 600 Austrian corpses, frozen stiff, which the
summer sun had rescued from the shroud of
snow.

In the middle of March 1916 the guns began to
sound again on the Isonzo. Gorizia and the Doberdo
plateau were bombarded, and for a week or two there
were attacks and counter-attacks. But the spring
floods made progress difficult, and the only result
of the action was to inspire the Austrian Staff with
a firm belief that General Cadorna contemplated a
great offensive in this quarter as soon as summer had
come. The chief activity of the early spring was in
the hill country. The night of 17th April
April 17, saw one of the great mining exploits of
1916. the campaign. West of the Falzarego
Pass, which runs from Cortina to Bozen, stands a
bold, round-topped spur, just inside the Austrian
frontier, which commands all the western road. It is
called the Col di Lana, and in November 1915 its
summit was taken by Colonel Peppino Garibaldi.
But the summit could not be held, and while the
Italians controlled the greater part of the mountain,
the Austrians kept their foothold on the northern
slopes. It was resolved to blast the enemy from his
stronghold, and in the middle of January mining
operations were begun under the guidance of Don
Gelasio Caetani, a son of the Duke of Sermoneta
and a brother of Prince Teano. The tunnel took

three months to complete.   Before the end the
Austrians grew suspicious, and started countermining; but their direction was wrong.   On the
night of 17th April the Italian mine was exploded,
and the remnants of the Austrian position were
carried by infantry.   The crater thus formed was
150 feet wide and 50 feet deep.

About the same time a brilliant action was
fought far to the west, where the Adamello range
separates the streams that feed Lake Garda from
Italy.   The Austrians held the crest, and the Italians
were in position far down on the great Adamello
glacier, and on the rock ridges that cut it.   Colonel
Giordano, commanding an Alpini detachment, resolved to push the enemy from the crest.   On the
night of 11th April 300 Alpini left the Rifugio
Garibaldi on skis, and reached the *April* 11.
glacier in a whirlwind of snow.   The
place is 10,000 feet above the sea, and in April its
climate is Arctic.   After struggling on through the
night, they attacked the Austrian position in the
early morning, and drove them from the rocks of
the glacier.   This exploit was followed on 29th
April by a bigger movement.   In a *April* 29.
clear starlit night 2,000 Alpini followed
the same route, drove the Austrians from the main
crest, and, after severe fighting, in which they were
assisted by a battery of 6-inch guns which had been
brought up to the very edge of the glacier, dominated
the head of the Val di Genova, and so won a position on the flank of the Austrian lines in the Val
Giudicaria.   Colonel Giordano was promoted to
major-general, and fell a few weeks later in the
Trentino battles.

The Austrian front, under the command of the Archduke Eugene, was divided into three main sections. From the sea to Tolmino lay the 5th Army, under General Boroevitch von Bojna, including the 7th and 16th Corps. North from Tolmino to Carnia lay the 10th Army, under General von Rohr. The 14th (Tirol) Corps defended the Pusterthal line to the north of Cadore. In the Trentino itself lay two Austrian armies—those of Dankl and von Koevess: the whole under the command of the Archduke Charles, the heir to the Austrian throne. Between them these forces probably aggregated a million men, with 600,000 combatants in line. Throughout the winter there had been a gradual strengthening of one section of the front—that part of the Trentino between the Val Lagarina and the Val Sugana. Large numbers of batteries had been brought to the Folgaria and Lavarone plateaux south-west of the city of Trent. The infantry strength was also increased during April by picked troops from the whole Austrian front. The Italian Staff were aware of the concentration, but they anticipated no more than a local counter-attack, such as they had seen in April on the Isonzo. In that view they erred, for the Archduke Charles was preparing one of the major offensives of the war.

It is hard to be certain as to Austria's real purpose in the Trentino assault. One thing is clear—that Conrad von Hoetzendorff and his colleagues wholly underrated the capacity of Russia. There had grown up a tradition on the Eastern front that Russia was too weak in munitionment for any movement till late in the summer; otherwise no sane commander would have risked tying up some of his best troops in a mountain angle from which they could not quickly be extricated should the enemy threaten elsewhere. Austria took the view of von Falkenhayn, and von Falkenhayn thereby made a blunder which lost him his post. But having stated this, it is less easy to determine what Austria aimed at. In the Trentino she had accumulated a total of some 400,000 men, and out of that she had a striking force of fifteen picked divisions. The obvious objective for an enemy in the Trentino was the plain of Venetia, through which ran the two railway lines which were the main communications of the Isonzo front. The northern ran by Brescia, Verona, Vicenza, and Castelfranco to Udine ; the southern, by Mantua and Padua to Montfalcone. If one was cut, the Isonzo army would be crippled and compelled to retreat ; if both fell, it would be in deadly danger. But it is difficult to believe that, knowing the size of Cadorna's potential reserves, Austria still seriously thought of undertaking such an enterprise with fifteen first-line divisions.

A more probable explanation is that Austria wished to forestall that great Isonzo attack which the months of March and April had led her to fear. She may even have meditated herself a movement from Gorizia and the Carso, for it would appear from the evidence at our disposal that she looked on that north-eastern plain as the Achilles-heel of Italy. But her immediate purpose was to alarm Cadorna about his communications, and upset whatever plans he had made for the summer campaign. It was in essence the motive of Verdun, and the gossip may be dismissed which represented Austria as taking the bit between her teeth, and undertaking the adventure in defiance of the German Staff. She was, on the contrary, loyally playing the German game—to forestall by an immediate assault the combined Allied offensive which was Germany's greatest peril. As at Verdun, the army of attack was commanded by an heir-apparent, for dynasties and military interests were interwoven in Teutonic strategy. The Archduke Charles in his address to his troops described the enterprise as a " *Straf-expedition* " ; but that does not invalidate the view that its aim was offensive-defensive, and not purely offensive—prevention rather than conquest. Young princes since the beginning of time have hankered after grandiosity.

To understand what followed, we must examine in some detail the Italian position in the Southern Trentino at the beginning of May. From a point just south of Rovereto in the Val Lagarina it ran eastward up the Val Terragnolo, north of the mountain mass called Pasubio. Thence it stretched north-eastward just inside the Austrian frontier, facing the enemy lines on the Folgaria plateau. From the hill called Soglio d'Aspio it went due east and then north, just outside the old frontier line, to the Cima Manderiolo, from which point it ran north across the valley of the Brenta to Monte Collo, north-west of Borgo. Thence it passed north-east to the Val Calamento. The front is worth study, for it had elements of dangerous weakness. On the extreme left the position at the north end of the Zugna ridge —the peak called Zugna Torta—was a salient exposed to the enemy's fire from three sides. The left centre and centre were also precarious, being commanded by the admirable Austrian gun positions on the Folgaria and Lavarone plateaux. The whole front was really a string of advanced posts which any resolute attack must speedily push in. The true Italian front was the second line, which ran from the Zugna ridge to the Pasubio *massif*, along the hills north of the Val Posina to the Upper Astico, across the north and higher part of the Sette Communi plateau, reaching the Val Sugana east of Borgo, at the glen of the little river Maso. Here, again, the left centre was badly situated, for behind it there were long bare slopes falling to the Posina and Astico valleys.

Obviously the main peril came on the flanks, for in the Val Lagarina and the Val Sugana there were roads and railways to support an enemy advance. In these valleys the defensive positions were good ; but there was always the danger that they might be turned by a thrust of the enemy's centre through the intervening mountains. A glance at the map will show where the danger lay. There were three roads along which troops and guns could move. One—the best—ran from the Val Lagarina up the Vallarsa to Chiese, and thence by a good pass to the town of Schio just above the plain. Another ran from the Folgaria plateau down the glen of the Astico to the little town of Arsiero. A third ran from the Lavarone plateau down the Val d'Assa to the town of Asiago. Schio, Arsiero, and Asiago were all connected by light railways with the trunk line running through Vicenza, and Asiago was only eight miles from Valstagna in the valley of the Lower Brenta. To get the Schio road the Austrians must carry Pasubio, which commanded it. To win Arsiero was easier, but in order to debouch from it

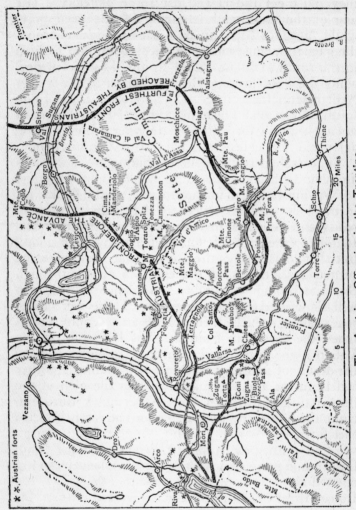

The Austrian Offensive in the Trentino.

they must get the ridge just south of it, the last line of the mountain defence. In the same way, while Asiago offered an easy prey, to make use of the gain they must clear the Sette Communi plateau to the south of it—so called from its seven villages, which long ago were a German settlement. In any great assault these three points—Pasubio, the ridge south of the Val Posina, and the Sette Communi upland—would form the last rallying ground of the defence. If they fell, the road to the plains was open.

The Italian front, held by the 1st Army at the moment of attack, was desperately short of guns, and its lines had by no means been skilfully drawn. General Roberto Brusati, who was in command, believed in the coming assault, but did not make adequate preparation to meet it. He received from Cadorna certain reinforcements, but he altogether miscalculated the weight of artillery which could be brought to bear on him. In April Cadorna himself moved his headquarters to the 1st Army, and investigated the position. Brusati was removed from his post, and succeeded by General Pecori-Giraldi, who proceeded to a drastic reorganization. Especially, Cadorna strengthened the flanks in the Val Lagarina and Val Sugana, which were obviously the vital points. But before the work could be completed the Archduke Charles had launched his attack.

The great bombardment began on 14th May. Over 2,000 guns, of which at least 800 were heavies, opened on a front of thirty miles. The Italian front line was blasted away, and *May* 14. from the 15-inch naval guns and the 420's in the Folgaria and Lavarone positions shells were thrown

into Asiago itself. The Italian advanced lines fell
back at once in the centre, but resisted fiercely on
the flanks at Zugna and west of Borgo. On the

May 15–16. 15th and 16th there was a severe struggle
on the Zugna ridge, and on the 18th
the Italian left retired from Zugna
Torta towards the Coni Zugna crest farther south.

May 17. Next day all the section from Monte
Maggio to Soglio d'Aspio was abandoned, and on the following day, the 19th, the

May 19. centre in the upper glen of the Astico
was driven from the position Monte
Toraro-Monte Campomolon-Spitz Tonezza. Things
went better on the right, but the defeat of the
centre meant that the Arsiero plateau must fall.
That day the Italian line ran from Coni Zugna over
the Pasubio *massif*, and then—waveringly—north of
the Val Posina and across the Sette Communi tableland to the Val Sugana.

On 20th May Cadorna decided to withdraw his
centre to a position well in the rear. The north side

May 20. of the Val Posina was no place to hold,
so the Italians fell back to the southern
ridge, and to a line in the Sette Communi east of
the Val d'Assa. This withdrawal was completed by

May 24. the 24th in good order; but the Austrian
advance did not allow the defence time
to prepare its new ground. Many prisoners had been
lost in the past days, and the casualties were heavy;
though the enemy had also suffered severely whenever
he came out from the shelter of his guns. By the

May 25. 25th the Austrians were violently attacking Coni Zugna and Pasubio, and had
made of the latter a salient, since they had pushed

up the Rovereto-Schio road between it and Coni
Zugna as far as the hamlet of Chiese under the
Buole Pass. If the advance continued, Pasubio
must fall; and if Pasubio fell, the whole Italian centre
south of the Val Posina was turned, and the way
was open to the Venetian plains.

Meantime Cadorna had summoned his reserves,
a new army, to assemble in and around Vicenza.
This was the 5th Army, which had been already
concentrated between the Tagliamento and the
Isonzo for the offensive against Gorizia. In ten
days it arrived on the skirts of the hills—a total of
little less than half a million men. But it could not
arrive before 2nd June—and to be ready so soon
was a splendid feat of organization and transport—
and it was necessary for Pecori-Giraldi to hold the
fort for the critical last week of May. Some local
reserves were brought to aid him, including one
division, which in a single night was moved by motor
from Carnia to Pasubio.

By the 25th, while Pasubio and the Posina position were threatened, the Italian right in the Val
Sugana had managed to retire in good order east of
Borgo to its prepared line on the east bank of the
Maso torrent. But the right centre in the Sette
Communi was in hard case. On the 25th and 26th
it was driven off all the heights east of the Val
d'Assa. On the 27th the Austrians were *May 27–*
south of the Galmarara, a tributary of *28.*
the Assa on the left bank. On the 28th
they had occupied the mountain called Moschicce,
just north of Asiago.

While things were going thus ill on the right
centre, the Italian left was fighting the action which

marked the critical point in the whole advance. For days a desperate struggle raged for Coni Zugna and Pasubio, and especially for the Pass of Buole, which would give the enemy access to the Lower Adige. There, in spite of the Austrian mastery in guns, the Italians—principally the 37th Division— managed to remain in their makeshift trenches till they could get to grips with the bayonet. Again and again the waves of attack rolled forward, broke, and ebbed. On 30th May came the climax. The May 30. Austrian infantry in masses assaulted the Pass of Buole ; but the defence did not yield one yard. On that day 7,000 Austrians fell, and in the week's fighting some 40 per cent. of their effectives perished. By their fortitude at this supreme moment the Italians had blunted the point of the whole Austrian spear-thrust.

But the battle was still far from its end. The enemy now endeavoured to take Pasubio, attacking on three sides—from the ridge of Col Santo, from Chiese, and from the Val Terragnolo by the Borcole Pass. His superiority in men was at least fourfold, and in guns far greater. But the resolute defence did not break. For three weeks in the snow of the ridges they battled heroically against odds, till the assault slackened, weakened, and then died away.

Meantime the Italian centre was scarcely less highly tried. The battleground lay in two sections —the left along the ridge which runs from Pasubio south of the Posina, the right across the Sette May 25. Communi tableland. On 25th May the Austrians took Bettale, on the Posina, and the height of Cimone, which dominates Ar-

siero. On the 28th they were across the Posina,
and fighting for the southern ridge, the *May* 28.
last line of defence before the plains.
On 30th May they won the peak of Pria Fora, one
of the points on the ridge, and to the *May* 30.
east were on the heights just north of
Arsiero. By that day the Italians had evacuated
both Arsiero and Asiago, and at the latter place
the enemy was east of the Val Campomolon, and
within four miles of the Val Sugana, well to the rear
of the Italian front in that valley. In the centre he
was all but looking down on Schio. On 1st June
an Austrian Army Order informed the *June* 1.
troops that only one mountain remained
between them and the Venetian plain. Three days
later the Italians were driven east of the Val Canaglia, to the south-east of Arsiero. The enemy was
only eighteen miles from Vicenza and the trunk line.

But on 3rd June General Cadorna announced
that the Austrian offensive had been checked. He
had got his new army ; moreover, the *June* 3.
troops already in line had taken the
measure of the enemy. The Italian position now
ran from Zugna Torta to Pasubio, then well south
of the Posina to the Astico, south-east of Arsiero,
east of the Val Canaglia, along the southern rim of
the Asiago plateau to east of the Val Campomolon,
and then north along the edge of the tableland that
drops to the Val Sugana. While the new army was
preparing its attack, a ceaseless struggle went on on
the Posina heights and in the Sette Communi. In
the first sector the enemy sought to reach Schio and
the plains, and in the second to turn the Italian right
in the Val Sugana. If this fighting represented the

great effort of the Austrian offensive, it was not less the supreme effort of the heavily-tried defence. On

June 4. the night of 4th June Ciove, the last Italian position south of the Posina, was violently assailed; and again on 12th June, when the whole ridge was blasted by the great guns. On the

June 13. 13th the attack was renewed without success; but the Italian brigade which held the place lost 70 per cent. of its strength. In the Sette Communi the main points of attack were Monte Cengio, the Val Canaglia, and the Val Frenzele, where the enemy was within four miles of Valstagna in the Val Sugana. On 15th June,

June 15- 17. and for the two days following, the Genoese troops on Monte Pau, the southern edge of the Sette Communi, repulsed what proved to be the last of the great Austrian assaults. The action declined into an artillery duel, and a week later Cadorna had begun to move forward in his counter-offensive.

The Austrian attack in the Trentino had deferred—but not for long—Italy's main offensive plan, and in so far it had succeeded in its purpose. It had been costly to the defence, and had shown some of the bloodiest combats of the war. Shelling with great guns among those peaks was a desperate business; for whereas elsewhere there was deep soil to limit the effects of the percussion, there among rock walls the result was as shattering as on the deck of a steel battleship. The test proved and tempered Italy's resolution. It awoke those sections of the people who were still apathetic to the realities of war, and—as is usual in a democracy when things go wrong—it led to the formation of a new Ministry. Signor Salandra was defeated, and a Cabinet was formed under Signor Boselli, with Baron Sonnino still in charge of Foreign Affairs. Through the whole Italian army went a wave of honest pride, which is the due of those who have suffered much and held their ground. No better preparation could have been sought for the coming offensive.

But the vital consequences of the Austrian attack were to be found in the field of general strategy. She had crowded her men and guns into a deep salient, served by few railways, and some hundreds of miles from her main battleground. In grips there with a determined enemy, she could not easily or quickly break off the battle should danger threaten elsewhere. And danger, deadly and unlooked for, speedily threatened. For on Sunday, 4th June, the day after Cadorna *June* 4. proclaimed the check of the invasion, Brussilov had launched his thunderbolts on the Galician front.

CHAPTER CV.

THE SECOND BATTLE OF VERDUN.

Position of Battle after 9th April—Petain succeeds Langle de
Cary—Nivelle succeeds Petain—Lull during April—French
Position on 1st May—Attacks on Hills 304 and 287—Crest
of Hill 304 lost—Attack on Mort Homme—Summit relin-
quished—New French Position—The French Attack on Fort
Douaumont — General Mangin's Division — Destruction of
German Kite Balloons—French 129th Regiment take the Fort
—Bavarians retake it—Final Attack on Mort Homme—
Cumières taken and retaken—Position on Left Bank at End
of May—Germans take Vaux Fort—Major Raynal's heroic
Defence—Thiaumont Fort taken—Fleury Village entered—
French retake Thiaumont—End of the Great Battle—Fight-
ing during July and August—The Meaning of Verdun for
Germany and for France.

THE First Battle of Verdun ended on 9th April
with the complete defeat of the German purpose. Defeat, indeed, had befallen the Imperial Crown Prince weeks before, ever since the
April 9. merciless usury of Petain had forced his
enemy to pay a price in excess of any
possible gain. Verdun had long ago passed out of
the sphere of pure strategy into that of politics. It
had become a fatal magnet, drawing to itself the
German strategic reserves, not for military ends,
but because the High Command had burned its
boats and could not retire. They had staked their
reputation on the capture of the little city, and

without grave loss of credit could not break off the action. Towards the end of April the French Staff believed that the battle was virtually over ; but they overestimated the capacity of their opponents for the rigour of the military game. Germany dared not take the heroic course—her commitments were too deep ; and a second battle was about to begin, not less desperate than the first, in which her sole purpose was, by blind blows on a narrow front, to wear down the French strength. The significance of Verdun itself had long since gone. It mattered very little for the main interests of the campaign whether or not a German soldier set foot in its shattered streets. Germany's own hope was to weaken what she still believed to be the waning man-power of France, and to forestall the combined Allied attack which since Christmas had been her nightmare.

In April General Petain succeeded Langle de Cary as commander of the central *secteur*, from Soissons to Verdun. His promotion to one of the three group commands was a well-deserved tribute to his superb achievement. He was succeeded in the command of the 2nd Army by General Nivelle, who, like Petain, had at the outbreak of war been only a colonel, in command of the 5th Infantry Regiment. Three months later he had become a brigadier, in February 1915 he commanded the 6th Division, and a little later became a general of division, in command of the 3rd Corps.

As we have seen, during April there was no great action in the Verdun section, but only minor attacks and counter-attacks and an intermittent bombard-

ment. At the end of the month the French line lay
as follows. From Avocourt, in the west, it ran
through the eastern fringes of the Avocourt Wood
covering the famous redoubt, along the slope of Hill
287, and across the northern slopes of Hill 304;
dipped into the ravine of the Esnes branch of
the Forges brook; climbed the western slopes of
Mort Homme, covering the summit; then fell back
to the south of the Goose's Crest, and reached the
Meuse at Cumières. On the right bank of the river
the line ran on the south side of the Côte du Poivre,
through the wood of Haudromont, along the south
side of the Douaumont ridge, just short of the crest;
dipped into the Vaux glen, passing through the
western skirts of Vaux village, and then ran south
along the eastern scarp of the Heights of the Meuse,
covering Vaux Fort.

The position on the left bank was curious, and
demands a moment's consideration. At Hills 287
and 304 the French front was in the shape of a
horseshoe facing north, with the ends in Avocourt
Wood and in the gully of the Esnes brook, and
the centre flung well forward on the north side of
the ridge. East of Mort Homme the position was
reversed. There the German front was the horseshoe facing south, having one end in the Esnes
gully, and the other north of Cumières, while the
centre bulged over the crest well into the Wood
of Cumières. Obviously this position, in the shape
of the letter S lying on its side, exposed both sides
to the danger of flanking attacks, and it was the
object of the German command to straighten it out.
Such a straightening would give them Hill 304 and
Mort Homme, which had been the key-points of

the first battle in this section. But at the end of
April these had not the importance they bore in
early March. The main French position was now
well behind, towards the Charny ridge. It should
be remembered that on the left bank of the Meuse
the Germans were still fighting for positions cor-
responding to those which they had won on the
right bank in the first week of the battle. The Hill
304–Mort Homme line was paralleled on the east
by the Louvemont ridge. Charny was the line
parallel to Douaumont.

The Second Battle of Verdun divides itself
naturally into three main episodes. First came the
attempt of the German right wing to carry Hill 304
and Mort Homme, and press the French back on
their last position—an attempt which succeeded in
its immediate but failed in its ultimate purpose.
The second, simultaneous with the first operation,
was a vigorous counter-attack by the French on the
Douaumont ridge. The third—the last phase of
the battle—was a concentrated German assault from
Douaumont against the last line covering Verdun,
which gave them the Fort of Vaux, the work of
Thiaumont, and for a moment the village of Fleury,
and brought them within four miles of the walls
of Verdun.

After a week of inaction there began on the
3rd of May a steady and violent bombardment of
the north slope of Hill 304, more than *May* 3.
a hundred German batteries concen-
trating on the front between Hill 287 and the Esnes
brook. Not only were the French front lines bombarded, but the crest of the slope behind them
became one mass of spouting volcanoes, which re-

sulted in changing the shape of the sky-line to an observer looking north from Verdun. All that night the fire continued ; the trenches were obliterated, and the defence sheltered as best it could in shell holes. There was a lull on the morning *May 4.* of the 4th, and then the artillery began again, and continued with increasing fury till the afternoon. At four o'clock reconnoitring parties of German infantry advanced, and were beaten back by French rifle fire. At five o'clock the enemy made a massed attack. Most of the French advanced troops had been buried, their rifles broken, and their machine guns put out of action by the bombardment. The result was that the Germans occupied a considerable stretch of the first lines north of Hill 304. That same day the French had themselves attacked at Mort Homme, and pushed their left horn forward.

On the night of the 4th there was a brilliant French counter-attack at Hill 304, led by Lieutenant-Colonel Odent, who fell in the action. It pushed the enemy back at the point of danger which he held just above the Esnes ravine. On the 5th the *May 5.* German bombardment moved a little westward, and attacked Hill 287 and the ragged little coppice called the Camard Wood, just south of the Haucourt-Avocourt road. There lay the French 66th Regiment of Infantry, one of whose captains has described that devastating fire. It began at four o'clock in the morning, and lasted till 3.30 p.m. " The dug-out in which I was was hewn out of solid rock, but it swayed like a boat on a stormy sea, and you could not keep a candle alight in it. The Camard Wood that morning had had the appearance of a wood, though all tattered and broken; but by the evening it had lost all semblance of anything but a patch of earth." At 3.30 p.m. the enemy's infantry attacked; but the heroic 66th and 32nd Regiments had still a sting left in them. With their rifle fire they halted the advancing waves, and then small parties of gallant men leaped from the rubble of their trenches and charged with the bayonet. It was sufficient to halt the enemy's advance. That night and the next day there was a lull, except for the steady bombardment.

On Sunday, 7th May, came a more formidable assault. It was delivered on all three sides of Hill 304, from the Wood of Avocourt, from the direction of Haumont, and in the *May 7.* ravine of the Esnes stream between Hill 304 and Mort Homme. An intense bombardment began at dawn, and a barrage cut off all communication with the rear. The front on Hill 304 was held on the left by the French 114th Regiment and on the right by the 125th, the men of La Vendée and Poitou. The Germans attacked with the equivalent of an army corps, by far the most considerable attempt yet made in this part of the front. Five times during that Sunday they advanced, and five times they were thrown back. In the last attack they carried the communication trench east of Hill 304, and pushed up the ravine. The French promptly counter-attacked, and after a stern struggle lasting well into the darkness they recovered the communication trench, and by the morning of the 8th were able to consolidate their line. But that day's fighting had altered the position. The crest of

Hill 304 was so bare and shell-swept that it could not be retained, and the French line now ran just south of it, though they had advanced posts still on the summit ridge. That same day there was an action on the right bank of the Meuse, between Haudromont Wood and Douaumont, where the Germans won a slight advantage. North of Thiaumont Farm they carried the French first line for 500 yards on both sides of the Fleury-Douaumont road.

Thereafter for some days the fighting on the left bank became desultory. On 17th May the *May* 17. Germans, after their usual fashion, having failed in their frontal attack on Hill 304, set themselves to turn it from the direction of Avocourt Wood. The action began at six in the evening, and very soon it spread over the whole front from Avocourt to the Meuse. On the 18th *May* 18. there were repeated attacks on the west flank of Hill 304, and also on the northeast from the Esnes glen. On the 20th the bombardment became especially severe on *May* 20. Mort Homme. It will be remembered that while the Germans held Hill 265 the French held the true summit, Hill 295, but held it as a salient, for their flanks fell back sharply on both sides of it. About two in the afternoon the German infantry attacked the salient from north-east and north-west, and carried the French front lines. In the eastern part they were driven out again ; but in the west they held their ground, and pushed on towards the French second line along the slopes of Mort Homme directly overlooking the Esnes brook. These attacks were delivered with great

resolution, with large numbers of men, and with
utter recklessness of loss. By Sunday, 21st May,
the summit of Mort Homme had passed   *May* 21.
from French hands, and their line now
lay along the southern slopes. That same day the
enemy won some ground south of Hill 287, and
made stupendous efforts to push his way up the

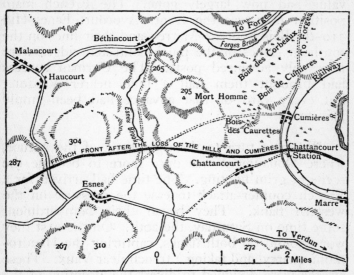

The Hill 287, Hill 304, Mort Homme, Cumières Position.

Esnes glen. But the impetus had slackened, and
the French were comfortable enough in their new
positions.

That fight for Mort Homme was one of the
most costly incidents of the whole battle. The
Germans between Avocourt and Cumières used at
least five divisions, partly drawn from the famous
1st Bavarian Corps, which had lately been on the

British front. Their losses were incalculable. The ravine of the Esnes was cumbered with dead, and there were slopes on Hill 304 and on Mort Homme where the ground was raised several metres by mounds of German corpses. The French casualties were high, but small in proportion to the enemy's. The two crests were lost, but their value had now largely gone. The French main position now was the front—Avocourt–Esnes–Hill 310–the Bois Bourrus–Marre—and their lines on the southern slopes of the much-contested ridges were now only advanced posts. The German success had brought them half a mile nearer Verdun ; but every yard of that advance had been amply paid for.

We must turn to the right bank of the Meuse, where Douaumont was once more to become the scene of grim fighting. The time had arrived for a French counter-attack to ease the pressure on the western flank. They began their bombardment some time on Saturday, the 20th. On the 21st they won ground on both flanks, capturing the Haudromont quarry, and taking a trench near Vaux. These attacks were designed to divert the attention of the enemy from the massing of troops on the French centre, opposite Douaumont Fort. The troops chosen for the principal attack were the 5th Division of the 3rd Corps, the men of Normandy, who on 3rd April had retaken the Caillette Wood. It was one of the most famous of French divisions, commanded by General Mangin, who had been with Marchand on his great African journey ; had fought under Lyautey in Morocco ; and had won great

honour in the Labyrinth fighting of 1915. On 21st
April he had issued an order to his men : " You
are about to reform your depleted ranks. Many of
you will return home, and will bear with you to
your families the warlike ardour and the thirst for
vengeance which inspire you. But there is no rest
for us French so long as the barbarous enemy treads
the sacred soil of our fatherland. There is no peace
for the world till the monster of Prussian militarism
has been laid low. Therefore prepare yourselves
for new battles, when you will have full confidence
in your superiority over an enemy whom you have
so often seen to flee and surrender before your
bayonets and grenades. You are certain of that
now. Any German who enters a trench of the
5th Division is dead or a prisoner ; any ground
seriously attacked by the 5th Division is captured ground. You march under the wings of
Victory."

The assault was fixed for Monday, 22nd May.
As the sun rose the German kite balloons appeared
in regular lines over the horseshoe of
upland. But at 8 a.m. a French airplane *May* 22.
squadron was seen hovering above the German
" sausages." They had with them a bomb, now
used for the first time, which in falling burst into
a shower of lesser bombs, each of which in turn
gave out minute particles of a burning chemical. In
a few minutes six of the German kite balloons had
exploded in flames. The infantry, waiting in the
trenches, watched the spectacle with joy. " We
have now bandaged the Boches' eyes," said one to
another. The Germans, scenting the new peril,
kept up a ceaseless fire of shrapnel, to which the

French replied, till the firmament twanged like a taut fiddle-string. At ten minutes to twelve precisely the men of the 10th Brigade of the 3rd Division leaped from their trenches.

The whole operation had been most skilfully planned. The French were close up to the fort, only some 350 yards distant. The Germans had dug trench lines south of it, but it would appear that these and the wire entanglements had been

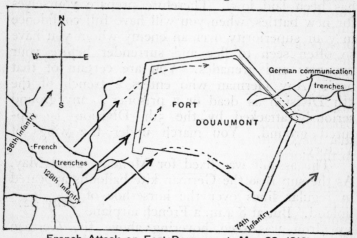

French Attack on Fort Douaumont, May 22, 1916.

largely destroyed by the French fire. The 129th Regiment of Infantry were directed against the fort itself, while on the left the 36th Regiment and on the right the 74th Regiment moved in support. The French streamed from their cover in open order, and with unfaltering resolution made straight for the fort. The 129th Regiment in ten minutes was into the south-west angle of the defence. At noon precisely a Bengal light was burned, and the

watchers behind knew that the centre had won its
objective.

On the left the 36th Regiment stormed all the
German trenches up to the Douaumont-Fleury
road. Inside the fort the 129th pushed on, fighting
from yard to yard of the honeycombed debris.
They took all the western and southern parts, and
the north side up to the northern angle. Engineers
were put in to organize the defence, and machine-
gun battalions were brought up to hold the captured bastions. In the first hour over a hundred
prisoners were sent back from the fort. The only
hitch was on the right, where the 74th Regiment
found a harder task. Their left had advanced
rapidly ; but their right was hung up by the cross-
fire from the German trenches, where the bombardment had been less effective. The result was
that the Germans were able to maintain themselves
in the north-eastern corner.

All day the fighting in the fort went on. The
French by the evening held two-thirds of the position, and had consolidated their defence. The
counter-attack did not come till darkness had
fallen. About 10 p.m. great masses of German
troops assembled east of Haudromont Wood, and a
furious bombardment was directed on the French
lines west of the fort. An infantry attack followed,
which won a little ground. In the fort itself the
new garrison won some yards during the darkness.
From daybreak on the 23rd there was a *May 23.*
steady bombardment, and many infantry
attacks on the position. But the 129th Regiment,
though losing heavily, clung to their gains, and
when next morning the whole brigade was relieved,

it had the proud consciousness that it had yielded
not an inch of the ground it had won.
May 24. On that day, however, two fresh Bavarian
divisions came up in the cover of the ravines in the
Wood of La Vauche and the Bezonvaux Glen, and
attacked in front and in flank. It was not Nivelle's
plan to continue a costly struggle beyond the point
which in his eyes marked the profitable limit. The

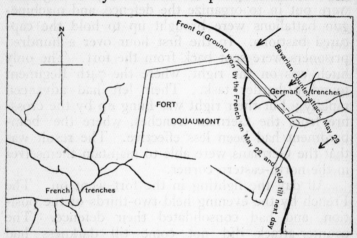

FORT
DOUAUMONT

Front of Ground won by the French on May 22, and held till next day

Bavarian counter attack, May 23

German trenches

French trenches

N

Counter-attack on Fort Douaumont, May 25th.

fort was retaken by the Germans, but the French
managed to retain on its east and west flanks some
of the trenches they had won.

Meantime the battle had waxed hotter on its
western flank. On Tuesday, the 23rd, the Germans
made a great effort to debouch from the
May 23. new positions they had won at Mort
Homme, and to straighten their front. Under a
terrific curtain fire from the French heavy guns they

attempted to push their left wing between the
Meuse and the hill into Cumières, and to advance
their right wing up the Esnes ravine. Again and
again they failed, for they could not establish themselves close enough to the French to forbid the
latter the use of their high-explosive barrage. But
at last, in the Esnes glen, largely by means of liquid
fire, they managed to carry the French front trenches.
During the night the German left, debouching from
the woods of Cumières and Caurettes, and pushing
along the Meuse bank, managed to gain a footing
in Cumières village. This, it will be remembered,
they had temporarily achieved before in the great
attack of April 9th. The place became a slaughter-
house, and the day of Wednesday, 24th *May 24.*
May, was one of the bloodiest since the
opening of the battle. By the evening the enemy
had won all Cumières, and had pushed his infantry
along the railway line almost to Chattancourt Station. A French counter-attack drove him back
to Cumières, the fighting being desperate in the
thickets and the low ground between the railway
and the river. The French main position was now
defined as Chattancourt—the south slopes of Hill
304—the south slopes of Hill 287—and Avocourt.
Both Mort Homme and Hill 304 were lost.

Till the end of the month the struggle continued.
On the evening of Friday, the 26th, the French,
attacking from the east, got into the *May 26–*
skirts of Cumières village. On Sunday *28.*
evening, the 28th, there was an abortive
German attack from the Crows' Wood against the
French trenches on the south slopes of Mort Homme.
After that there came a great bombardment, which

lasted through most of Monday, the 29th—the hundredth day of the battle. At three in the afternoon of that day German forces, estimated at the strength of two corps, attacked all along the front between Avocourt and the river, in a great attempt to drive the French from their position on the south slopes of Hill 304 and Mort Homme. There were now five fresh divisions in action—two of them being from the general reserve at Cambrai, and two from the 6th Army—and the enemy's immediate aim was to carry the salient between Mort Homme and Cumières. It was the last great effort on the western side, and it won only the ground which artillery fire had made untenable. The French first-line trenches south of the Caurettes Wood were obliterated. There was also a big attack from Cumières towards Chattancourt, which French counter-attacks drove back to its old line. In those days there was seen what was up to date the heaviest bombardment of the whole campaign. Both in number of shells and in casualties in a limited area all records were surpassed. But no result was obtained. On the last day of May the French position was unbroken ; they had not even been forced back upon their main defences; and the road to Verdun by the left bank of the Meuse was as firmly held as when, on 2nd March, the guns first opened from the Wood of Forges.

May 29.

May 31.

The battle was to end as it had begun—on the Heights of the Meuse. While the struggle had been furious at Mort Homme the Germans had made certain useful gains on the right bank. On 25th

May they had carried Haudromont quarry and extended their hold across the upper part of
Thiaumont ravine. On the 27th they *May* 25.
pushed their right wing to the south-west border of
that part of the big Haudromont Wood
which was called indiscriminately the *May* 27.
Wood of Thiaumont and the Wood of Nawé. On
Monday, the 29th, the heavy guns began
near Vaux a "preparation" which warned *May* 29.
Nivelle of what was coming. With mathematical
exactness the German effort had swung from flank
to flank, and the failure which was presently announced on the left bank meant a new effort on
the right. There they were within five miles of
Verdun, and the recapture of Douaumont Fort and
their possession of the rest of the Douaumont crest
gave them direct observation over all the intervening ground. From about the same position which
they held on 26th February they were to make, after
a hundred days, their final effort to gain what they
had promised themselves to win in four.

The German plan was an advance in front and
flank to turn the inner fortified line which defended
the city, and to make the flanking movement possible
they must first carry the fort of Vaux. That fort,
since Douaumont was lost, had become the key-point
of the French defence on the plateau. Its fire covered
the glen of Vaux, and all the eastern approaches
to the great fort of Souville. For twenty-six
hours the enemy guns played on the
French lines, and then on 1st June their *June* 1.
infantry carried the remains of the Caillette Wood,
won the ground south of Vaux Pond, and fought
their way into the Fumin Wood. At the same time

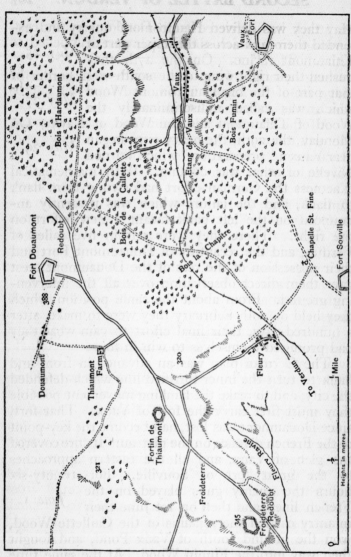

Second Battle of Verdun.—Ground over which the Germans advanced from Douaumont and Vaux.

an attack was delivered from Damloup in the east, a village from which the French were compelled to retire. The German aim was to make two converging assaults—from the north-west along the ridge from the Fumin Wood, and from the south-east up the gully from Damloup.

All the day of Friday, the 2nd, and Saturday, the 3rd, the contest continued. Wave after wave of Bavarian infantry surged up the hillsides, only to be mown down by the French fire. *June 2–5.* The fort had long ago been smashed by the heavy guns, for since March the enemy had directed on it a daily average of 8,000 shells ; but in the deep cellars the little garrison, under Major Raynal, continued their resistance. The place was as bare and open as a target buoy at sea, and after the 2nd, when the Germans won the Fumin ridge, there was no direct communication between the defence and the French lines.

This isolation had not been achieved without a desperate struggle. Scattered sections of trench, which till occupied prevented complete envelopment, were held by detachments of the 101st Regiment for three days, under torrents of bombs and a fire of high explosives which observers likened to a tropical downpour. It was not till 9 p.m. on 5th June that this gallant remnant retired from a fight which began early on the morning of 1st June.

By the 2nd, as we have seen, the fort was cut off from news, for no dispatch-bearer could cross the zone of death. The defence tried to establish a system of signals, but the troops a mile away could not see them. A volunteer managed to make his way out, and, by shifting the position of the

signallers at the other end, established some kind
of communication. A young officer named Bessett
also made his way out with a report, and returned
to join his comrades. Another most gallant man,
a stretcher-bearer of the 124th Division called
Vanier, worked patiently among the wounded,
dressing their wounds and hiding them in crevices
among the ruins. When there were no more wounded
to tend he went out to fetch water, for thirst was the
supreme torment. Four hundred men had taken
refuge in the fort, and the garrison numbered 150;
the air was thick with fumes and dust; every throat
was parched, and every drop of water had to be
brought from a distance through a land churned
by great shells into the likeness of a yeasty sea.

For five days Major Raynal and his men performed the patently impossible. Presently the
enemy won the outer walls; but the main building
was still defended, and a machine gun in every
cranny made it death for the invaders to enter the
courtyard. The fight was now largely subter-
ranean. The enemy let down baskets of grenades
to a level with the loopholes, and tried to swing
them through the openings so as to explode inside.

June 6. The limit of human endurance came on
Tuesday, the 6th. Raynal sent his last
message : " We are near the end. Officers and men
have done their whole duty. *Vive la France !* "
Vanier, that incomparable *brancardier*, managed to
escape with a few wounded through a grating; and,
after perilous adventures while crawling through the
enemy's ground, most of the party reached the
French lines. " Better dead than the Boches' prisoner " was Vanier's greeting to his colonel. That was

the last news from the fort. Raynal was removed to Mainz, and permitted by his captors to retain his sword. He was made Commander of the Legion of Honour by the French Republic, and at a special review at the Invalides the insignia of his new honour was conferred upon his wife.

The capture of Vaux Fort saw the beginning of a furious German assault upon the whole section from Thiaumont eastwards. The direct objective was Fort Souville, which had now become the main outwork of Verdun. The French front on 7th June ran from Hill 321 below the Côte du Poivre and the Côte de Froide Terre, *June 7.* through the *fortin* of Thiaumont, along the slopes defined by the woods of Chapitre, Fumin, and Laufée, and then south along the fringes of the hills east of Eix. Between the Côte de Froide Terre and the plateau where stood the forts of Souville and Tavannes was a deep-cut hollow, down which ran the road from Vaux to Verdun. The village of Fleury lay on the western lip of this ravine. The easiest and most open approach to Souville was by way of Fleury and the western ridge, for on the east the woods gave strong defensive positions.

For four days there was a lull. Then on the night of Sunday, the 11th, after a bombardment, the enemy managed to *June 11.* gain a little ground in the Fumin Wood. Next day the assault was on the other flank, delivered by a division and a half of Ba- *June 12.* varian and Pomeranian troops. A bit of the French line on Hill 321 west of Thiaumont was captured, and the enemy was within 3¾ miles of Verdun. All through the week Thiaumont and the adjacent slopes

of Hills 321, 316, and 320 were the theatre of heavy
fighting. The great effort came on Friday, 23rd

June 23.   June. At eight o'clock in the morning
a hundred thousand men were flung
against a front of three miles. The French right
stood firm, but the left was driven back between
Hill 320 and Hill 321, and Thiaumont Fort fell.
Meantime the German centre, coming down the
ravine from the Wood of Caillettes, attacked Fleury
village, and got into its outskirts; but a French
counter-attack, admirably timed, drove back the
invaders. The position in the evening was that
the German centre stood out in a wedge towards
Fleury, some eight hundred yards in advance of
their general front.

That day General Nivelle, foreseeing the last
desperate effort, issued an order to his army: " The
hour is decisive. The Germans, hunted down on
all sides, are launching wild and furious attacks on
our front, in the hope of reaching the gates of Verdun before they themselves are assailed by the united
forces of the Allies. You will not let them pass, my
comrades. The country demands this further supreme effort. The army of Verdun will not allow
itself to be intimidated by shelling, or by the German infantry whom for four months it has beaten
back. The army of Verdun will keep its fame un-
tarnished." His confidence was not misplaced; but
the last week of June saw a mad crescendo in the
German assault. On 24th June the enemy again

June 24.   got into Fleury, and the two sides faced
each other in its streets. Meantime the
advance from Hills 320 and 321 on the Froide
Terre ridge was firmly held, and the French made

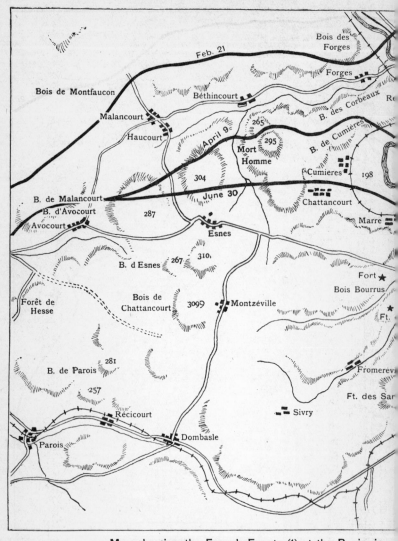

Map showing the French Fronts (1) at the Beginning
of the Battle, April 9th; and (3) on June 3

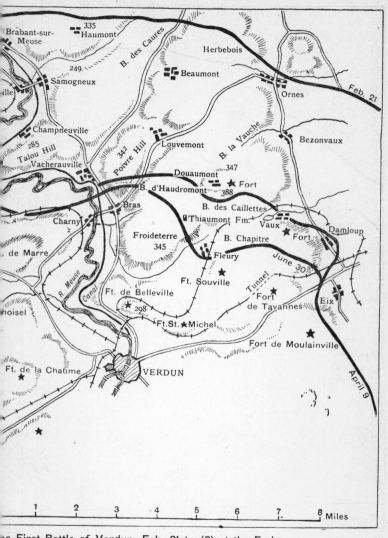

the First Battle of Verdun, Feb. 21st; (2) at the End
in the Final Stage of the Second Battle.

some small progress towards Thiaumont. On the last day of June, about ten in the morning, with a brilliant effort they pushed through the German barrage, regained Thiau- *June 30.* mont Fort, and held it against all counter-attacks.

The rest of the story may be briefly told. During July and August the Verdun volcano had moments of eruption, but the centre of gravity had moved elsewhere. The Germans at the beginning of July were still in Fleury, and on the 12th of the month their centre delivered an attack *July 12.* on a 3,000 yards front from Fleury to the Chapitre Wood with the effectives of six regiments, and gained a little ground at the Chapelle St. Fine, 1,000 yards north-west of Souville. On Tuesday, 3rd August, it was the turn of *Aug. 3.* the French to counter-attack. On Thursday they regained Fleury village, pushed their left well along Hill 320 to the south-east of Thiaumont, and increased the number of prisoners captured since 1st August to 1,750. This meant that the German central wedge was now flattened in. During August the fighting swayed backwards and forwards, and on Tuesday, 8th August, the Germans were back in small parts of Thiaumont, *Aug. 8.* and a day or two later again entered Fleury. From the latter place they were promptly ejected, and from Thiaumont they were ousted a few days later. The initiative was now wholly in the hands of Nivelle. Whatever the enemy won he won at great cost, and he held his gains only so long as the French cared to permit him.

The recapture of Thiaumont work on the last

day of June, the 130th day of the struggle, may be
taken as the logical end of the Battle of Verdun.
The fighting which followed was the backwash of
the great action, the last desperate efforts of a
baffled enemy who had lost all strategic purpose,
and the first forward movement of the triumphant
defence. The confession of defeat came two months
later, when von Falkenhayn, the originator of the
policy, was dismissed from office, and all Germany
saw in his retirement the penalty of this particular
failure. The battle—by far the greatest single action
fought in this campaign or any other—had more
than served its purpose. It had sucked in and
destroyed the bulk of Germany's free strategic
reserves. It had tided over the months of waiting
while France's allies were completing their preparations. The scene was about to change from the
shattered Verdun uplands to the green hills of
Picardy, and the main battle was on the eve of
transference from the Meuse to the Somme. Even
as the weary and dusty *fantassins* scrambled over the
debris of Thiaumont, a hundred miles to the north-
west on a broad front the infantry of France and
Britain were waiting to cross their parapets.

The citadel by the Meuse had been for Germany
a will-o'-the-wisp to lead her to folly and death.
But as the weeks passed it became for France also
a watchword, an oriflamme to which all eyes could
turn, a mystic symbol of her resolution. It was a
sacred place, and its wardenship was the test of her
devotion. Mankind must have its shrines, and that
thing for which much blood has been spilled becomes holy in our eyes. Over Verdun, as over
Ypres, there will brood in history a strange *aura*,

the effluence of the supreme sacrifice, the splendid
resolution, the unyielding fortitude of the tens of
thousands who died before her gates. Her little
hills are consecrated for ever by the immortal dead.

> " Heureux ceux qui sont morts sur un dernier haut lieu
>   Parmi tout l'appareil des grandes funérailles ;
>   Heureux ceux qui sont morts pour les cités charnelles,
>   Car elles sont le corps de la cité de Dieu." *

* Charles Péguy.

APPENDICES

APPENDIX I.

CTESIPHON AND KUT.

SIR JOHN NIXON'S DISPATCH.

WAR OFFICE, May 10, 1916.

THE following dispatch from General Sir John Nixon, K.C.B., on the operations in Mesopotamia in October, November, and December 1915, has been forwarded by the Government of India for publication :—

General Headquarters,
I.E.F. " D," 17th January 1916.

From

General Sir John Nixon, K.C.B., A.D.C., General Commanding Indian Expeditionary Force " D,"

To

The Chief of the General Staff,

Army Headquarters,

India.

SIR,

I have the honour to forward a report on the operations in Mesopotamia during the months of October, November, and December 1915.

2. In my last dispatch I described events up to October 5th. On that date the Turkish Army under Nur-Ed-Din, which had been defeated at Kut-Al-Amarah, had reached a previously prepared position astride the Tigris at Ctesiphon, where it received reinforcements ; and our advanced troops under Major-General Townshend reached Aziziyah (30 miles east of Ctesiphon).

3. During the next six weeks reinforcements, supplies, and transport animals were brought up to Kut and Aziziyah preparatory to a further advance up the Tigris. These preliminary movements were inevitably slow on account of the difficulties of navigation during the low water season, which delayed the passage of shipping.

4. Throughout this period of preparation frequent skirmishes took place with the enemy, who had pushed out advanced detachments to Zeur and Kutunie, seven and fourteen miles respectively above Aziziyah.

5. The Cavalry Brigade and one Infantry Brigade advanced from Aziziyah on 11th November, and occupied Kutunie without opposition.

On the 18th November General Townshend had concentrated the whole of his force and the shipping at Kutunie.

6. On the 19th November the advance was continued, moving by both banks of the river, and Zeur was occupied. The enemy's advanced troops withdrew towards Ctesiphon after offering slight opposition. On 20th November the force on the left bank reached Lajj (nine miles from Ctesiphon); the shipping and the right bank detachment arrived on the 21st, the latter crossing the river and joining the main body on the left bank.

7. The Turkish position at Ctesiphon lay astride the Tigris, covering the approach to Baghdad, which is situated some eighteen miles to the north-west. The defences had been under construction for some months. They consisted of an extensive system of entrenchments forming two main positions. On the right bank the front position extended from the river for about three miles in a S.W. direction ; the second-line trenches lying some five miles further upstream. On the left bank a continuous line of entrenchments and redoubts stretched from the river for six miles to the north-east, the left flank terminating in a large redoubt. On this bank the second line was about two miles behind the front position and parallel to it for three miles from the Tigris, thence it

BELLOC'S GENERAL SKETCH OF THE EUROPEAN WAR

Vol. 1. THE FIRST PHASE
Price $1.50 Net

Vol. 2. THE SECOND PHASE
Price $1.50 Net

Postage, 15c a copy extra.

A series of volumes in which Mr. Belloc will expound the main lines of the history of the War. The volumes will be published at intervals of several months. Mr. Belloc's articles have attracted universal attention. By his lectures in the United Kingdom he has also performed a work of great public usefulness in helping to give to the nation generally much interesting information regarding military matters. Of his writings, so great an authority as Mr. Spencer Wilkinson, the Oxford professor of military history, has written: "They reveal a thorough knowledge of war and a military judgment of a high order, as well as an unrivalled grip of the geography of the theatre of the war in all its significance." In this series the author will explain the main movements of the war with a fullness and certainty which is only made possible by the fact that a conerable period has elapsed since the military operations under discussion actually took place.

The **first volume** deals with the causes of the war, the strength in men and munitions of the various combatants and the preliminary operations, encounters, etc. The terminal date is September 5, 1914.

The **second volume** treats of the Battle of the Marne, which marked the defeat of the great initial German strategy, and which may well rank among the decisive battles of the world.

The account which is given is the first full tactical study to be published in France or Great Britain. He continues the story down to the failure of the German attempt to break through in West Flanders. The book is illustrated with many plans. It is a narrative written by a military student of worldwide reputation for the delight and instruction of the civilian reader.

NELSON'S HISTORY OF THE WAR

By John Buchan. Vols. 1—XI. ready.

A History of the War told in a straightforward narrative, with full and authoritative details. The early volumes have been repeatedly reprinted, and it has been hailed by the Press in England, France, and Canada, as the most illuminating guide yet issued to the present struggle. It is published monthly, bound in cloth, with numerous maps and plans. The following volumes are now ready, price 45 cents per volume, postpaid.

Vol. I. From the Beginning of the War to the Fall of Namur. 23 Maps and Plans.

Vol. II. From the Battle of the Marne to the German Retreat to the Aisne. 19 Maps and Plans.

Vol. III. The Battle of the Aisne and the Events down to the fall of Antwerp. 23 Maps and Plans.

Vol. IV. The Great Struggle in West Flanders, the two Attacks upon Warsaw, and the Fighting at Sea down to the Battle of the Falkland Islands. 43 maps and plans.

Vol. V. The War of Attrition in the West, the Campaign in the Near East, the Fighting at Sea down to the Blockade of Britain. 25 maps.

Vol. VI. The Campaign on the Niemen and the Narew, the Struggle in the Carpathians, Neuve Chapelle, and the First Attempt upon the Dardanelles. 21 maps and plans.

Vol. VII. The Second Battle of Ypres (in which the Canadian Division played such an heroic part), to the beginning of the Balkan Campaign. 27 maps and plans.

Vol. VIII. The Midsummer Campaigns and the Battles on the Warsaw Salient.

Vol. IX. The Italian War, the Campaign in Gallipoli, and the Russian Retreat from the Warsaw Salient.

Vol. X. The Russian Stand and the September offensive in the West.

Vol. XI. The struggle for the Dvina and the great invasion of Serbia.

Vol. XII. The Retreat from Bagdad, the Evacuation of Gallipoli, and the Derby report. (Ready in three weeks.)

"Students of the History of the Great War have come to look for the regular appearance of Mr. Buchan's admirable little volumes. . . . Each new volume tells the story in the same remarkable detail, and with the same balanced judgment and literary charm which have distinguished each part of this well-planned and well-written history."—Army and Navy Gazette.

NELSON'S SPECIAL ATLAS OF THE WORLD-WIDE WAR

(Ready 3 weeks. New Edition)
Postpaid for 30 cents

A new and much improved edition, entirely remodelled, illustrating the past history of the War and providing the likely maps for its future development.

NELSON'S COLLAPSIBLE METAL BOOK STANDS

These stands are quite invaluable and are in use by booksellers all over the Dominion. Price $1.50 net. Send in your order now.

THE CHILDREN'S STORY OF THE WAR

Vol I. Sir Edward Parrott, LL.D.
Price $1.25

The first volume of this book (which has been published in monthly parts) is bound in red cloth. The volume gives a general sketch of European history leading up to the causes of the war, and brings the narrative of fighting down to the landing of the British Army in France. The story is simply told for children, and has been largely introduced into schools throughout Great Britain and the Empire generally. The volume is also profusely illustrated.

THE CHILDREN'S STORY OF THE WAR

Vol. II. Price $1.25

In this volume the fascinating story by Sir Edward Parrott is continued to the Battle of the Marne. Numerous illustrations and colored frontispiece.

THE CHILDREN'S STORY OF THE WAR

Vol. III. Price $1.25

From the first Battle of Ypres down to the end of the year 1914.

The above publication is also issued in monthly parts. Number 18 now ready.

JU-JITSU SELF DEFENCE

By W. Bruce Sutherland. Price 45c.

Ju-Jitsu, the Japanese style of wrestling, is rapidly making its way into this country. The book deals specially with the application of Ju-Jitsu movements to self defence. The author is a well known Scottish physical instructor, who has been engaged recently in training military and police recruits.

turned northwards to the Dialah River. Close to the Tigris, on the left bank and midway between the two defensive lines, was situated the Arch of Ctesiphon—a prominent landmark.

A mile in rear of the second line of trenches a bridge of boats connected the two wings of the Turkish Army. Further in rear, the Dialah River, near its junction with the Tigris, was bridged at two points, and entrenchments commanded the crossings.

During General Townshend's concentration at Aziziyah accurate information had been obtained by aerial observation regarding the position of the Turkish defences.

8. The officers employed in these reconnaissances displayed the same intrepidity and devotion to duty that has been commented on in previous dispatches. Unfortunately, during the actual period of the battle at Ctesiphon, a series of accidents deprived the Royal Flying Corps of several officers and machines. Among those forced to descend within the enemy's lines was Major H. L. Reilly, a Flight Commander of exceptional ability, who has much distinguished service to his credit.

BATTLE OF CTESIPHON.

9. It was reported that the enemy had over 13,000 regular troops and 38 guns in the Ctesiphon position. There were reports of the early arrival of further reinforcements. Though information on this point was indefinite and lacked confirmation, it was advisable that there should be no delay in attacking and defeating Nur-Ed-Din before the arrival of possible reinforcements.

10. General Townshend, after a night march from Lajj, on 21st–22nd November attacked the hostile position on the left bank at the centre and on the north-east flank. A severe fight lasted throughout the day, resulting in the capture of the front position and more than 1,300 prisoners.

Our troops pressed on and penetrated to the second line, capturing eight guns and establishing themselves in the enemy's trenches. Here they were subjected to heavy counter-attacks by fresh troops. The captured guns changed hands several times. Finally they had to be abandoned, as shortly before nightfall it was found necessary, owing to diminished numbers, to order the withdrawal of our troops from the forward positions to which they had penetrated back to the first position.

11. On the 23rd November our troops were reorganized in the position they had captured, and the work of collecting the numerous casualties was continued.

Owing to heavy losses in killed and wounded it was inadvisable to renew the offensive.

There is no doubt that the Turkish troops who had fought on the previous day were in no condition to resume the fight. The battlefield was littered with their killed and wounded, and many of the trenches were choked with dead. The 45th Turkish Division, which had held the front trenches, was practically destroyed. But reinforcements came up, and heavy attacks were made all along General Townshend's line throughout the night 23rd–24th November. These were repulsed, and the enemy must have lost heavily.

12. On the 24th November wounded and prisoners were evacuated from Ctesiphon to Lajj, where the shipping flotilla was banked in ; and General Townshend consolidated the position he had taken up on the battlefield. His left flank, which had been near the Ctesiphon Arch, in advance of the main position, moved back into the general alignment. Owing to the interruption of a water channel, which had supplied the trenches on the north-east flank, our troops there suffered from want of water ; so the right flank was brought nearer the river. This movement was successfully effected under the cover of an offensive movement pushed out from the centre of the position. The enemy displayed little activity throughout this day, except for shell fire. Most of this came from guns on the right bank, which prevented the steamers advancing upstream from Lajj.

13. On the 25th November the remainder of the wounded were sent back to Lajj. Up to this time it appeared from hostile movements to their rear—reported by air reconnaissance—that the Turks contemplated a retirement from their remaining positions. But apparently they received fresh reinforcements on the 25th. During the afternoon large columns were seen advancing down the left bank and also inland, as if to turn our right flank, while hostile cavalry threatened our rear.

DOWNSTREAM TO KUT.

14. General Townshend was nine miles from his shipping and source of supplies at Lajj, faced by superior forces of fresh troops. He decided to avoid an engagement, and, under cover of night, withdrew to Lajj.

Here he remained during the 26th.

15. A position so far from bases of supply, with a vulnerable line of communication along the winding shallow river, was unfavourable for defence. It was necessary to withdraw further downstream to a more secure locality until conditions might enable a resumption of the offensive.

16. General Townshend withdrew unmolested during the night of 27th–28th to Aziziyah.

On the 29th the Cavalry Brigade, under Brigadier-General Roberts, east of Kutunie engaged and drove back the enemy's advanced mounted troops, who were attacking a stranded gunboat. The 14th Hussars and the 7th (Hariana) Lancers made a successful charge. Some 140 casualties were inflicted on the enemy.

17. On the morning of 30th, continuing the retirement, the main force halted at Umm Al Tubal ; a mixed brigade under Major-General Sir C. Melliss pushing on towards Kut to deal with hostile mounted troops which had interrupted the passage of steamers at Chubibat, about twenty-five miles below Kut.

18. The troops had to remain at Umm Al Tubal as the ships were in difficulties in shoal water in this vicinity, and the enemy's whole force came up during the night. They attacked in great strength at daylight on 1st December.

A fierce fight ensued, the Turks losing heavily from our artillery fire at a range of 2,500 yards. General Townshend took advantage of a successful counter-attack made by the Cavalry Brigade against a column which attempted to envelop his right flank, to break off the fight and retire by echelons of Brigades. This was carried out in perfect order under a heavy shell fire, and by midday the enemy had been shaken off. General Townshend reports that it was entirely due to the splendid steadiness of the troops and to the excellence of his Brigadiers that he was able to repulse the enemy's determined attacks and extricate his force from the difficult situation in which it was placed.

The mixed Brigade, commanded by General Melliss, consisting of :—

30th Infantry Brigade,

1/5th Hants (Howitzer) Battery R.F.A., and 16th Cavalry, which had been dispatched to Chubibat on the morning of 30th November, was recalled on the night of 30th November–1st December. This Brigade marched eighty miles in three days, including the battle of December 1st. At the end of it their valour and discipline was in no way diminished and their losses did not include a single prisoner.

19. After a march of 30 miles, Shadi was reached on the night of the 1st–2nd December, and on the morning of 3rd December General Townshend was installed at Kut-Al-Amarah, where, it was decided, his retirement should end.

WORK OF NAVAL FLOTILLA.

20. The Naval Flotilla on the Tigris operated on the left flank of the troops throughout the operations that have been described.

From November 22nd to November 25th the gunboats from positions below Bustan (two miles east of Ctesiphon) were engaged against hostile artillery, particularly against concealed guns on the right bank, which prevented ships from moving above Bustan.

21. During the retreat from Ctesiphon to Kut the gunboats under Captain Nunn, D.S.O., Senior Naval Officer, rendered valuable services in protecting the steamers and barges and in assisting when they grounded. The naval gunboats were employed at this work day and night, frequently under fire from snipers on both banks.

Owing to numerous loops and twists in the course of the river, it was impossible for the flotilla to remain in touch with the troops during the retirement.

22. On the evening of the 28th November *Shaitan* went aground about eight miles above Aziziyah and could not be refloated. Throughout November 29th, *Firefly* and *Shushan* salved *Shaitan's* guns and stores under heavy sniping from both banks, until the situation was relieved in the afternoon by the action of the Cavalry Brigade which has already been referred to.

The hull of *Shaitan* eventually had to be abandoned, as the Turks opened fire with guns on the ships which had remained behind.

23. On the occasion of the Turkish attack on the morning of December 1st, at Umm Al Tubal, *Firefly* and *Comet* made good practice with lyddite at a large body of Turks at a range of 3,000 yards. The ships came under a heavy and accurate shell fire, and at .7 a.m. a shell penetrated the boiler of *Firefly*, disabling her. H.M.S. *Comet* (Captain Nunn) took *Firefly* in tow, and in endeavouring to turn in the narrow river, both ships took the ground. *Firefly* was got clear and sent drifting downstream ; but *Comet* would not move from the bank, against which she had been wedged by *Firefly*.

24. *Sumana* came up and made several unsuccessful attempts to drag *Comet* off the bank. The enemy's fire in-

creased in intensity ; they brought up several field guns to short range ; the ships were surrounded by Turkish troops and fired on at a range of 50 yards. *Comet* and *Firefly* were badly damaged and on fire. They were abandoned after the guns had been rendered useless, and the crews were taken on board *Sumana*, which succeeded in effecting her escape.

Subsequently *Sumana* did most valuable work in salving shipping which had got into difficulties further downstream.

25. Throughout these operations Captain Nunn, Lieutenant Eddis, who was wounded, and all officers and men of the Naval Flotilla behaved with great coolness and bravery under most trying circumstances.

GENERAL TOWNSHEND AND HIS TROOPS.

26. The valour of the troops who fought under General Townshend at the battle of Ctesiphon is beyond praise. The 6th Division exhibited the same dauntless courage and self-sacrifice in the attack that has distinguished it throughout the campaign in Mesopotamia.

The dash with which the Indian troops (enlisted from all parts of India) have attacked a stubborn foe in well-entrenched positions, I attribute largely to the confidence with which they have been inspired by the British battalions of the Force.

When forced by greatly superior numbers to act on the defensive, and during the retreat to Kut, under the most trying conditions, the troops responded to the calls made on them with admirable discipline and steadiness.

They proved themselves to be soldiers of the finest quality.

27. These fine troops were most ably commanded by Major-General C. V. F. Townshend, C.B., D.S.O. I have a very high opinion indeed of this officer's capabilities as a commander of troops in the field. He was tried very highly, not only at the battle of Ctesiphon, but more especially during the retirement that ensued. Untiring, resourceful, and even more cheerful as the outlook grew darker, he possesses, in my opinion, very special qualifications as a commander.

He is imperturbable under the heaviest fire, and his judgment is undisturbed.

PREPARING FOR THE SIEGE.

28. With great regret, I have been forced, by reasons of ill-health, to resign the command of the British Forces in Mesopotamia—an appointment I have had the honour of holding during the past nine months.

In order to complete the record of events during my period in command, I will now give a brief narrative of the operations on the Tigris from the time that General Townshend's Force reached Kut-Al-Amarah on December 3rd until the date of my departure from Mesopotamia.

29. When General Townshend reached Kut on December 3rd, measures were taken to withstand a siege until the arrival of relief from reinforcements which were coming from overseas.

Defences were improved. Shipping was dispatched to Basrah, evacuating the sick and wounded, and also the Turkish prisoners (1,350 were captured at Ctesiphon, and all were safely brought away in the retreat).

The armed tug *Sumana* was the only vessel left at Kut.

The Cavalry Brigade and a convoy of transport animals were marched down to Ali Al Gharbi before the enemy could effect an investment.

The cavalry left on December 6th. On that day the enemy closed on the northern front, and by December 7th the investment of Kut was complete.

30. The cavalry at Ali Al Gharbi was reinforced with infantry and guns from Basrah. Behind this advanced detachment a force under the command of Major-General F. J. Aylmer, V.C., was collected on the line Amarah-Ali Al Gharbi for the relief of Kut as soon as its concentration was completed.

31. The entrenched camp at Kut is contained in a " U "

shaped loop of the Tigris ; the town stands at the most southerly end of the peninsula so formed. The northern defences are some 3,200 yards from the town ; the peninsula is about a mile in width.

A detached post was established at a small village on the right bank of the river opposite Kut. East of the town was a bridge of boats, covered by a bridgehead detachment on the right bank.

BOMBARDED AND INVESTED.

32. On December 8th, the enemy carried out a heavy bombardment from three sides, and Nur-Ed-Din Pasha called upon General Townshend to surrender.

33. On December 9th, our detachment on the right bank, covering the bridge, was forced to retire before a heavy attack. The enemy occupied the right bank at the bridgehead.

During the night, December 9th–10th, the bridge was successfully demolished by a party gallantly led by Lieutenant A. B. Matthews, R.E., and Lieutenant R. T. Sweet, 2/7th Gurkha Rifles.

34. During the following days Kut was subjected to a continuous bombardment, and several attacks were beaten off. The enemy's losses were heavy, especially in the abortive attacks on December 12th, when, it is estimated, their casualties amounted to 1,000.

35. Operations were then conducted on the lines of regular siege warfare. A redoubt at the north-east corner of the defences became the special objective of Turkish shell fire and sapping operations.

36. On the night of December 14th–15th a successful sortie was made against trenches facing the detached post on the right bank, and on the night December 17th–18th two sorties, from the redoubt previously referred to, cleared the enemy's nearest trenches. About thirty Turks were bayoneted and ten were captured.

37. Heavy fire was concentrated on the redoubt during

the night December 23rd–24th and throughout the 24th. The parapet was breached and the Turks effected an entrance, but they were driven out by a counter-attack, leaving 200 dead behind. Attacks were renewed later, and throughout the night of December 24th–25th a fierce struggle took place around the redoubt. The enemy again effected a lodgment, but by morning they had been ejected and the assault was finally defeated.

38. No decisive attacks have been attempted by the Turks since their failure at Christmas, which, it is reported, cost them about 2,000 casualties.

39. On December 28th a movement of troops, which was continued for several days, took place from the Turkish main camp (six miles above Kut) to Shaikh Saad—which had been occupied by enemy mounted troops for some time.

THE RELIEF COLUMN.

40. On January 4th, General Aylmer's leading troops, under Major-General Younghusband, advanced from Ali Al Gharbi towards Shaikh Saad, moving by both banks.

General Younghusband's column got in touch with the enemy on the morning of January 6th. The Turks were entrenched astride the Tigris, three and a half miles east of Shaikh Saad. An attempt to turn the Turkish right flank did not succeed owing to presence of hostile cavalry and Arabs in superior force on this flank.

41. General Aylmer arrived on morning of January 7th with the remainder of his force, and ordered a general attack ; Major-General Younghusband commanding on the left bank and Major-General Kemball on the right bank.

Very heavy fighting lasted throughout the day. By evening the enemy's trenches on the right bank had been captured and some 600 prisoners and two guns taken.

On the left bank our troops were entrenched opposite the enemy, who still held their positions on that bank. Attempts to turn their left flank had been checked by counter enveloping movements from the north.

42. The troops were very fatigued next day and little progress was made.

On January 9th the Turks were forced to abandon their remaining positions, and retired upstream, followed by General Aylmer's force. But heavy rain now fell, making the alluvial soil of the roads almost impassable, and prevented active operations for the next two days. It is estimated that the enemy's losses during the three days' fighting at Shaikh Saad amounted to 4,500.

43. The enemy fell back about ten miles, to the Wadi— a tributary which joins the Tigris on the left bank. They took up a new position behind the Wadi and on the right bank of the Tigris, opposite the mouth of the Wadi.

44. General Aylmer concentrated his whole force on the left bank and attacked the Wadi positions on the 13th. After hard fighting the Turks were driven out on the 14th, and retired five miles further west and entrenched across a defile bounded on the north by a marsh and on the south by the Tigris. They were followed to this position by General Aylmer's force.

45. Throughout these operations the weather was very bad. The heavy rain and high wind caused great discomfort to the troops and made movement by land and by river most difficult. Up to January 17th there was no improvement in the weather, and active operations were at a standstill.

COMMANDS AND STAFF.

46. As, owing to ill-health, I am about to relinquish command of Indian Expeditionary Force " D," I desire to place on record my warm appreciation of the able and devoted assistance afforded me by the Staff at General Headquarters and Officers of the various Administrative Services and Departments.

I wish specially to bring forward the names of the following officers who have rendered very valuable services :—Major-General G. V. Kemball has proved himself to be a very gallant officer and has the true offensive spirit. As a commander of troops in the field I consider him to be a leader of great ability and power.

I am indebted to Major-General M. Cowper for the assistance which his knowledge of administrative staff work and organization has afforded me.

Major (temporary Lieutenant-Colonel) W. H. Beach is at all times a hard-working, capable, and thoroughly reliable Staff Officer whose services have been invaluable to me. As head of the Intelligence Branch he has shown exceptional powers of insight and organization.

Major (temporary Lieutenant-Colonel) H. R. Hopwood has performed his important duties in a highly satisfactory manner. He is thoroughly capable and full of tact and resource ; in fact, possesses all the qualities that go to make a good Staff Officer.

Major R. A. Cassels has in the field proved himself to be a bold and resourceful Staff Officer, and the manner in which he has acquitted himself of duties falling to hand outside the ordinary scope of his work is highly satisfactory and of value to the State.

Major W. C. Croly, R.A.M.C., has been in medical charge of the Staff at General Headquarters and has shown himself always the right man in the right place, and to have taken the keenest interest in his work and care of those whom he had in charge. To my Personal Staff I am under great obligations for their willing and able assistance in quarters, on the march, and in the fight, and I draw attention to the recommendations for rewards which I have already made.

Captain L. G. Williams.
Captain E. J. Nixon,
Lieutenant G. B. Walker.

MEDICAL SERVICES.

The Medical Services have had to face very trying and unusual conditions. On more than one occasion the number and severity of the casualties have thrown the greatest strain on them, but the organization and efficiency of the arrangements have ensured as speedy an evacuation of the wounded as the means placed at their disposal permitted. In this connection I wish to bring forward the name of Surgeon-General H. G. Hathaway.

The work of the Royal Engineers has been excellently carried out under the able direction of Brigadier-General J. C. Rimington, and I take this opportunity of expressing my appreciation of the valuable assistance rendered by this branch of the service as a whole.

The British General Hospital has throughout been in charge of Lieutenant-Colonel D. J. Collins, R.A.M.C., whose zeal, energy, and organizing power have rendered it a model hospital of its kind. Credit is also due to Lieutenant-Colonel G. B. Irvine, I.M.S., for his devoted and careful supervision of the Indian General Hospital.

I have before expressed my indebtedness to Major-General K. S. Davison and his Staff, and I must now do so again for their able and efficient management of the lines of communication under the most difficult and trying circumstances. In Captain J. C. Macrae he has a good and able Staff Officer.

It must be remembered that as a port Basrah has no facilities for the discharge of stores or the disembarkation of troops and animals. The officers of the Royal Indian Marine consequently have had no easy task in improvising wharves and berths, and dealing with the large number of transports which have recently arrived and have had to be unloaded with the utmost expedition. They have, nevertheless, overcome these many difficulties, and the greatest credit is due to them for what they have accomplished.

The officers and crews of the Tigris steamers belonging to

Messrs. Lynch Brothers and of the other river craft have always displayed gallantry of a high order in bringing their ships on, often under heavy fire, and it is not too much to say that without this assistance, and the indefatigable manner in which they have worked, the movements of troops and supplies would not have been possible.

I cannot praise too highly the work done by the Telegraph and Postal Departments, the state of completeness of which has done much to promote the general efficiency of the force.

All demands made on the Telegraph Department have been rapidly and effectively met at the cost of much hard labour under trying conditions and at great personal risk, which reflects the greatest credit on Mr. L. Bagshawe and the important department over which he presides.

The exigencies of the field service have thrown a great strain on the Postal Department, but owing to the hard work done and the excellent organization built up by Mr. E. Clerici and his staff the results have been most satisfactory.

TRIBUTE TO SIR P. COX.

Finally, I am very grateful to Lieutenant-Colonel Sir P. Z. Cox for his able co-operation and willing assistance. The Force has largely profited by his deep knowledge of local conditions and peoples, and by the tact and bold resource which he has displayed in all he has undertaken.

The names of the following officers, all of whom have performed good service, are brought to the notice of His Excellency the Commander-in-Chief in India :—

Booth, Brevet Major F.

Branson, Captain L. H.

Dick, Major R. N.

Duffy, Deputy Commissary and Captain T. A.

Goad, Lieutenant-Commander C. R., R.I.M.

Greenstreet, Major C. B. L.

Gribbon, Major W. H.

Hamilton, Captain W. H., I.M.S.

Huddleston, Commander (temporary Captain) W. B.

Kinch, Lieutenant A. T., R.I.M.

Marsh, Lieutenant B. C., R.I.M.

More, Captain J. C.

Mowat, Captain J. S.

Parsley, Sec. Lieutenant W. C.

Queripel, Major (temporary Lieutenant-Colonel) L. H., D.S.O.

Shah, Lieutenant A. S.

Thompson, Captain R. C.

Whittall, Captain G. E.

Winter, Major (temporary Lieutenant-Colonel) C. B.

47. As soon as postal communication is established with General Townshend I have no doubt that he will have further names to bring to notice.

I have the honour to be,

Sir,

Your obedient servant,

JOHN NIXON, General,

Commanding Indian Expeditionary Force, " D."

APPENDIX II.

THE END OF THE SENUSSI RISING.

SIR JOHN MAXWELL'S DISPATCH.

Army Headquarters, Cairo.
London, 9th April 1916.

MY LORD,

On 1st March I submitted a report on the Force in Egypt up to the 31st January 1916. I now have the honour to supplement that report up to 19th March 1916, the date on which I handed over command to General Sir A. J. Murray, K.C.B., K.C.M.G., C.V.O., D.S.O., Commander-in-Chief, Mediterranean Expeditionary Force.

The present Dispatch describes the operations under Major-General W. E. Peyton, C.B., C.V.O., D.S.O., for the re-occupation of Sollum. I also venture to submit herewith, for Your Lordship's favourable consideration, the names of those officers, non-commissioned and men, who have especially distinguished themselves during the period covered by this dispatch.

> I have the honour to be
> Your Lordship's obedient servant,
> J. G. MAXWELL, General.

THE RE-OCCUPATION OF SOLLUM.

My last Dispatch ended with the successful engagement at Hazalin, and General Wallace's resignation of the command of the Western Frontier Force, on grounds which have already been explained.

General Peyton's assumption of command on the 9th February practically coincided with the final reorganization of the force, and the provision of sufficient camel transport to render the column completely mobile. Henceforth it was possible to follow up any success, instead of having to return to Matruh after each engagement. This meant that the re-occupation of Sollum, which had already received War Office sanction, was now a possibility, and preparations were pushed on as rapidly as possible.

Information from various sources was to the effect that the main hostile force, with certain reinforcements, was in the neighbourhood of Barrani, and that another smaller body was in the Camp at Sollum. It was clear that if the country was to be pacified these forces must be beaten. Two courses were open to me :—

(i) To attack at Barrani, and simultaneously to land a force at Sollum by sea.

(ii) To move by land, to supply the force by sea at Barrani, and to arrange for naval co-operation at any point which might be necessary.

The Navy were, as always, prepared to give me every assistance in whichever course I might decide to adopt.

On the one hand, Sollum Bay is completely commanded by encircling heights, and, as it would be necessary to remove the mines which had been laid at the entrance, surprise would be impossible. On the other hand, the country between Barrani and Sollum was known to be almost devoid of water, and the physical difficulties to be overcome would certainly be great.

After visiting Matruh, and going into the question on the spot with General Wallace, who had not yet left, and with Commander Eyres Monsell, Royal Navy, I decided to utilize the land route only ; supplies to be put by sea into Barrani and Sollum as soon as possible after their re-occupation by us.

APPENDIX II. 231

These were my instructions to General Peyton when he left Cairo to take over command. As you are already aware, he carried them out, with the assistance of the Navy, to my complete satisfaction.

Just as the preparations for the advance were approaching completion, news was received that a hostile force had occupied the Baharia Oasis on the 11th February. This oasis lies some 200 miles south-west of Cairo and about 100 miles from the rich and thickly populated districts of Fayum and Minia. The strength of this force, which was discovered by an air reconnaissance on the day of its arrival, was said to be about 500 men; it was increased on the following day to about 1,000. Further reinforcements are known to have arrived from the west, and the more southerly oases of Farafra and Dakhla had both been occupied by the 27th. All reports are to the effect that an orderly form of government has been set up—indeed in most cases the Egyptian officials are believed to be carrying on their ordinary duties, but a few Copts have been induced to embrace the Moslem faith. This move of the enemy had, of course, been foreseen, and I had obtained War Office sanction to organize a command, under Major-General J. Adye, C.B., for the defence of the southern provinces of Egypt. This command had recently come into being, and General Adye was able to establish his headquarters at Beni Suef and to arrange for a thorough system of patrols from the Fayum to the neighbourhood of Assiut and the south, with a small guard on the important bridge over the Nile at Nag Hamadi. Subsequently, as our successful operations cleared the situation in the north, and the centre of gravity began to shift southward, General Adye was able to strengthen and to extend his defensive line until, at the moment of handing over my command to Sir A. Murray, his most southerly detachment was at Esna.

Meanwhile I had withdrawn the Civil Officials from the Kharga Oasis as soon as it was known that Dakhla was in the enemy's hands. I had the choice of occupying and protecting that oasis or of withdrawing from it everything which would be of value to the enemy, and contenting myself with occasional patrols. The strategical importance of these oases is, of course, very obvious, but in view of the uncertainty as to what troops would be under my command at any moment I considered that any enterprise distant from the Nile Valley would be out of place, and I restricted General Adye to purely defensive measures, with, however, instructions to prepare a small mobile column with which he could strike at the enemy should he approach the cultivation.

All this time the oases were kept under constant observation by means of aeroplanes. Very long flights were necessary, and to reduce them as much as possible a system of advanced depôts in the desert was started. The credit for originating this system is due to Lieut. (now Captain) Van Rynefeld, R.F.C., and to Mr. Jennings Bramley, of the Sudan Civil Service, and was first put into practice on the occasion of the flight to Qara mentioned in my previous Dispatch.

Such was the situation when I handed over my command on the 19th March.

Meanwhile the preparations for the advance in the North were steadily proceeding. An advanced depôt was established at Unjeila on the 16th February, and on the 20th February General Peyton dispatched a force, under Brig.-General H. T. Lukin, C.M.G., D.S.O., consisting of one squadron Royal Bucks Hussars, Queen's Own Dorset Yeomanry, Notts Battery, R.H.A., 1st South African Brigade, less the 2nd and 4th Battalions, a detachment 1/6th Royal Scots, and two field ambulances, with orders to establish itself at Barrani, and thus to secure the second stepping-stone on the way to Sollum.

On the following day the hostile forces were located by air reconnaissance at Agagia, some fourteen miles south-east of Barrani. Reports by surrendered Bedouin confirmed the accuracy of this information, and added that both Nuri Bey and Gaafer Pasha were in the camp, although Sayed Ahmed himself had left for Siwa.

As General Peyton considered that the advanced force was sufficiently strong to overthrow any opposition which it was likely to encounter, he ordered General Lukin to continue his march and to attack so soon as he was within striking distance of his enemy.

In accordance with this order the original March programme was adhered to, and on the 24th February General Lukin camped at the Wadi Maktil. The 25th was to be a day of rest preliminary to a night approach and attack at dawn on the 26th. However, as on all previous occasions, Gaafer Pasha again showed that he was by no means disposed passively to await attack, and at 5.30 p.m. on the 25th two field guns and at least one machine gun opened fire upon the camp. The action which followed was without importance, as the enemy's artillery was soon silenced, and the threatened attack was repelled with a loss to ourselves of one man killed and one wounded. Nevertheless it had been sufficient to bring about a change in General Lukin's plans, and the night march was abandoned in favour of daylight operations.

A Yeomanry reconnaissance sent out at daylight on the 26th found that the position occupied by the enemy on the previous evening had been vacated during the night, but aerial reconnaissance and officers' patrols discovered him in his old position near Agagia. Having collected sufficient information to enable him to form his plans, General Lukin moved out at 9.30 a.m. with his whole force except for a small detachment left to guard his camp. By 10.15 a.m. the Yeomanry had seized a hillock 4,000 yards north of the enemy's position, and three-quarters of an hour later the attack was developed. In the centre the 3rd South African Infantry advanced on a front of about 1,700 yards ; the Yeomanry (less one squadron) and two armoured cars operated on the right flank with orders to pursue the moment the enemy should break ; on the left was the remaining squadron with two more armoured cars. The 1st South African Infantry and two armoured cars formed the general reserve.

As the attack developed the enemy opened a fairly heavy fire with rifles and machine guns, and two or three field guns distributed their fire over the field. The 3rd South African Infantry moved forward with admirable steadiness. Then, acting exactly as on previous occasions, the enemy's infantry, moving very rapidly, attempted an outflanking movement against General Lukin's left. This was met by a company from the reserve sent up in echelon behind the threatened flank, and the counter-attack at once faded away.

As soon as the danger was over General Lukin, acting with admirable promptitude, withdrew his squadron from his left flank and sent it to strengthen his main pursuing force on his right, and there is little doubt that this quick decision did much to ensure the success of the subsequent operations. As the firing line was now within 500 yards of the position, General Lukin threw into the fight the greater portion of his reserves, including his last two armoured cars, and at the same time sent a staff officer to warn Colonel Souter, of the Dorset Yeomanry, to be ready for his opportunity. In the face of this vigorous action the enemy was compelled to evacuate his position, and, in exact accordance with the plans, the fight was taken up by the cavalry. The rest of the story may be told in the words of Colonel Souter's report :—

" About 1 p.m. I received a message from the G.O.C. saying that he wished me to pursue and to cut off the enemy if possible. It was my intention to let the enemy get clear of the sandhills, where there might have been wire or trenches, and then to attack him in the open. I therefore pursued on a line parallel to, and about 1,000 yards west of, the line of retreat, attacking with dismounted fire wherever the horses wanted an easy. About 2 p.m. I saw for the first time the whole retreating force extend for about a mile with a depth of 300 to 400 yards. In front were the camels and baggage, escorted by irregulars, with their proper fighting force (Muhafizia) and maxims forming their rear and flank guard. I decided to attack mounted. About 3 p.m. I dismounted for the last time to give my horses a breather and to make a careful examination of the ground over which I was about to move. By this time the Dorset Regiment was complete, and as the squadron of the Bucks Yeomanry had gone on ahead and could not be found, I attacked with Dorsets alone. The attack was made in two lines, the horses galloping steadily and well in hand. Three maxims were brought into action against us, but the men were splendidly led by their squadron and troop leaders, and their behaviour was admirable. About 50 yards from the position I gave the order to charge, and with one yell the Dorsets hurled themselves upon the enemy, who immediately broke. In the middle of the enemy's lines my horse was killed under me, and, by a curious chance, his dying strides brought me to the ground within a few yards of the Senussi General, Gaafer Pasha."

At this moment Colonel Souter was alone, except for Lieutenant Blaksley and Yeoman Brown, both of the Dorset Yeomanry, who had also had their horses shot under them. Around them about 50 fit or lightly wounded enemy, and the situation was distinctly threatening until the arrival of the machine-gun section decided the issue. Gaafer Pasha and his staff were then escorted from the field to a place of safety.

For this happy result great credit is due to Colonel Souter, whose resolution and coolness stood him in great stead at a very critical moment. His name has already been submitted to Your Lordship for reward.

Colonel Souter adds—

" It is difficult accurately to express the effect of this cavalry charge on the enemy. Throughout the day he had fought with extreme boldness, but when the horses got into him he had only one thought, and that was to get away."

The losses in this remarkable exploit were severe, but they were justified by both the moral and material result achieved. One squadron was deprived of all its leaders, two being killed and two having their horses killed under them. Without their officers' control the men carried on too far, and it was this squadron that suffered most of the casualties. The enemy's losses were also heavy, and it is most improbable that anything would have induced them to stand up to well-handled cavalry again.

This action on the 26th completed the first stage of General Peyton's advance on Sollum, for Barrani was occupied without further opposition on the 28th February. The next stage was to bring up the remainder of his force and to put sufficient stores into Barrani to enable the advance to be continued. This was a naval operation. For various reasons the advance had been begun some days earlier than I had intended or than the Navy had been led to expect. The Australian Train, which had worked splendidly, was required for duty elsewhere, and, although 2,000 transport camels had been provided, we were still dependent upon the supply ships. Fortunately, these had been provided and stocked in ample time, and Captain Burmester, R.N., and Commander Eyres Monsell were, in fact, able to put supplies into Barrani about a week earlier than the date originally given to them.

The remainder of the South African Infantry Brigade and the second Mounted Brigade, together with the two sections of the Hong Kong and Singapore Mountain Battery, were accordingly brought from Mersa Matruh, and the whole force was assembled at Barrani by the 8th March.

After their defeat at Agagia on the 26th February the enemy retreated westwards towards Sollum, and the Egyptian Bedouin (Aulad Ali) began to desert him in large numbers and to appeal to General Peyton for pardon. A number of prominent Sheikhs came into his camp, but the necessity of pushing on the operations made it impossible to enter into lengthy negotiations for the moment. Air reconnaissance and native report established the fact that the enemy had re-occupied their old camps at Bir Warr and Msead, which had been Sayed Ahmed's headquarters before the opening of hostilities, and it was possible that reinforcements might be coming up from Cyrenaica.

From Barrani to Sollum two possible routes were open to General Peyton. One, following the Khedival road along the coast line ; the other climbing on to the inland plateau by the Nagb Medean or some other of the various passes, and then following along the higher ground towards the camp at Msead. Tactically and strategically the latter route was undoubtedly to be preferred, since at Sollum the escarpment rises sheerly from the shores of the bay, and to climb it there in the face of opposition must entail heavy loss of life. As is usual in African campaigning, the water question was as important as either tactics or strategy. In this case all information was to the effect that a good supply could be found in the wells at Augerin, and that there were large cisterns at the Nagb Medean and Siwiat. This meant that by careful use of the reserve water park which had been organized, and by moving in two bodies, the whole force could use the inland road by the plateau.

The first column, which comprised all the infantry and slow moving troops, left Barrani on the 9th March, under General Lukin, with orders to secure a foothold on the plateau, using the Nagb Medean. The second column, comprised of mounted troops, horses and camels, was to leave two days later and to reach Augerin on the day after the Nagb Medean had been secured. That is to say, that the whole force would have been concentrated at Augerin with its outposts in the high ground ready to make its final and decisive attack upon Bir Warr and Msead. This plan was upset by the discovery, on 12th March, that previous reports as to water were far too optimistic. The supply at Augerin was found to be quite inadequate, and the cisterns at Medean and Siwiat were both reported to be dry. Some reconsideration, therefore, became

necessary. The situation at that moment was as follows :—
The armoured cars had reached the plateau, using the most
westerly pass near Alim er Rabia. Telephone conversation
cleverly intercepted at Barrani by a Turkish-speaking operator
showed that the enemy was anxious, and in two minds whether
to fight or fly ; and Captain Blunt, R.E., had discovered a
cistern at Alim Tejdid containing sufficient water for two
battalions for one night. General Peyton was still rightly
averse to risking the losses which he would suffer if compelled
to attack the Sollum heights from the coastline, especially
as he had already made good a footing on the plateau. On
the other hand, the water on the inland route was only sufficient for a portion of his troops. He therefore decided to
send two battalions of infantry, the armoured cars, his camel
corps company, and his mountain guns under General Lukin
along the top of the escarpment, while the remainder of his
force was to move by the coast. At midnight on the 13th/14th
General Lukin was at Siwiat, the remaining infantry was at
Alim Tejdid, and the mounted troops at Bagbag. On the
morning of the 14th both columns moved towards Sollum ;
at 9 a.m. aeroplane reconnaissance reported that the enemy
was evacuating his camps. The mounted troops under
General Peyton then joined General Lukin's column on the
high ground, and, as the aeroplane had discovered a hostile
force some 20 miles to the west, the armoured cars, under
Major the Duke of Westminster, were sent on in pursuit.

The result of this pursuit has already been fully reported.
It resulted, as Your Lordship is aware, in the capture of all
the enemy's guns and machine guns, together with about 40
prisoners, including three Turkish officers, and in inflicting on
the enemy a loss of 50 killed and many wounded. Our loss in
this exceptionally successful affair was one British officer
slightly wounded.

By the re-occupation of Sollum and this pursuit by the
armoured cars, the defeat of the northern column operating
against Egypt was made complete. In little more than three

weeks General Peyton's force had cleared the country of the enemy for 150 miles, had captured his commander, had taken all his artillery and machine guns, and had driven his scattered forces far beyond the Egyptian frontier.

Nevertheless, one more object remained to be achieved. It was known that somewhere in Cyrenaica the Senussi held some 95 British prisoners, survivors from the *Tara* and *Moorina*, which had been torpedoed in November. After thorough examination of prisoners taken on the 14th, Captain Royle came to the conclusion that these prisoners could be found at a place some 75 miles west of Sollum. It was decided to make the attempt, and, as has also already been reported, it also was a complete success. The task was again entrusted to the light armoured car battery, under Major the Duke of Westminster, accompanied by the motor ambulances. The distance travelled was 120 miles, and the fact that the rescue was effected without any loss of life does not, in my opinion, detract in any way from the brilliance of the exploit. To lead his cars through perfectly unknown country against an enemy of unknown strength was a feat which demanded great resolution, and which should not be forgotten even in this war, where deeds of rare daring are of daily occurrence.

With the rescue of the prisoners and the safe return of the armoured cars, the campaign in the west came to an end, and I think it may fairly be claimed that seldom has a small campaign been so completely successful or had such far-reaching results.

The effect of this success has been to remove the anxiety which was at one time felt as to the possibility of hostile outbreaks in Egypt itself, where agitation was known to be rife. The attitude of the people in Alexandria, and more especially of the very large Bedouin population of the Behera province, has completely changed, and any prestige which we have lost through the evacuation of Sollum has been more than recovered. Moreover, through his failure as a temporal leader, Sayed

Ahmed has lost much of the influence which was attached to him as a spiritual head.

On the west the Aulad Ali, who had been induced to throw in their lot with the Senussi in the belief that they would soon be able to raid the rich lands of the Delta, have been reduced to a state of starvation, and are now surrendering in such large numbers that feeding them has become so serious a problem that it has been necessary to establish a special branch of the administration for their protection and control.

On the east, the failure of the Turks to carry out their threat to attack Egypt and seize the Suez Canal has similarly resulted in a loss of credit and prestige. In the south, scattered forces still hold the oases, and the inherent difficulties of desert campaigning will make them troublesome to deal with ; but the failures in east and west have, it may fairly be claimed, had the result of establishing our hold upon Egypt more firmly than ever, and of convincing all the more enlightened of the people that they can gain nothing by intriguing with our enemies.

APPENDIX III.

THE SITUATION FOLLOWING THE SINKING OF THE " SUSSEX."

I.—THE AMERICAN NOTE OF APRIL 18, 1916.

YOUR EXCELLENCY,

I have not failed to communicate without delay, tele-graphically, to my Government your Excellency's Note of the 10th inst., concerning certain attacks of German sub-marines, and especially concerning the disastrous explosion which destroyed the French steamer *Sussex* on March 24 in the English Channel. In accordance with the instructions of my Government, I now have the honour to communicate to your Excellency the following answer :—

Through advices now in possession of the United States Government the facts in the *Sussex* case are completely established, and for the conclusions which my Government has deduced from these advices it finds confirmation in the circumstances set forth in your Excellency's Note of the 10th inst. On March 24, 1916, at about 2.50 in the afternoon, the unarmed steamer *Sussex*, with 325 or more passengers aboard, among whom were a number of American citizens, was torpedoed during her passage from Folkestone to Dieppe. The *Sussex* was never armed ; she was a ship which, as is well known, was regularly employed only for the transport of passengers across the English Channel. She did not follow the route pursued by troop transports or munition ships. About 80 passengers, non-combatants of every age and both sexes, including citizens of the United States, were killed or wounded.

A careful, thorough, scientific, impartial examination by officers of the United States Navy and Army has conclusively established the fact that the *Sussex* was torpedoed without warning or challenge to surrender, and that the torpedo with which she was struck was of German make. In the view of the United States Government these facts, from beginning to end, made the conclusion that the torpedo was discharged from a German submarine inevitable. It now finds this conclusion fortified by the expositions in your Excellency's Note. A complete representation of the facts is appended on which the United States Government has based its conclusion. After careful examination of the Note of the Imperial Government of April 10 the United States Government regrets to have to say that it has derived the impression, from the representations and proposals of this Note, that the Imperial Government has failed to appreciate the seriousness of the situation which has arisen, not only out of the attack on the *Sussex*, but out of the whole method and character of submarine warfare as they appear in consequence of the unrestricted maintenance of the practice of indiscriminate destruction of merchantmen of every kind, nationality, and designation during a period exceeding 12 months by commanders of German submarines.

If the sinking of the *Sussex* had been an isolated case, that would enable the Government of the United States to hope that the officer responsible for the deed arbitrarily exceeded his instructions, or in criminal negligence failed to observe the prescribed measures of precaution, and that satisfaction might be done to justice by his appropriate punishment, associated with a formal disavowal of his conduct and the payment of appropriate compensation by the Imperial Government. But although the attack on the *Sussex* was evidently indefensible and caused so tragic a loss of human life that it appears as one of the most terrible examples of the inhumanity of the submarine warfare as waged by the commanders of German vessels, it unhappily stands not alone.

On the contrary, the Government of the United States is compelled by the most recent events to conclude that it is only one instance, although one of the gravest and most disturbing, of the deliberate method and spirit with which merchantmen of every kind, nationality, and designation are indiscriminately destroyed, and which has become the more unmistakable the more the activity of German submarines has increased in intensity and extension in recent months.

The Imperial Government will remember that when it announced in February 1915 its intention to treat the waters of Great Britain and Ireland as a war area and destroy all merchantmen in enemy possession found within this danger zone, and when it warned all ships, both of neutrals and belligerents, to avoid the waters thus proscribed or enter them at their own peril, the Government of the United States protested earnestly. It assumed the standpoint that such a policy could not be followed without permanent, serious, and evident violation of recognized international law, especially if submarines should be employed as its instruments, because the rules of international law, rules resting on the principles of humanity and established for the protection of the life of non-combatants at sea, could not, in the nature of things, be observed by such vessels. It based its protest on the fact that persons of neutral nationality and ships of neutral owners would be exposed to the most extreme and intolerable dangers, and that, under the then existing circumstances, the Imperial Government could establish no justifiable claim to close a part of the high seas.

The international law, which here applies and upon which the United States Government based its protest, is not of recent origin or based on purely arbitrary principles established by agreement. On the contrary, it rests on obvious principles of humanity and has long been in force, with the approval and the express assent of all civilized nations. The Imperial Government insisted, notwithstanding, on prosecuting the policy announced, while it expressed the hope that the existing dangers, at least for neutral ships, would be restricted to a minimum by instructions given to the commanders of its submarines, and assured the United States Government that it would apply every possible precaution to respect the rights of neutrals and protect the lives of non-combatants.

In pursuit of this policy of submarine warfare against its enemy's trade, so announced and begun despite the solemn protest of the United States Government, the Imperial Government's submarine commanders have practised a procedure of such reckless destruction as made it more and more clear during recent months that the Imperial Government has found no way to impose upon them such restrictions as it had hoped and promised. The Imperial Government has repeatedly and solemnly assured the United States Government that passenger ships, at least, would not be thus treated, and yet it has repeatedly allowed its submarine commanders to disregard these assurances with impunity. Even in February of this year it announced that it regarded armed merchantmen in enemy possession as part of the armed naval forces of its adversaries and would treat them as warships, while it bound itself, at least implicitly, to warn unarmed vessels and guarantee the lives of their passengers and crews; but their submarine commanders have freely disregarded even this restriction.

Neutral ships, even neutral ships *en route* from neutral port to neutral port, have been destroyed, just as hostile ships, in steadily increasing number. Attacked merchantmen have sometimes been warned and challenged to surrender before being fired on or torpedoed, sometimes the most scanty security has been granted to their passengers and crews of being allowed to enter boats before the ship was sunk; but repeatedly no warning has been given, and not even refuge in boats was granted to passengers on board. Great ships like the *Lusitania* and the *Arabic*, and pure passenger ships like the *Sussex*, have been attacked without any warning, often before they were aware they were in the presence of an armed enemy ship, and the life of non-combatants, passengers, and crews was indiscriminately destroyed in a manner which the Government of the United States could only regard as wanton and lacking every justification. Indeed, no sort of limit was set to the further indiscriminate destruction of merchantmen of every kind and nationality outside the waters which the Imperial Government has been pleased to indicate as within the war zone. The list of Americans who lost their lives on the vessels thus attacked and destroyed has increased month by month, until the terrible number of the victims has risen to hundreds.

The United States Government has adopted a very patient attitude, and at every stage of this painful experience of tragedy upon tragedy has striven to be guided by well-considered regard for the extraordinary circumstances of an unexampled war, and to allow itself to be directed by feelings of sincerest friendship for the people and Government of Germany. It has accepted the successive explanations and assurances of the Imperial Government as naturally made in full sincerity and good faith, and has desired not to abandon the hope that it would be possible for the Imperial Government to regulate and supervise the actions of the commanders of its naval forces in a way which will bring their conduct into consonance with the recognized principles of humanity embodied in international law. It has made every concession to the new circumstances for which no precedents exist, and was willing to wait till the facts were unmistakable and susceptible of only one explanation. It owes it now to the just appreciation of its own rights to declare to the Imperial Government that this moment has arrived.

To its pain, it has become clear to it that the standpoint which it adopted from the beginning is inevitably right—namely, that the employment of submarines for the destruction of enemy trade is of necessity, owing to the character of the ships employed and the methods of attack which their use involves, completely irreconcilable with the principles of humanity, with the long-existing, undisputed rights of neutrals, and with the sacred privileges of non-combatants. If it is still the intention of the Imperial Government to wage further war mercilessly and indiscriminately with submarines against merchantmen without respect for what the Government of the United States must regard as the sacred and indisputable rules of international law and the generally recognized dictates of humanity, the United States Government will be finally forced to the conclusion that there is only one course it can take. If the Imperial Government should not now, without delay, proclaim and make effective renunciation of its present methods of submarine warfare against passenger and cargo ships, the United States Government can have no other choice than to break off completely diplomatic relations with the German Government.

The United States Government views such a step with the greatest reluctance, but it feels itself compelled to adopt it in the name of humanity and of the rights of neutral nations.

I seize this opportunity to renew to your Excellency the assurance of my most distinguished esteem.

(Signed) GERARD.

II.—THE GERMAN REPLY, MAY 4.

The German Government has handed over to the proper naval authorities for further investigation the evidence concerning the *Sussex*, as communicated by the United States Government. Judging by the results which that investigation has hitherto yielded, the German Government is alive to the possibility that the ship mentioned in the Note of April 10 as torpedoed by a German submarine is actually identical with the *Sussex*.

The German Government begs to reserve further communications on the matter until certain points which are of decisive importance for establishing the facts of the case have been ascertained. Should it turn out that the commander of the submarine was wrong in assuming the vessel to be a man-of-war, the German Government will not fail to accept the consequences resulting therefrom. In connection with the case of the *Sussex*, the United States Government made a series of statements the gist of which is the assertion that the incident is to be considered but one instance of a deliberate method of indiscriminate destruction of vessels of all sorts, of all nationalities, and of all designations by German submarine commanders. The German Government must emphatically repudiate this assertion, and thinks it of little avail to enter into details in the present stage of affairs, more particularly as the Government of the United States omitted to substantiate the assertion by reference to concrete facts. The German Government will only state that it has as far as possible instituted a far-reaching restraint upon the use of the submarine weapon solely in consideration of neutrals' interests, in spite of the fact that these restrictions were necessarily of advantage to Germany's enemies. No such consideration has ever been shown to neutrals by Great Britain and her Allies.

The German submarine forces have had in fact orders to conduct submarine warfare in accordance with the general principles of search and destruction of merchant vessels recognized by International Law, the sole exception being the conduct of warfare against enemy trade carried on by enemy freight-ships encountered in the war zone surrounding Great Britain. With regard to these, no assurances have ever been given to the Government of the United States. No such assurance * was contained in the declaration of February 8, 1916.

The German Government cannot admit any doubt that

* This was the declaration in which Germany announced her intention to treat all armed merchantmen as belligerent ships. The American Note about the *Sussex* claimed that in this declaration Germany had bound herself, " at least implicitly, to warn unarmed vessels, and guarantee the lives of their passengers and crews."

these orders were given and executed in good faith. Errors actually occurred. In no kind of warfare can they be avoided altogether. Allowances must be made in the conduct of naval warfare against an enemy resorting to all kinds of ruses whether permissible or illicit. But, apart from the possibility of errors, naval warfare, just like warfare on land, implies unavoidable dangers for neutral persons and goods entering the fighting zone. Even in cases where naval actions are confined to ordinary forms of cruiser warfare, neutral persons and goods repeatedly come to grief. The German Government has repeatedly and explicitly pointed out the dangers from mines that have led to the loss of numerous ships.

The German Government made several proposals to the United States Government in order to reduce to a minimum for American travellers and goods the inherent dangers of naval warfare. Unfortunately the Government of the United States decided not to accept the proposals.* Had it accepted them, the Government of the United States would have been instrumental in preventing a greater part of the accidents that American citizens have met with in the meantime. The German Government still stands by its offer to come to an agreement along these lines.

As the German Government has repeatedly declared, it cannot dispense with the use of the submarine weapon in the conduct of warfare against enemy trade. The German Government, however, has now decided to make a further concession, adapting the methods of submarine warfare to the interests of neutrals. In reaching this decision the German Government is actuated by considerations which are above the level of disputed question.

The German Government attaches no less importance to the sacred principles of humanity than the Government

* The offer was a proposal that a reasonable number of neutral ships under the American flag should be used for carrying passengers, and that these, if conspicuously marked, and if reasonable notice of their departures were given to Germany, would be respected.

of the United States. Again, it fully takes into account the fact that both Governments for many years co-operated in developing International Law in conformity with these principles, the ultimate object of which has aways been to confine warfare on sea and land to the armed forces of the belligerents, and to safeguard as far as possible non-combatants against the horrors of war.

But although these considerations are of great weight, they alone would not, in the present circumstances, have determined the attitude of the German Government ; for, in answer to the appeal by the Government of the United States on behalf of the sacred principles of humanity and International Law, the German Government must repeat once more with all emphasis that it was not the German but the British Government which, ignoring all accepted rule of International Law, extended this terrible war to the lives and property of non-combatants, having no regard whatever for the interests and rights of neutrals and non-combatants that through this method of warfare have been severely injured. In self-defence against the illegal conduct of British warfare, while fighting a bitter struggle for national existence, Germany had to resort to the hard but effective weapon of submarine warfare.

As matters stand, the German Government cannot but reiterate its regret that sentiments of humanity, which the Government of the United States extends with such fervour to the unhappy victims of submarine warfare, have not been extended with the same feeling to the many millions of women and children, who, according to the avowed intention of the British Government, are to be starved, and who by sufferings are to force the victorious armies of the Central Powers into an ignominious capitulation. The German Government, in agreement with the German people, fails to understand this discrimination, all the more as it has repeatedly and explicitly declared itself ready to use the submarine weapon in strict conformity with the rules of International Law as recognized before the outbreak of war, if Great Britain is likewise ready to adapt her conduct of warfare to these rules.

The several attempts which have been made by the Government of the United States to prevail upon the British Government to act accordingly failed because of the flat refusal on the part of the British Government. Moreover, Great Britain ever since has again and again violated International Law, surpassing all bounds and outraging neutral rights. The latest measure adopted by Great Britain of declaring German bunker coal contraband, and of establishing conditions under which alone English bunker coal can be supplied to neutrals, is nothing but an unheard-of attempt by way of exaction to force neutral tonnage into the service of the British trade war.

The German people knows that the Government of the United States has the power to confine war to the armed forces of belligerent countries in the interests of humanity and the maintenance of International Law. The Government of the United States would have been certain of attaining that end had it been determined to insist, against Great Britain, on incontestable rights to the freedom of the seas. But, as matters stand, the German people is under the impression that the Government of the United States, while demanding that Germany, who is struggling for her existence, shall restrain the use of her effective weapon, and while making compliance with these demands the condition for the maintenance of relations with Germany, confines itself to protests against the illegal methods adopted by Germany's enemies. Moreover, the German people knows to what considerable extent her enemies are supplied with all kinds of war materials from the United States.

It will, therefore, be understood that the appeal made by the Government of the United States to the sentiment of humanity and the principles of International Law cannot under the circumstances meet with the same hearty response from the German people which such an appeal would otherwise always be certain to find here. If the German Government nevertheless resolved to go the limit of the concessions demanded, it is not alone being guided by the friendship connecting two great nations for over a hundred years, but also by the thought of the great doom which threatens the entire civilized world should this cruel and sanguinary war be extended and prolonged.

The German Government is conscious of Germany's strength. Twice within the past few months she has announced before the world her readiness to make peace on a basis safeguarding Germany's vital interests, thus indicating that it is not Germany's fault if peace is still withheld from the nations of Europe. The German Government feels all the more justified in declaring that the responsibility could not be borne before the forum of mankind and history if after 21 months' duration of war the submarine question under discussion between the German Government and the Government of the United States were to take a turn seriously threatening the maintenance of peace between these two nations.

As far as lies with the German Government, it wishes to prevent things from taking such a course. The German Government, moreover, is prepared to do its utmost to confine the operations of war for the rest of its duration to the fighting forces of the belligerents, thereby also ensuring the freedom of the seas—a principle upon which the German Government believes itself to be now, as before, in agreement with the Government of the United States.

The German Government, guided by this idea, notifies the Government of the United States that the German naval forces receive the following orders for submarine warfare in accordance with the general principles of visit, search, and destruction of merchant vessels recognized by International Law. Such vessels, both within and without the area declared as a naval war zone, shall not be sunk without warning, and without saving human lives, unless the ship attempts to escape or offer resistance.

But neutral vessels cannot expect that Germany, forced to fight for her existence, shall for the sake of neutral interests restrict the use of her effective weapon if the enemy is permitted to continue to apply at will methods of warfare violating the rules of International Law. Such a demand would be incompatible with the character of neutrality, and the German Government is convinced that the Government of the United States does not think of making such a demand, knowing that the Government of the United States has repeatedly declared that it is determined to restore the principle of the freedom of the seas from whatever quarter it has been violated.

Accordingly, the German Government is confident that in consequence of the new orders issued to her naval forces the Government of the United States will now also consider all impediments removed which may have been in the way of mutual co-operation towards restoration of the freedom of the seas during the war, as suggested in the Note of July 23, 1915, and it does not doubt that the Government of the United States will now demand and insist that the British Government shall forthwith observe the rules of International Law universally recognized before the war, as are laid down in the Notes * presented by the Government of the United States to the British Government on December 28, 1914, and November 5, 1915.

Should the steps taken by the Government of the United States not attain the object it desires—viz., to have the laws of humanity followed by all belligerent nations—the German Government would then be facing a new situation in which it must reserve for itself a complete liberty of decision.

* The Note of December 28, 1914, was a friendly remonstrance against our alleged improper interference with neutral trade. The Note of November 5, 1915, was a protest against our interference with commerce to Germany and adjacent countries based upon three main grounds :—(1) That our reading of the law of contraband was wrong ; (2) that our " blockade " instituted by the Order in Council of March 11, 1915, was illegal ; and (3) that our suggestion that American shipping might protect itself through our Prize Courts was illusory.

III.—THE AMERICAN REPLY, MAY 8.

The note of the Imperial Government under date May 4 has received the careful consideration of the Government of the United States. It is especially noted, as indicating the purpose of the Imperial Government for the future, that " it is prepared to do its utmost to confine the operation of war for the rest of its duration to the fighting forces of the belligerents," and is determined to impose upon all its commanders at sea the limitations recognized by the rules of International law, upon which the Government of the United States has insisted.

Throughout the months which have elapsed since the Imperial Government announced on February 4, 1915, its submarine policy, now happily abandoned, the Government of the United States has been constantly guided and restrained by motives of friendship in its patient efforts to bring to an amicable settlement the critical questions arising out of that policy. Accepting the Imperial Government's declaration of its abandonment of a policy which has so seriously menaced the good relations of the two countries, the Government of the United States will rely upon the scrupulous execution henceforth of the now altered policy of the Imperial Government, such as will remove the principal danger to the interruption of good relations existing between the United States and Germany.

The Government of the United States feels it necessary to state that it takes for granted that Germany does not intend to imply that the maintenance of its newly-announced policy is in any way contingent upon the course or result of diplomatic negotiations between the Government of the United States and any other belligerent Government, notwithstanding the fact that certain passages in the Imperial Government's Note of the 4th inst. might appear to be susceptible of that construction.

In order, however, to avoid any possible misunderstanding,

the Government of the United States notifies the Imperial Government that it cannot for a moment entertain, much less discuss, the suggestion that respect by the German naval authorities for the rights of citizens of the United States upon the high seas should in any way, or in the slightest degree, be made contingent upon the conduct of any other Government as affecting the rights of neutrals and non-combatants. The responsibility in such matters is single, not joint; absolute, not relative.

APPENDIX IV.

SPRING ON THE BRITISH FRONT.

SIR DOUGLAS HAIG'S FIRST DISPATCH.

WAR OFFICE,
LONDON, S.W., 29th May 1916.

THE following Dispatch has been received by the Secretary of State for War from General Sir Douglas Haig, G.C.B., Commander-in-Chief, the British Forces in France :—

General Headquarters, 19th May 1916.
MY LORD,

1. I have the honour to report the operations of the British Forces serving in France and Belgium since 19th December 1915, on which date, in accordance with the orders of His Majesty's Government, I assumed the Chief Command.

During this period the only offensive effort made by the enemy on a great scale was directed against our French Allies near Verdun. The fighting in that area has been prolonged and severe. The results have been worthy of the high traditions of the French Army, and of great service to the cause of the Allies. The efforts made by the enemy have cost him heavy losses both in men and in prestige, and he has made these sacrifices without gaining any advantage to counterbalance them.

During this struggle my troops have been in readiness to co-operate as they might be needed, but the only assistance asked for by our Allies was of an indirect nature—viz., the relief of the French troops on a portion of their defensive front. This relief I was glad to be able to afford.

Its execution on a considerable front, everywhere in close touch with the enemy, was a somewhat delicate operation; but it was carried out with complete success, thanks to the cordial co-operation and good will of all ranks concerned and to the lack of enterprise shown by the enemy during the relief.

A CONTINUOUS STRUGGLE.

2. On the British front no action on a great scale, such as that at Verdun, has been fought during the past five months; nevertheless our troops have been far from idle or inactive. Although the struggle, in a general sense, has not been intense, it has been everywhere continuous, and there have been many sharp local actions.

The maintenance and repair of our defences alone, especially in winter, entails constant heavy work. Bad weather and the enemy combine to flood and destroy trenches, dugouts, and communications; all such damages must be repaired promptly, under fire, and almost entirely by night.

Artillery and snipers are practically never silent, patrols are out in front of the lines every night, and heavy bombardments by the artillery of one or both sides take place daily in various parts of the line. Below ground there are continual mining and countermining, which, by the ever-present threat of sudden explosion and the uncertainty as to when and where it will take place, cause perhaps a more constant strain than any other form of warfare. In the air there is seldom a day, however bad the weather, when aircraft are not busy reconnoitring, photographing, and observing fire. All this is taking place constantly at any hour of the day or night, and in any part of the line.

3. In short, although there has been no great incident of historic importance to record on the British front during the period under review, a steady and continuous fight has gone

APPENDIX IV. 257

on, day and night, above ground and below it. The com-
parative monotony of this struggle has been relieved at short
intervals by sharp local actions, some of which, although in-
dividually almost insignificant in a war on such an immense
scale, would have been thought worthy of a separate dispatch
under different conditions; while their cumulative effect,
though difficult to appraise at its true value now, will doubt-
less prove hereafter to have been considerable.

One form of minor activity deserves special mention—
namely, the raids or " cutting out parties " which are made
at least twice or three times a week against the enemy's line.
They consist of a brief attack, with some special object, on a
section of the opposing trenches, usually carried out at night
by a small body of men. The character of these operations—
the preparation of a road through our own and the enemy's
wire—the crossing of the open ground unseen—the penetration
of the enemy's trenches—the hand-to-hand fighting in the darkness and the uncertainty as to the strength of the opposing
force—give peculiar scope to the gallantry, dash, and quickness of decision of the troops engaged ; and much skill and
daring are frequently displayed in these operations.

The initiative in these minor operations was taken, and
on the whole has been held, by us ; but the Germans have
recently attempted some bold and well-conceived raids against
our lines, many of which have been driven back, although
some have succeeded in penetrating, as has been reported by
me from time to time.

4. Of the numerous local actions alluded to, the total
number, omitting the more minor raids, amounts to over 60
since December 19th, of which the most important have been :—

The operations at The Bluff ; the Hohenzollern Redoubt,
and at St. Eloi ; the mining operations and crater fighting in
the Loos salient and on the Vimy Ridge ; and the hostile gas
attacks north of Ypres in December, and opposite Hulluch
and Messines in April.

The most recent local operations worthy of mention are the
XIV.   17

capture of some 500 yards of our trenches by the Germans at the Kink, on the 11th May, and the capture by us of 250 yards of their trenches near Cabaret Rouge, on the night of the 15th–16th May.

5. As an illustration of the nature of these local operations it will suffice to describe two or three of the most important.

YPRES AND THE BLUFF.

During the period 8th to 19th February the enemy displayed increased activity in the Ypres salient, and carried out a series of infantry attacks, preceded, as a rule, by intense bombardment, and by the explosion of mines. These attacks may, no doubt, be regarded as a subsidiary operation, designed partly to secure local points of vantage, but probably also to distract attention from the impending operations near Verdun, which began on the 21st February.

After several days' heavy shelling over the whole of our line in this area, the first attack took place on 12th February, at the extreme left of our line to the north of Ypres. A bombing attack was launched by the Germans in the early morning, and they succeeded in capturing our trenches. Our counter-attack, however, which was immediately organized, enabled us to clear our trenches of the enemy, and to pursue him to his own. After a period of further bombardment on both sides, the German fire again increased in intensity against our trenches and the French line beyond them ; and in the evening a second attempt was made to rush our extreme left—this time entirely without success. Smaller attempts against other trenches in the neighbourhood were made at the same time, but were immediately repulsed by rifle and machine-gun fire. Throughout the operations our position in this part of the line remained intact, except that two isolated trenches of no tactical importance were captured by the enemy a day or two later ; they were subsequently obliterated by our artillery fire. Throughout this fighting the French on our immediate left rendered us the prompt and valuable assistance which we have at all times received from them.

Another series of German attacks was launched about the same time in the neighbourhood of Hooge, to the east of Ypres. The enemy had pushed out several saps in front of his trenches, and connected them up into a firing line some 150 yards from our lines. During the whole of the 13th February he heavily bombarded our front-line trenches in this neighbourhood, and completely destroyed them. On the following afternoon an intense bombardment of our line began, and the enemy exploded a series of mines in front of our trenches, simultaneously launching infantry attacks against Hooge and the northern and southern ends of Sanctuary Wood. Each of these attacks was repulsed by artillery, machine-gun, and rifle fire.

Further to the south, however, the enemy was more successful. On the northern bank of the Ypres-Comines Canal there is a narrow ridge, 30 to 40 feet high, covered with trees—probably the heap formed by excavation when the canal was dug—which forms a feature of the flat-wooded country at the southern bend of the Ypres salient. It runs outward through our territory almost into the German area, so that our trenches pass over the eastern point of it, which is known as The Bluff. Here also our trenches were almost obliterated by the bombardment on the afternoon of the 14th, following which a sudden rush of hostile infantry was successful in capturing these and other front-line trenches immediately north of The Bluff—some 600 yards in all. Two of these trenches were at once regained, but the others were held by the enemy, in the face of several counter-attacks. On the night of the 15th–16th we made an unsuccessful counter-attack, with the object of regaining the lost trenches. An advance was begun across the open on the north side of the canal, combined with grenade attacks along the communication trenches immediately north of The Bluff. The night was very dark, and heavy rain had turned the ground into a quagmire, so that progress was difficult for the attacking force, which was unable to consolidate its position in the face of heavy machine-gun and rifle fire. After the failure of this attack it was decided to adopt slower and more methodical methods of recapturing the lost trenches, and nothing of special importance occurred in the Ypres salient during the rest of the month, although both sides displayed rather more than the usual activity.

The recapture of The Bluff took place after the enemy had held it for seventeen days. After several days' preliminary bombardment by our artillery, the assault was carried out at 4.29 a.m. on the 2nd March. Measures taken to deceive the enemy were successful, and our infantry effected a complete surprise, finding the enemy with their bayonets unfixed, and many of them without rifles or equipment. About 50 Germans took refuge in a crater at the eastern end of The Bluff, and these put up a brief resistance before taking refuge in the tunnels they had constructed, in which they were captured at leisure. Otherwise our right hand attacking party, whose objective was The Bluff, met with little opposition.

The front line of the centre attack, reaching its assigned objective without much opposition, swept on past it and seized the German Third Line at the eastern side of the salient. This line was not suitable to hold permanently, but it proved useful as a temporary covering position while the captured trenches in rear were being consolidated, and at nightfall the covering party was withdrawn unmolested. The later waves of our centre attack met and captured, after some fighting, several Germans coming out of their dug-outs.

The left attacking party, at the first attempt, failed to reach the German trenches; but those who had penetrated to the German line on the right realized the situation, and brought a Lewis gun to bear on the enemy's line of resistance, completely enfilading his trenches, and thus enabling the left company to reach its goal.

Thus our objective, which included a part of the German line, as well as the whole of the front lost by us on the 14th February, was captured, and is still held by us. Several counter-attacks were destroyed by our fire. The enemy's trenches were found full of dead as a result of our bombardment, and five officers and 251 other ranks were captured.

The support of the Heavy and Field Artillery, and a number of trench mortars, contributed largely to the success of the operation.

ST. ELOI.

6. On the 27th March our troops made an attack with the object of straightening out the line at St. Eloi, and cutting away the small German salient which encroached on the semi-circle of our line in the Ypres salient to a depth of about 100 yards over a front of some 600 yards. The operation was begun by the firing of six very large mines ; the charge was so heavy that the explosion was felt in towns several miles behind the lines, and large numbers of the enemy were killed. Half a minute after the explosion our infantry attack was launched aiming at the German Second Line. The right attack met with little opposition, and captured its assigned objective ; but the left attack was not so successful, and a gap was left in possession of the Germans, through which they entered one of the craters. The following days were spent by both sides in heavy bombardment and in unsuccessful attacks, intended on our part to capture the remaining trenches, and on the part of the Germans to drive us from the positions we had occupied. In the very early morning of April 3rd we succeeded in re-capturing the crater and the trenches still held by the enemy, thereby securing the whole of our original objective. We had, moreover, captured five officers and 195 men in the first attack on March 27th, and five officers and 80 men in the attack on April 3rd. The work of consolidating our new position, however, proved extremely difficult, owing to the wet soil, heavy shelling, and mine explosions ; though pumps were

brought up and efforts at draining were instituted, the result achieved was comparatively small. By dint of much heavy work the Brigade holding these trenches succeeded in reducing the water in the trenches by 2 feet by the morning of the 5th. This state of affairs could not, even so, be regarded as satisfactory ; and during the 5th the enemy's bombardment increased in intensity, and the new trenches practically ceased to exist. On the morning of the 6th the enemy attacked with one battalion supported by another ; he penetrated our new line, and gained the two westernmost craters. It is difficult to follow in detail the fighting of the next three weeks, which consisted in repeated attacks by both sides on more or less isolated mine craters, the trench lines having been destroyed by shell fire. Great efforts were made to maintain communication with the garrisons of these advanced posts, and with considerable success. But there were periods of uncertainty, and some misconception as to the state of affairs arose. On the 11th it was reported to me that we had recaptured all that remained of the position won by us on the 27th March and 3rd April. This report, probably due to old craters having been mistaken for new ones, was subsequently found to be incorrect. The new craters, being exposed to the enemy's view and to the full weight of his artillery fire, have proved untenable, and at the present time our troops are occupying trenches roughly in the general line which was held by them before the 27th.

GERMAN GAS ATTACKS.

7. On the night of the 29th–30th April the enemy carried out a gas attack on a considerable scale near Wulverghem, on a front of 3,500 yards. The operation was opened by heavy rifle and machine-gun fire under cover of which the gas was released. Immediately afterwards a heavy " barrage," or curtain of artillery fire, was placed on three parts of this area, and eight infantry attacks were launched. Of these attacks

only two penetrated our trenches ; one was immediately repelled, while the other was driven out by a counter-attack
after about 40 minutes' occupation. The enemy's object
would appear to have been the destruction of mine shafts, as
a charge of gun-cotton was found unexploded in a disused
shaft, to which the enemy had penetrated. But if this was
his object he was completely unsuccessful.

Similar attacks were made by the Germans in front of
Vermelles, to the south of La Bassée, on the 27th and 29th
April, the discharge of a highly concentrated gas being accompanied by bombardment with lachrymatory and other shells
and the explosion of a mine. On the first occasion two
minor infantry attacks penetrated our trenches, but were
driven out almost immediately ; on the second occasion a
small attack was repulsed, but the more serious advance
which appears to have been intended was probably rendered
impossible by the fact that a part of the enemy's gas broke
back over his own lines, to the visible confusion of his
troops, who were massing for the attack.

COMMENDATION OF UNITS.

8. While many other units have done excellent work
during the period under review, the following have been specially brought to my notice for good work in carrying out or
repelling local attacks and raids :—

3rd Divisional Artillery.
17th Divisional Artillery.
1st Canadian Divisional Artillery.
62nd Brigade, Royal Field Artillery.
B Battery, 153rd Brigade, Royal Field Artillery.
83rd Battery, Royal Field Artillery (Lahore).
22nd Canadian (Howitzer) Brigade.
24th Heavy Battery, Royal Garrison Artillery.
115th Heavy Battery, Royal Garrison Artillery.

122nd Heavy Battery, Royal Garrison Artillery.
3rd Siege Battery, Royal Garrison Artillery.
12th Siege Battery, Royal Garrison Artillery.
9th Field Company, Royal Engineers.
56th Field Company, Royal Engineers.
70th Field Company, Royal Engineers.
77th Field Company, Royal Engineers.
1st (Cheshire) Field Company, Royal Engineers.
170th Tunnelling Company, Royal Engineers.
172nd Tunnelling Company, Royal Engineers.
173rd Tunnelling Company, Royal Engineers.
253rd Tunnelling Company, Royal Engineers.
12th Divisional Signal Company, Royal Engineers.
24th Trench Mortar Battery.
76/1st Trench Mortar Battery.
No. 2 Squadron, Royal Flying Corps.
No. 6 Squadron, Royal Flying Corps.
2nd Battalion, Grenadier Guards.
1st Battalion, Coldstream Guards.
2nd Battalion, Irish Guards.
1st Battalion, Welsh Guards.
11th (Service) Battalion, The Royal Scots (Lothian Regiment).
1st Battalion, the Queen's (Royal West Surrey Regiment).
7th (Service) Battalion, The King's Own (Royal Lancaster Regiment).
8th (Service) Battalion, The King's Own (Royal Lancaster Regiment).
1st Battalion, Northumberland Fusiliers.
12th (Service) Battalion, Northumberland Fusiliers.
1st Battalion, Royal Warwickshire Regiment.
8th Battalion, Royal Warwickshire Regiment (Territorial).
8th (Service) Battalion, Royal Fusiliers (City of London Regiment).
9th (Service) Battalion, Royal Fusiliers (City of London Regiment).
4th (Extra Reserve) Battalion, The King's Liverpool Regiment.

1/8th (Irish) Battalion, The King's Liverpool Regiment (Territorial).

7th (Service) Battalion, Lincolnshire Regiment.

1/4th Battalion, Suffolk Regiment (Territorial).

7th (Service) Battalion, Suffolk Regiment.

8th (Service) Battalion, Somerset Light Infantry.

7th (Service) Battalion, Bedfordshire Regiment.

1/4th Battalion, The Prince of Wales's Own (West Yorkshire Regiment) (Territorial).

2nd Battalion, Lancashire Fusiliers.

11th (Service) Battalion, Lancashire Fusiliers.

15th (Service) Battalion, Lancashire Fusiliers.

17th (Service) Battalion, Lancashire Fusiliers.

2nd Battalion, Royal Welsh Fusiliers.

15th (Service) Battalion, Royal Welsh Fusiliers.

8th (Service) Battalion, King's Own Scottish Borderers.

7th (Service) Battalion, Royal Inniskilling Fusiliers.

9th (Service) Battalion, Royal Inniskilling Fusiliers.

10th (Service) Battalion, Royal Inniskilling Fusiliers.

1/6th Battalion, Gloucestershire Regiment (Territorial).

1st Battalion, East Lancashire Regiment.

7th (Service) Battalion, East Surrey Regiment.

8th (Service) Battalion, East Surrey Regiment.

9th (Service) Battalion, West Riding Regiment.

2nd Battalion, The Border Regiment.

7th (Service) Battalion, The Border Regiment.

11th (Service) Battalion, The Border Regiment.

7th (Service) Battalion, Royal Sussex Regiment.

8th (Service) Battalion, Royal Sussex Regiment.

8th (Service) Battalion, South Staffordshire Regiment.

1st Battalion, Dorsetshire Regiment.

1/4th Battalion, Oxfordshire and Buckinghamshire Light Infantry (Territorial).

1st Battalion, Northamptonshire Regiment.

5th (Service) Battalion, Northamptonshire Regiment.

6th (Service) Battalion, Northamptonshire Regiment.

1st Battalion, The King's (Shropshire Light Infantry).

1st Battalion, Duke of Cambridge's Own (Middlesex Regiment).

2nd Battalion, Duke of Cambridge's Own (Middlesex Regiment).

2nd Battalion, King's Royal Rifle Corps.

6th (Service) Battalion, The Duke of Edinburgh's (Wiltshire Regiment).

18th (Service) Battalion, Manchester Regiment.

1st Battalion, The Prince of Wales's (North Staffordshire Regiment).

8th (Service) Battalion, The Prince of Wales's (North Staffordshire Regiment).

17th (Service) Battalion, Highland Light Infantry.

8th (Service) Battalion, Seaforth Highlanders (Ross-shire Buffs, The Duke of Albany's).

1st Battalion, The Gordon Highlanders.

2nd Battalion, The Royal Irish Rifles.

9th (Service) Battalion, The Royal Irish Rifles.

1st Battalion, Princess Victoria's (Royal Irish Fusiliers).

2nd Battalion, Princess Louise's (Argyll and Sutherland Highlanders).

9th (Service) Battalion, Royal Munster Fusiliers.

3rd Battalion, The Rifle Brigade (The Prince Consort's Own).

5th Canadian Infantry Battalion.

7th Canadian Infantry Battalion.

29th Canadian Infantry Battalion.

49th Canadian Infantry Battalion.

9. The activity described above has its counterpart in rear of our lines in the training which is carried out continuously. During the periods of relief all formations, and especially the newly created ones, are instructed and practised in all classes of the present and other phases of warfare. A large number of schools also exist for the instruction of individuals especially in the use and theory of the less familiar weapons, such as bombs and grenades.

There are schools for young staff officers and regimental

officers, for candidates for commissions, etc. In short, every effort is made to take advantage of the closer contact with actual warfare, and to put the finishing touches, often after actual experience in the trenches, to the training received at home.

10. During the period under review the forces under my command have been considerably augmented by the arrival of new formations from home, and the transfer of others released from service in the Near East. This increase has made possible the relief of a French Army, to which I have already referred, at the time of the Battle of Verdun. Among the newly arrived forces is the " Anzac " Corps. With them, the Canadians, and a portion of the South African Overseas Force which has also arrived, the Dominions now furnish a valuable part of the Imperial Forces in France.

Since the date of the last Dispatch, but before I assumed command, the Indian Army Corps left this country for service in the East. They had given a year's valuable and gallant service under conditions of warfare which they had not dreamt of, and in a climate peculiarly difficult for them to endure. I regret their departure, but I do not doubt that they will continue to render gallant and effective service elsewhere, as they have already done in this country.

THE ROYAL FLYING CORPS.

11. I take this opportunity to bring to notice the admirable work which the Royal Flying Corps has continued to perform, in spite of much unfavourable weather, in carrying out reconnaissance duties, in taking photographs—an important aid to reconnaissance which has been brought to a high pitch of perfection—and in assisting the work of our Artillery by registering targets and locating hostile batteries. In the performance of this work they have flown in weather when no hostile aeroplane ventured out, and they have not hesitated to fly low, under fire of the enemy's guns, when their duties

made it necessary to do so. They have also carried out a series of bombing raids on hostile aerodromes and points of military importance. A feature of the period under review has been the increased activity of the enemy's aircraft, in suitable weather. But the enemy's activity has been mainly on his own side of the line, and has aimed chiefly at interrupting the work carried out by our machines. In order to carry out the work in spite of this opposition, which was for a time rendered more effective by the appearance in December of a new and more powerful type of enemy machine, it has been necessary to provide an escort to accompany our reconnaissance aeroplanes, and fighting in the air, which was formerly exceptional, has now become an everyday occurrence.

The observers, no less than the pilots, have done excellent service, and many fine feats have been performed by both. Developments on the technical side of the Air Service have been no less remarkable and satisfactory than the progress made on the purely military side. Much inventive genius has been displayed ; and our equipment for photography, wireless telegraphy, bomb-dropping, and offensive action generally has been immensely improved, while great skill has been shown in keeping the flying machines themselves in good flying condition.

THE ROYAL ENGINEERS.

12. The continuance of siege warfare has entailed for the Royal Engineers work of a particularly arduous and important kind, extending from the front trenches to the Base Ports.

In the performance of this work the Officers, Non-Commissioned Officers, and men of the Field Companies and other units of the Corps have continued to exhibit a very high standard of skill, courage, and devotion to duty.

13. The work of the Tunnelling Companies calls for special mention. Increased mining activity on the part of the enemy has invariably been answered with enterprise combined with

untiring energy on the part of our miners, who, in carrying out duties always full of danger, have shown that they possess in the highest degree the qualities of courage, perseverance, and self-sacrifice. Their importance in the present phase of warfare is very great.

OTHER SERVICES.

14. The excellent work done by the Corps of Military Police is worthy of mention. This Corps is inspired by a high sense of duty, and in the performance of its share in the maintenance of discipline it has shown both zeal and discretion.

15. All branches of the Medical Services deserve the highest commendation for the successful work done by them, both at the Front and on the Lines of Communication. The sick rate has been consistently low ; there has been no serious epidemic, and enteric fever, the bane of armies in the past, has almost completely disappeared owing to preventive measures energetically carried out.

The results of exposure incidental to trench warfare during the winter months were to a very great extent kept in check by careful application of the precautions recommended and taught by regimental Medical Officers.

The wounded have been promptly and efficiently dealt with, and their evacuation to the Base has been rapidly accomplished.

The close co-operation which has existed between the officers of the Regular Medical Service of the Army and those members of the civil medical profession, who have patriotically given their valuable services to the Army, has largely contributed to the prevention of disease, and to the successful treatment and comfort of the sick and wounded.

As part of the Medical Services, the Canadian Army Medical Corps has displayed marked efficiency and devotion to duty.

16. The Commission of Graves Registration and In-

quiries has, since it first undertook this work, eighteen months ago, registered and marked over 50,000 graves. Without its labours many would have remained unidentified. It has answered several thousand inquiries from relatives, and supplied them with photographs. Flowers and shrubs have been planted in most of the cemeteries which are sufficiently far removed from the firing line, and all cemeteries which it is possible to work in during the daytime are now being looked after by non-commissioned officers and men of this unit.

17. The valuable nature of the work performed by the officers of the Central Laboratory and the Chemical Advisers with the Armies in investigations into the nature of the gases and other new substances used in hostile attacks, and in devising and perfecting means of protecting our troops against them, is deserving of recognition. The efforts of these officers materially contributed to the failure of the Germans in their attack of 19th December 1915, as well as in the various gas attacks since made.

18. The stream of additional personnel and material arriving from England, and the move of complete formations to and from the East during the period under review, have thrown a great deal of work on our Base Ports and on the Advanced Base. The staff and personnel at these stations have coped most ably with the work of forwarding and equipping the various units passing through their hands, and I desire to bring their good work to notice.

19. The large increases made to our forces have necessitated a great expansion in the resources of our Lines of Communication, and I have been greatly struck by the forethought shown by the Administrative Services in anticipating the requirements of the Armies in the Field and in the provision made to satisfy these requirements.

The Base Ports have been developed to the utmost possible extent, advanced Depôts have been provided, and communications have been improved to ensure punctual distribution to the troops.

Labour has been organized in order to develop local resources, especially in the matter of timber for defences and hutting, and stone for road maintenance, whereby considerable reductions have been made possible in the shipments from over sea.

Economy has attended the good methods adopted, and the greatest credit is due to all concerned for the results obtained.

20. I desire to acknowledge here the valuable assistance rendered by the naval transport officers on the Lines of Communications. They have worked with and for the Army most untiringly, efficiently, and with the utmost harmony.

I also desire to acknowledge the indebtedness of the Army to the Royal Navy for their unceasing and uniformly successful care in securing the safety of our transport service on the seas.

21. I wish to acknowledge the work done in the reproduction of maps by the Ordnance Survey Department. Over 90 per cent. of the maps used in this country are reproduced and printed in England by the Ordnance Survey, and the satisfactory supply is largely due to the foresight and initiative displayed by this Department. I can now count on obtaining an issue of as many as 10,000 copies of any map within one week of sending it home for reproduction.

22. I have forwarded under a separate letter the names of the Officers, Non-Commissioned Officers, and Men whom I wish to bring to notice for gallant and distinguished service.

23. I cannot close this Dispatch without some reference to the work of my predecessor in Command, Field-Marshal Viscount French. The Field-Marshal, starting the war with our small Expeditionary Force, faced an enemy far superior in numbers and fully prepared for this great campaign. During the long and anxious time needed for the improvisation of the comparatively large force now serving in this country, he overcame all difficulties, and before laying down his responsibilities he had the satisfaction of seeing the balance

of advantage swing steadily in our favour. Those who have served under him appreciate the greatness of his achievement.

> I have the honour to be,
>> Your Lordship's most obedient Servant,
>> D. HAIG, General,
> Commander-in-Chief, The British Forces in France.

APPENDIX V.

THE BATTLE OF JUTLAND.

Dispatch of Sir John Jellicoe and Sir David Beatty.

Admiralty, 6th July 1916.

The following Dispatch has been received from Admiral Sir John Jellicoe, G.C.B., G.C.V.O., Commander-in-Chief, Grand Fleet, reporting the action in the North Sea on 31st May 1916 :—*

Iron Duke,
24th June 1916.

Sir,

Be pleased to inform the Lords Commissioners of the Admiralty that the German High Sea Fleet was brought to action on 31st May 1916, to the westward of the Jutland Bank, off the coast of Denmark.

The ships of the Grand Fleet, in pursuance of the general policy of periodical sweeps through the North Sea, had left its bases on the previous day, in accordance with instructions issued by me.

In the early afternoon of Wednesday, 31st May, the 1st and 2nd Battle-cruiser Squadrons, 1st, 2nd, and 3rd Light-cruiser Squadrons and destroyers from the 1st, 9th, 10th, and 13th Flotillas, supported by the 5th Battle Squadron, were, in accordance with my directions, scouting to the southward of the Battle Fleet, which was accompanied by the 3rd Battle-

---

* All times given in this report are Greenwich mean time.

cruiser Squadron, 1st and 2nd Cruiser Squadrons, 4th Light-cruiser Squadron, 4th, 11th, and 12th Flotillas.

The junction of the Battle Fleet with the scouting force after the enemy had been sighted was delayed owing to the southerly course steered by our advanced force during the first hour after commencing their action with the enemy battle-cruisers. This was, of course, unavoidable, as had our battle-cruisers not followed the enemy to the southward the main fleets would never have been in contact.

The Battle-cruiser Fleet, gallantly led by Vice-Admiral Sir David Beatty, K.C.B., M.V.O., D.S.O., and admirably supported by the ships of the Fifth Battle Squadron under Rear-Admiral Hugh Evan-Thomas, M.V.O., fought an action under, at times, disadvantageous conditions, especially in regard to light, in a manner that was in keeping with the best traditions of the service.

The following extracts from the report of Sir David Beatty give the course of events before the Battle Fleet came upon the scene :—

" At 2.20 p.m. reports were received from *Galatea* (Commodore Edwyn S. Alexander-Sinclair, M.V.O., A.D.C.), indicating the presence of enemy vessels. The direction of advance was immediately altered to S.S.E., the course for Horn Reef, so as to place my force between the enemy and his base.

" At 2.35 p.m. a considerable amount of smoke was sighted to the eastward. This made it clear that the enemy was to the northward and eastward, and that it would be impossible for him to round the Horn Reef without being brought to action. Course was accordingly altered to the eastward and subsequently to north-eastward, the enemy being sighted at 3.31 p.m. Their force consisted of five battle-cruisers.

" After the first report of the enemy, the 1st and 3rd Light-cruiser Squadrons changed their direction, and, without waiting for orders, spread to the east, thereby forming a screen in advance of the Battle-cruiser Squadrons and 5th Battle Squadron by the time we had hauled up to the course of approach. They engaged enemy light cruisers at long range. In the meantime the 2nd Light-cruiser Squadron had come in at high speed, and was able to take station ahead of the battle-cruisers by the time we turned to E.S.E., the course on which we first engaged the enemy. In this respect the work of the Light-cruiser Squadrons was excellent, and of great value.

" From a report from *Galatea* at 2.25 p.m. it was evident that the enemy force was considerable, and not merely an isolated unit of light cruisers, so at 2.45 p.m. I ordered *Engadine* (Lieutenant-Commander C. G. Robinson) to send up a seaplane and scout to N.N.E. This order was carried out very quickly, and by 3.8 p.m. a seaplane, with Flight Lieutenant F. J. Rutland, R.N., as pilot, and Assistant Paymaster G. S. Trewin, R.N., as observer, was well under way ; her first reports of the enemy were received in *Engadine* about 3.30 p.m. Owing to clouds it was necessary to fly very low, and in order to identify four enemy light cruisers the seaplane had to fly at a height of 900 feet within 3,000 yards of them, the light cruisers opening fire on her with every gun that would bear. This in no way interfered with the clarity of their reports, and both Flight Lieutenant Rutland and Assistant Paymaster Trewin are to be congratulated on their achievement, which indicates that seaplanes under such circumstances are of distinct value.

" At 3.30 p.m. I increased speed to 25 knots, and formed line of battle, the 2nd Battle-cruiser Squadron forming astern of the 1st Battle-cruiser Squadron, with destroyers of the 13th and 9th Flotillas taking station ahead. I turned to E.S.E., slightly converging on the enemy, who were now at a range of 23,000 yards, and formed the ships on a line of bearing to clear the smoke. The 5th Battle Squadron, who had conformed to our movements, were now bearing N.N.W., 10,000 yards. The visibility at this time was good, the sun behind us and the wind S.E. Being between the enemy and his base, our situation was both tactically and strategically good.

" At 3.48 p.m. the action commenced at a range of 18,500 yards, both forces opening fire practically simultaneously. Course was altered to the southward, and subsequently the mean direction was S.S.E., the enemy steering a parallel course distant about 18,000 to 14,500 yards.

" At 4.8 p.m. the 5th Battle Squadron came into action and opened fire at a range of 20,000 yards. The enemy's fire now seemed to slacken. The destroyer *Landrail* (Lieutenant-Commander Francis E. H. G. Hobart), of 9th Flotilla, who was on our port beam, trying to take station ahead, sighted the periscope of a submarine on her port quarter. Though causing considerable inconvenience from smoke, the presence of *Lydiard* (Commander Malcolm L. Goldsmith) and *Landrail* undoubtedly preserved the battle-cruisers from closer submarine attack. *Nottingham* (Captain Charles B. Miller) also reported a submarine on the starboard beam.

" Eight destroyers of the 13th Flotilla, *Nestor* (Commander the Hon. Edward B. S. Bingham), *Nomad* (Lieutenant-Commander Paul Whitfield), *Nicator* (Lieutenant Jack E. A. Mocatta), *Narborough* (Lieutenant-Commander Geoffrey Corlett), *Pelican* (Lieutenant-Commander Kenneth A. Beattie), *Petard* (Lieutenant-Commander Evelyn C. O. Thomson), *Obdurate* (Lieutenant-Commander Cecil H. H. Sams), *Nerissa* (Lieutenant-Commander Montague C. B. Legge), with *Moorsom* (Commander John C. Hodgson), and *Morris* (Lieutenant-Commander Edward S. Graham), of 10th Flotilla, *Turbulent* (Lieutenant-Commander Dudley Stuart), and *Termagant* (Lieutenant-Commander Cuthbert P. Blake), of the 9th Flotilla, having been ordered to attack the enemy with torpedoes when opportunity offered, moved out at 4.15 p.m., simultaneously with a similar movement on the part of the enemy destroyers. The attack was carried out in the most gallant manner, and with great determination. Before arriving at a favourable position to fire torpedoes, they intercepted an enemy force consisting of a light cruiser and fifteen destroyers. A fierce engagement ensued at close quarters, with the result that the enemy were forced to retire on their battle-cruisers, having lost two destroyers sunk, and having their torpedo attack frustrated. Our destroyers sustained no loss in this engagement, but their attack on the enemy battle-cruisers was rendered less effective, owing to some of the destroyers having dropped astern during the fight. Their position was therefore unfavourable for torpedo attack.

" Nestor, Nomad, and Nicator, gallantly led by Commander the Hon. Edward B. S. Bingham, of Nestor, pressed home their attack on the battle-cruisers and fired two torpedoes at them, being subjected to a heavy fire from the enemy's secondary armament. Nomad was badly hit, and apparently remained stopped between the lines. Subsequently Nestor and Nicator altered course to the S.E., and in a short time, the opposing battle-cruisers having turned 16 points, found themselves within close range of a number of enemy battleships. Nothing daunted, though under a terrific fire, they stood on, and their position being favourable for torpedo attack fired a torpedo at the second ship of the enemy line at a range of 3,000 yards. Before they could fire their fourth torpedo, Nestor was badly hit and swung to starboard, Nicator altering course inside her to avoid collision, and thereby being prevented from firing the last torpedo. Nicator made good her escape, and subsequently rejoined the Captain (D), 13th Flotilla. Nestor remained stopped, but was afloat when last seen. Moorsom also carried out an attack on the enemy's battle fleet.

" Petard, Nerissa, Turbulent, and Termagant also pressed home their attack on the enemy battle-cruisers, firing torpedoes after the engagement with enemy destroyers. Petard reports that all her torpedoes must have crossed the enemy's line, while Nerissa states that one torpedo appeared to strike the rear ship. These destroyer attacks were indicative of the spirit pervading His Majesty's Navy, and were worthy of its highest traditions. I propose to bring to your notice a recommendation of Commander Bingham and other Officers for some recognition of their conspicuous gallantry.

" From 4.15 to 4.43 p.m. the conflict between the opposing battle-cruisers was of a very fierce and resolute character. The 5th Battle Squadron was engaging the enemy's rear ships, unfortunately at very long range. Our fire began to tell, the accuracy and rapidity of that of the enemy depreciating considerably. At 4.18 p.m. the third enemy ship was seen to be on fire. The visibility to the north-eastward had become considerably reduced, and the outline of the ships very indistinct.

" At 4.38 p.m. *Southampton* (Commodore William E. Goodenough, M.V.O., A.D.C.) reported the enemy's Battle Fleet ahead. The destroyers were recalled, and at 4.42 p.m. the enemy's Battle Fleet was sighted S.E. Course was altered 16 points in succession to starboard, and I proceeded on a northerly course to lead them towards the Battle Fleet. The enemy battle-cruisers altered course shortly afterwards, and the action continued. *Southampton*, with the 2nd Light-cruiser Squadron, held on to the southward to observe. They closed to within 13,000 yards of the enemy Battle Fleet, and came under a very heavy but ineffective fire. *Southampton's* reports were most valuable. The 5th Battle Squadron were now closing on an opposite course and engaging the enemy battle-cruisers with all guns. The position of the enemy Battle Fleet was communicated to them, and I ordered them to alter course 16 points. Led by Rear-Admiral Evan-Thomas, in *Barham* (Captain Arthur W. Craig), this squadron supported us brilliantly and effectively.

" At 4.57 p.m. the 5th Battle Squadron turned up astern of me and came under the fire of the leading ships of the enemy Battle Fleet. *Fearless* (Captain (D) Charles D. Roper), with the destroyers of 1st Flotilla, joined the battle-cruisers, and, when speed admitted, took station ahead. *Champion*

(Captain (D) James U. Farie), with 13th Flotilla, took station on the 5th Battle Squadron. At 5 p.m. the 1st and 3rd Light-cruiser Squadrons, which had been following me on the southerly course, took station on my starboard bow ; the 2nd Light-cruiser Squadron took station on my port quarter.

" The weather conditions now became unfavourable, our ships being silhouetted against a clear horizon to the west-ward, while the enemy were for the most part obscured by mist, only showing up clearly at intervals. These conditions prevailed until we had turned their van at about 6 p.m. Between 5 and 6 p.m. the action continued on a northerly course, the range being about 14,000 yards. During this time the enemy received very severe punishment, and one of their battle-cruisers quitted the line in a considerably damaged condition. This came under my personal observation, and was corroborated by *Princess Royal* (Captain Walter H. Cowan, M.V.O., D.S.O.) and *Tiger* (Captain Henry B. Pelly, M.V.O.). Other enemy ships also showed signs of increasing injury. At 5.5 p.m. *Onslow* (Lieutenant-Commander John C. Tovey) and *Moresby* (Lieutenant-Commander Roger V. Alison), who had been detached to assist *Engadine* with the seaplane, rejoined the battle-cruiser squadrons and took station on the starboard (engaged) bow of *Lion* (Captain Alfred E. M. Chat-field, C.V.O.). At 5.10 p.m. *Moresby*, being 2 points before the beam of the leading enemy ship, fired a torpedo at a ship in their line. Eight minutes later she observed a hit with a torpedo on what was judged to be the sixth ship in the line. *Moresby* then passed between the lines to clear the range of smoke, and rejoined *Champion*. In corroboration of this, *Fearless* reports having seen an enemy heavy ship heavily on fire at about 5.10 p.m., and shortly afterwards a huge cloud of smoke and steam.

" At 5.35 p.m. our course was N.N.E., and the estimated position of the Battle Fleet was N. 16 W., so we gradually hauled to the north-eastward, keeping the range of the enemy at 14,000 yards. He was gradually hauling to the eastward, receiving severe punishment at the head of his line, and probably acting on information received from his light cruisers, which had sighted and were engaged with the Third Battle-cruiser Squadron.

" Possibly Zeppelins were present also. At 5.50 p.m. British cruisers were sighted on the port bow, and at 5.56 p.m. the leading battleships of the Battle Fleet, bearing north 5 miles. I thereupon altered course to east, and proceeded at utmost speed. This brought the range of the enemy down to 12,000 yards. I made a report to you that the enemy battle-cruisers bore south-east. At this time only three of the enemy battle-cruisers were visible, closely followed by battle-ships of the *Koenig* class.

" At about 6.5 p.m. *Onslow*, being on the engaged bow of *Lion*, sighted an enemy light cruiser at a distance of 6,000 yards from us, apparently endeavouring to attack with torpedoes. *Onslow* at once closed and engaged her, firing 58 rounds at a range of from 4,000 to 2,000 yards, scoring a number of hits. *Onslow* then closed the enemy battle-cruisers, and orders were given for all torpedoes to be fired. At this moment she was struck amidships by a heavy shell, with the result that only one torpedo was fired. Thinking that all his torpedoes had gone, the Commanding Officer proceeded to retire at slow speed. Being informed that he still had three torpedoes, he closed with the light cruiser previously engaged and torpedoed her. The enemy's Battle Fleet was then sighted, and the remaining torpedoes were fired at them and must have crossed the enemy's track. Damage then caused *Onslow* to stop.

" At 7.15 p.m. *Defender* (Lieutenant-Commander Lawrence R. Palmer), whose speed had been reduced to 10 knots, while on the disengaged side of the battle-cruisers, by a shell which damaged her foremost boiler, closed *Onslow* and took her in tow. Shells were falling all round them during this operation, which, however, was successfully accomplished. During the heavy weather of the ensuing night the tow parted twice,

but was re-secured. The two struggled on together until
1 p.m. 1st June, when *Onslow* was transferred to tugs. I
consider the performances of these two destroyers to be
gallant in the extreme, and I am recommending Lieutenant-
Commander J. C. Tovey, of *Onslow*, and Lieutenant-Commander L. R. Palmer, of *Defender*, for special recognition.
Onslow was possibly the destroyer referred to by the Rear-
Admiral Commanding 3rd Light-cruiser Squadron as follows :—
' Here I should like to bring to your notice the action of a
destroyer (name unknown) which we passed close in a disabled
condition soon after 6 p.m. She apparently was able to
struggle ahead again, and made straight for *Derfflinger* to
attack her.' "

PROCEEDINGS OF BATTLE FLEET AND THIRD BATTLE-CRUISER
SQUADRON.

On receipt of the information that the enemy had been
sighted, the British Battle Fleet, with its accompanying cruiser
and destroyer force, proceeded at full speed on a S.E. by S.
course to close the Battle-cruiser Fleet. During the two
hours that elapsed before the arrival of the Battle Fleet on
the scene the steaming qualities of the older battleships were
severely tested. Great credit is due to the engine-room
departments for the manner in which they, as always, responded to the call, the whole Fleet maintaining a speed in
excess of the trial speeds of some of the older vessels.

The Third Battle-cruiser Squadron, commanded by Rear-
Admiral the Hon. Horace L. A. Hood, C.B., M.V.O., D.S.O.,
which was in advance of the Battle Fleet, was ordered to
reinforce Sir David Beatty. At 5.30 p.m. this squadron
observed flashes of gunfire and heard the sound of guns
to the south-westward. Rear-Admiral Hood sent *Chester*
(Captain Robert N. Lawson) to investigate, and this ship
engaged three or four enemy light cruisers at about 5.45 p.m.
The engagement lasted for about twenty minutes, during

which period Captain Lawson handled his vessel with great skill against heavy odds, and, although the ship suffered considerably in casualties, her fighting and steaming qualities were unimpaired, and at about 6.5 p.m. she rejoined the Third Battle-cruiser Squadron.

The Third Battle-cruiser Squadron had turned to the north-westward, and at 6.10 p.m. sighted our battle-cruisers, the squadron taking station ahead of *Lion* at 6.21 p.m. in accordance with the orders of the Vice-Admiral Commanding Battle-cruiser Fleet. He reports as follows :—

" I ordered them to take station ahead, which was carried out magnificently, Rear-Admiral Hood bringing his squadron into action ahead in a most inspiring manner, worthy of his great naval ancestors. At 6.25 p.m. I altered course to the E.S.E. in support of the Third Battle-cruiser Squadron, who were at this time only 8,000 yards from the enemy's leading ship. They were pouring a hot fire into her and caused her to turn to the westward of south. At the same time I made a report to you of the bearing and distance of the enemy Battle Fleet.

" By 6.50 p.m. the battle-cruisers were clear of our leading Battle Squadron then bearing about N.N.W. 3 miles, and I ordered the Third Battle-cruiser Squadron to prolong the line astern and reduced to 18 knots. The visibility at this time was very indifferent, not more than 4 miles, and the enemy ships were temporarily lost sight of. It is interesting to note that after 6 p.m., although the visibility became reduced, it was undoubtedly more favourable to us than to the enemy. At intervals their ships showed up clearly, enabling us to punish them very severely and establish a definite superiority over them. From the report of other ships and my own observation it was clear that the enemy suffered considerable damage, battle-cruisers and battleships alike. The head of their line was crumpled up, leaving battleships as targets for the majority of our battle-cruisers. Before leaving us the Fifth Battle

Squadron was also engaging battleships. The report of
Rear-Admiral Evan-Thomas shows that excellent results
were obtained, and it can be safely said that his magnificent
squadron wrought great execution.

" From the report of Rear-Admiral T. D. W. Napier,
M.V.O., the Third Light-cruiser Squadron, which had maintained its station on our starboard bow well ahead of the
enemy, at 6.25 p.m. attacked with the torpedo. *Falmouth*
(Captain John D. Edwards) and *Yarmouth* (Captain Thomas
D. Pratt) both fired torpedoes at the leading enemy battle-
cruiser, and it is believed that one torpedo hit, as a heavy
underwater explosion was observed. The Third Light-
cruiser Squadron then gallantly attacked the heavy ships with
gunfire, with impunity to themselves, thereby demonstrating
that the fighting efficiency of the enemy had been seriously
impaired. Rear-Admiral Napier deserves great credit for
his determined and effective attack. *Indomitable* (Captain
Francis W. Kennedy) reports that about this time one of the
Derfflinger class fell out of the enemy's line."

Meanwhile, at 5.45 p.m., the report of guns had become
audible to me, and at 5.55 p.m. flashes were visible from ahead
round to the starboard beam, although in the mist no ships
could be distinguished, and the position of the enemy's Battle
Fleet could not be determined. The difference in estimated
position by " reckoning " between *Iron Duke* (Captain Frederic
C. Dreyer, C.B.) and *Lion*, which was inevitable under the
circumstances, added to the uncertainty of the general situation.

Shortly after 5.55 p.m. some of the cruisers ahead, under
Rear-Admirals Herbert L. Heath, M.V.O., and Sir Robert
Arbuthnot, Bt., M.V.O., were seen to be in action, and reports
received show that *Defence*, flagship (Captain Stanley V. Ellis),
and *Warrior* (Captain Vincent B. Molteno), of the First
Cruiser Squadron, engaged an enemy light cruiser at this
time. She was subsequently observed to sink.

At 6 p.m. *Canterbury* (Captain Percy M. R. Royds), which ship was in company with the Third Battle-cruiser Squadron, had engaged enemy light cruisers which were firing heavily on the torpedo-boat destroyer *Shark* (Commander Loftus W. Jones), *Acasta* (Lieutenant-Commander John O. Barron), and *Christopher* (Lieutenant-Commander Fairfax M. Kerr) ; as a result of this engagement the *Shark* was sunk.

At 6 p.m. vessels, afterwards seen to be our battle-cruisers, were sighted by *Marlborough* bearing before the starboard beam of the battle fleet.

At the same time the Vice-Admiral Commanding, Battle-cruiser Fleet, reported to me the position of the enemy battle-cruisers, and at 6.14 p.m. reported the position of the enemy Battle Fleet.

At this period, when the Battle Fleet was meeting the battle-cruisers and the Fifth Battle Squadron, great care was necessary to ensure that our own ships were not mistaken for enemy vessels.

I formed the Battle Fleet in line of battle on receipt of Sir David Beatty's report, and during deployment the fleets became engaged. Sir David Beatty had meanwhile formed the battle-cruisers ahead of the Battle Fleet.

The divisions of the Battle Fleet were led by :—

The Commander-in-Chief.

Vice-Admiral Sir Cecil Burney, K.C.B., K.C.M.G.

Vice-Admiral Sir Thomas Jerram, K.C.B.

Vice-Admiral Sir Doveton Sturdee, Bt., K.C.B., C.V.O., C.M.G.

Rear-Admiral Alexander L. Duff, C.B.

Rear-Admiral Arthur C. Leveson, C.B.

Rear-Admiral Ernest F. A. Gaunt, C.M.G.

At 6.16 p.m. *Defence* and *Warrior* were observed passing down between the British and German Battle Fleets under a very heavy fire. *Defence* disappeared, and *Warrior* passed to the rear disabled.

It is probable that Sir Robert Arbuthnot, during his

engagement with the enemy's light cruisers and in his desire
to complete their destruction, was not aware of the approach
of the enemy's heavy ships, owing to the mist, until he found
himself in close proximity to the main fleet, and before he
could withdraw his ships they were caught under a heavy
fire and disabled. It is not known when *Black Prince* (Captain Thomas P. Bonham), of the same squadron, was sunk,
but a wireless signal was received from her between 8 and 9
p.m.

The First Battle Squadron became engaged during deployment, the Vice-Admiral opening fire at 6.17 p.m. on a battleship of the *Kaiser* class. The other Battle Squadrons, which
had previously been firing at an enemy light cruiser, opened
fire at 6.30 p.m. on battleships of the *Koenig* class.

At 6.6 p.m. the Rear-Admiral Commanding Fifth Battle
Squadron, then in company with the battle-cruisers, had
sighted the starboard wing division of the Battle Fleet on the
port bow of *Barham*, and the first intention of Rear-Admiral
Evan-Thomas was to form ahead of the remainder of the Battle
Fleet, but on realizing the direction of deployment he was
compelled to form astern, a manœuvre which was well executed by the squadron under a heavy fire from the enemy
Battle Fleet. An accident to *Warspite's* steering gear caused
her helm to become jammed temporarily and took the ship
in the direction of the enemy's line, during which time she
was hit several times. Clever handling enabled Captain
Edward M. Phillpotts to extricate his ship from a somewhat
awkward situation.

Owing principally to the mist, but partly to the smoke,
it was possible to see only a few ships at a time in the enemy's
battle line. Towards the van only some four or five ships
were ever visible at once. More could be seen from the
rear squadron, but never more than eight to twelve.

The action between the Battle Fleets lasted intermittently
from 6.17 p.m. to 8.20 p.m. at ranges between 9,000 and
12,000 yards, during which time the British Fleet made

alterations of course from S.E. by E. to W. in the endeavour to close. The enemy constantly turned away and opened the range under cover of destroyer attacks and smoke screens as the effect of the British fire was felt, and the alterations of course had the effect of bringing the British Fleet (which commenced the action in a position of advantage on the bow of the enemy) to a quarterly bearing from the enemy battle line, but at the same time placed us between the enemy and his bases.

At 6.55 p.m. *Iron Duke* passed the wreck of *Invincible* (Captain Arthur L. Cay), with *Badger* (Commander C. A. Fremantle) standing by.

During the somewhat brief periods that the ships of the High Sea Fleet were visible through the mist, the heavy and effective fire kept up by the battleships and battle-cruisers of the Grand Fleet caused me much satisfaction, and the enemy vessels were seen to be constantly hit, some being observed to haul out of the line and at least one to sink. The enemy's return fire at this period was not effective, and the damage caused to our ships was insignificant.

THE BATTLE-CRUISERS IN THE VAN.

Sir David Beatty reports :—

" At 7.6 p.m. I received a signal from you that the course of the Fleet was south. Subsequently signals were received up to 8.46 p.m. showing that the course of the Battle Fleet was to the south-westward.

" Between 7 and 7.12 p.m. we hauled round gradually to S.W. by S. to regain touch with the enemy, and at 7.14 p.m. again sighted them at a range of about 15,000 yards. The ships sighted at this time were two battle-cruisers and two battleships, apparently of the *Koenig* class. No doubt more continued the line to the northward, but that was all that could be seen. The visibility having improved considerably as the sun descended below the clouds, we re-engaged at

7.17 p.m. and increased speed to 22 knots. At 7.32 p.m. my course was S.W., speed 18 knots, the leading enemy battleship bearing N.W. by W. Again, after a very short time, the enemy showed signs of punishment, one ship being on fire, while another appeared to drop right astern. The destroyers at the head of the enemy's line emitted volumes of grey smoke, covering their capital ships as with a pall, under cover of which they turned away, and at 7.45 p.m. we lost sight of them.

" At 7.58 p.m. I ordered the First and Third Light-cruiser Squadrons to sweep to the westward and locate the head of the enemy's line, and at 8.20 p.m. we altered course to west in support. We soon located two battle-cruisers and battleships, and were heavily engaged at a short range of about 10,000 yards. The leading ship was hit repeatedly by *Lion*, and turned away eight points, emitting very high flames and with a heavy list to port. *Princess Royal* set fire to a three-funnelled battleship. *New Zealand* (Captain John F. E. Green) and *Indomitable* report that the third ship, which they both engaged, hauled out of the line, heeling over and on fire. The mist which now came down enveloped them, and *Falmouth* reported they were last seen at 8.38 p.m. steaming to the westward.

" At 8.40 p.m. all our battle-cruisers felt a heavy shock as if struck by a mine or torpedo, or possibly sunken wreckage. As, however, examination of the bottoms reveals no sign of such an occurrence, it is assumed that it indicated the blowing up of a great vessel.

" I continued on a south-westerly course with my light cruisers spread until 9.24 p.m. Nothing further being sighted, I assumed that the enemy were to the north-westward, and that we had established ourselves well between him and his base. *Minotaur* (Captain Arthur C. S. H. D'Aeth) was at this time bearing north 5 miles, and I asked her the position of the leading battle squadron of the Battle Fleet. Her reply was that it was not in sight, but was last seen bearing

N.N.E. I kept you informed of my position, course, and speed, also of the bearing of the enemy.

" In view of the gathering darkness, and the fact that our strategical position was such as to make it appear certain that we should locate the enemy at daylight under most favourable circumstances, I did not consider it desirable or proper to close the enemy Battle Fleet during the dark hours. I therefore concluded that I should be carrying out your wishes by turning to the course of the Fleet, reporting to you that I had done so."

DETAILS OF BATTLE-FLEET ACTION.

As was anticipated, the German Fleet appeared to rely very much on torpedo attacks, which were favoured by the low visibility and by the fact that we had arrived in the position of a " following " or " chasing " fleet. A large number of torpedoes were apparently fired, but only one took effect (on *Marlborough*), and even in this case the ship was able to remain in the line and to continue the action. The enemy's efforts to keep out of effective gun range were aided by the weather conditions, which were ideal for the purpose. Two separate destroyer attacks were made by the enemy.

The First Battle Squadron, under Vice-Admiral Sir Cecil Burney, came into action at 6.17 p.m. with the enemy's Third Battle Squadron, at a range of about 11,000 yards, and administered severe punishment, both to the battleships and to the battle-cruisers and light cruisers, which were also engaged. The fire of *Marlborough* (Captain George P. Ross) was particularly rapid and effective. This ship commenced at 6.17 p.m. by firing seven salvos at a ship of the *Kaiser* class, then engaged a cruiser, and again a battleship, and at 6.54 she was hit by a torpedo and took up a considerable list to starboard, but reopened at 7.3 p.m. at a cruiser, and at 7.12 p.m. fired fourteen rapid salvos at a ship of the *Koenig* class, hitting her frequently until she turned out of the line. The manner in which this effective fire was kept up in spite of the disadvantages due to the injury caused by the torpedo was most creditable to the ship and a very fine example to the squadron.

The range decreased during the course of the action to 9,000 yards. The First Battle Squadron received more of the enemy's return fire than the remainder of the Battle Fleet, with the exception of the Fifth Battle Squadron. *Colossus* (Captain Alfred D. P. R. Pound) was hit but was not seriously damaged, and other ships were straddled with fair frequency.

In the Fourth Battle Squadron—in which squadron my flagship *Iron Duke* was placed—Vice-Admiral Sir Doveton Sturdee leading one of the divisions—the enemy engaged was the squadron consisting of the *Koenig* and *Kaiser* class and some of the battle-cruisers, as well as disabled cruisers and light cruisers. The mist rendered range-taking a difficult matter, but the fire of the squadron was effective. *Iron Duke*, having previously fired at a light cruiser between the lines, opened fire at 6.30 p.m. on a battleship of the *Koenig* class at a range of 12,000 yards. The latter was very quickly straddled, and hitting commenced at the second salvo and only ceased when the target ship turned away. The rapidity with which hitting was established was most creditable to the excellent gunnery organization of the flagship, so ably commanded by my Flag Captain, Captain Frederic C. Dreyer.

The fire of other ships of the squadron was principally directed at enemy battle-cruisers and cruisers as they appeared out of the mist. Hits were observed to take effect on several ships.

The ships of the Second Battle Squadron, under Vice-Admiral Sir Thomas Jerram, were in action with vessels of the *Kaiser* or *Koenig* classes between 6.30 and 7.20 p.m., and fired also at an enemy battle-cruiser which had dropped back apparently severely damaged.

During the action between the Battle Fleets the Second Cruiser Squadron, ably commanded by Rear-Admiral Herbert

L. Heath, M.V.O., with the addition of *Duke of Edinburgh* (Captain Henry Blackett) of the First Cruiser Squadron, occupied a position at the van, and acted as a connecting link between the Battle Fleet and the Battle-cruiser Fleet. This squadron, although it carried out useful work, did not have an opportunity of coming into action.

The attached cruisers *Boadicea* (Captain Louis C. S. Woollcombe, M.V.O.), *Active* (Captain Percy Withers), *Blanche* (Captain John M. Casement), and *Bellona* (Captain Arthur B. S. Dutton) carried out their duties as repeating-ships with remarkable rapidity and accuracy under difficult conditions.

The Fourth Light-cruiser Squadron, under Commodore Charles E. Le Mesurier, occupied a position in the van until ordered to attack enemy destroyers at 7.20 p.m., and again at 8.18 p.m., when they supported the Eleventh Flotilla, which had moved out under Commodore James R. P. Hawksley, M.V.O., to attack. On each occasion the Fourth Light-cruiser Squadron was very well handled by Commodore Le Mesurier, his captains giving him excellent support, and their object was attained, although with some loss in the second attack, when the ships came under the heavy fire of the enemy Battle Fleet at between 6,500 and 8,000 yards. The *Calliope* (Commodore Le Mesurier) was hit several times, but did not sustain serious damage, although, I regret to say, she had several casualties. The light cruisers attacked the enemy's battleships with torpedoes at this time, and an explosion on board a ship of the *Kaiser* class was seen at 8.40 p.m.

During these destroyer attacks four enemy torpedo-boat destroyers were sunk by the gunfire of battleships, light cruisers, and destroyers.

After the arrival of the British Battle Fleet the enemy's tactics were of a nature generally to avoid further action, in which they were favoured by the conditions of visibility.

At 9 p.m. the enemy was entirely out of sight, and the threat of torpedo-boat destroyer attacks during the rapidly approaching darkness made it necessary for me to dispose the Fleet for the night, with a view to its safety from such attacks, whilst providing for a renewal of action at daylight. I accordingly manœuvred to remain between the enemy and his bases, placing our flotillas in a position in which they would afford protection to the Fleet from destroyer attack, and at the same time be favourably situated for attacking the enemy's heavy ships.

NIGHT ATTACKS BY FLOTILLAS.

During the night the British heavy ships were not attacked, but the Fourth, Eleventh, and Twelfth Flotillas, under Commodore Hawkesley and Captains Charles J. Wintour and Anselan J. B. Stirling, delivered a series of very gallant and successful attacks on the enemy, causing him heavy losses.

It was during these attacks that severe losses in the Fourth Flotilla occurred, including that of *Tipperary*, with the gallant leader of the flotilla, Captain Wintour. He had brought his flotilla to a high pitch of perfection, and although suffering severely from the fire of the enemy, a heavy toll of enemy vessels was taken, and many gallant actions were performed by the flotilla.

Two torpedoes were seen to take effect on enemy vessels as the result of the attacks of the Fourth Flotilla, one being from *Spitfire* (Lieutenant-Commander Clarence W. E. Trelawny), and the other from either *Ardent* (Lieutenant-Commander Arthur Marsden), *Ambuscade* (Lieutenant-Commander Gordon A. Coles) or *Garland* (Lieutenant-Commander Reginald S. Goff).

The attack carried out by the Twelfth Flotilla (Captain Anselan J. B. Stirling) was admirably executed. The squadron attacked, which consisted of six large vessels, besides light cruisers, and comprised vessels of the *Kaiser* class, was taken by surprise. A large number of torpedoes was fired, including some at the second and third ships in the line ; those fired at the third ship took effect, and she was observed to blow up. A second attack made twenty minutes later by *Mænad* (Commander John P. Champion) on the five vessels still remaining, resulted in the fourth ship in the line being also hit.

The destroyers were under a heavy fire from the light cruisers on reaching the rear of the line, but the *Onslaught* (Lieutenant-Commander Arthur G. Onslow, D.S.C.) was the only vessel which received any material injuries. In the *Onslaught* Sub-Lieutenant Harry W. A. Kemmis, assisted by Midshipman Reginald G. Arnot, R.N.R., the only executive officers not disabled, brought the ship successfully out of action and reached her home port.

During the attack carried out by the Eleventh Flotilla, *Castor* (Commodore James R. P. Hawkesley), leading the flotilla, engaged and sank an enemy torpedo-boat destroyer at point-blank range.

Sir David Beatty reports :—

" The Thirteenth Flotilla, under the command of Captain James U. Farie, in *Champion*, took station astern of the Battle Fleet for the night. At 0.30 a.m. on Thursday, 1st June, a large vessel crossed the rear of the flotilla at high speed. She passed close to *Petard* and *Turbulent*, switched on searchlights and opened a heavy fire, which disabled *Turbulent*. At 3.30 a.m. *Champion* was engaged for a few minutes with four enemy destroyers. *Moresby* reports four ships of *Deutschland* class sighted at 2.35 a.m., at whom she fired one torpedo. Two minutes later an explosion was felt by *Moresby* and *Obdurate*.

" *Fearless* and the 1st Flotilla were very usefully employed as a submarine screen during the earlier part of the 31st May. At 6.10 p.m., when joining the Battle Fleet,

Fearless was unable to follow the battle cruisers without fouling the battleships, and therefore took station at the rear of the line. She sighted during the night a battleship of the *Kaiser* class steaming fast and entirely alone. She was not able to engage her, but believes she was attacked by destroyers further astern. A heavy explosion was observed astern not long after."

There were many gallant deeds performed by the destroyer flotillas ; they surpassed the very highest expectations that I had formed of them.

Apart from the proceedings of the flotillas, the Second Light-cruiser Squadron in the rear of the Battle Fleet was in close action for about 15 minutes at 10.20 p.m. with a squadron comprising one enemy cruiser and four light cruisers, during which period *Southampton* and *Dublin* (Captain Albert C. Scott) suffered rather heavy casualties, although their steaming and fighting qualities were not impaired. The return fire of the squadron appeared to be very effective.

Abdiel, ably commanded by Commander Berwick Curtis, carried out her duties with the success which has always characterized her work.

PROCEEDINGS ON 1ST JUNE.

At daylight, 1st June, the Battle Fleet, being then to the southward and westward of the Horn Reef, turned to the northward in search of enemy vessels and for the purpose of collecting our own cruisers and torpedo-boat destroyers. At 2.30 a.m. Vice-Admiral Sir Cecil Burney transferred his flag from *Marlborough* to *Revenge*, as the former ship had some difficulty in keeping up the speed of the squadron. *Marlborough* was detached by my direction to a base, successfully driving off an enemy submarine attack en route. The visibility early on 1st June (three to four miles) was less than on 31st May, and the torpedo-boat destroyers, being out of visual touch, did not rejoin until 9 a.m. The British Fleet remained in the proximity of the battlefield and near the line of approach to German ports until 11 a.m. on 1st June, in spite of the disadvantage of long distances from fleet bases and the danger incurred in waters adjacent to enemy coasts from submarines and torpedo craft. The enemy, however, made no sign, and I was reluctantly compelled to the conclusion that the High Sea Fleet had returned into port. Subsequent events proved this assumption to have been correct. Our position must have been known to the enemy, as at 4 a.m. the Fleet engaged a Zeppelin for about five minutes, during which time she had ample opportunity to note and subsequently report the position and course of the British Fleet.

The waters from the latitude of the Horn Reef to the scene of the action were thoroughly searched, and some survivors from the destroyers *Ardent* (Lieutenant-Commander Arthur Marsden), *Fortune* (Lieutenant-Commander Frank G. Terry), and *Tipperary* (Captain (D) Charles J. Wintour), were picked up, and the *Sparrowhawk* (Lieutenant-Commander Sydney Hopkins), which had been in collision and was no longer seaworthy, was sunk after her crew had been taken off. A large amount of wreckage was seen, but no enemy ships, and at 1.15 p.m., it being evident that the German Fleet had succeeded in returning to port, course was shaped for our bases, which were reached without further incident on Friday, 2nd June. A cruiser squadron was detached to search for *Warrior*, which vessel had been abandoned whilst in tow of *Engadine* on her way to the base owing to bad weather setting in and the vessel becoming unseaworthy, but no trace of her was discovered, and a further subsequent search by a light-cruiser squadron having failed to locate her, it is evident that she foundered.

Sir David Beatty reports in regard to the *Engadine* as follows :—

" The work of *Engadine* appears to have been most praise-worthy throughout, and of great value. Lieutenant-Commander C. G. Robinson deserves great credit for the skilful and seamanlike manner in which he handled his ship. He actually towed *Warrior* for 75 miles between 8.40 p.m., 31st May, and 7.15 a.m., 1st June, and was instrumental in saving the lives of her ship's company."

I fully endorse his remarks.

The Fleet fuelled and replenished with ammunition, and at 9.30 p.m. on 2nd June was reported ready for further action.

LOSSES.

The condition of low visibility under which the day action took place and the approach of darkness enhance the difficulty of giving an accurate report of the damage inflicted or the names of the ships sunk by our forces, but after a most careful examination of the evidence of all officers who testified to seeing enemy vessels actually sink, and personal interviews with a large number of these officers I am of opinion that the list shown in the enclosure gives the minimum in regard to numbers, though it is possibly not entirely accurate as regards the particular class of vessel, especially those which were sunk during the night attacks. In addition to the vessels sunk, it is unquestionable that many other ships were very seriously damaged by gunfire and by torpedo attack.

I deeply regret to report the loss of H.M. ships *Queen Mary*, *Indefatigable*, *Invincible*, *Defence*, *Black Prince*, *Warrior*, and of H.M. T.B.D's *Tipperary*, *Ardent*, *Fortune*, *Shark*, *Sparrowhawk*, *Nestor*, *Nomad*, and *Turbulent*, and still more do I regret the resultant heavy loss of life. The death of such gallant and distinguished officers as Rear-Admiral Sir Robert Arbuthnot, Bart., Rear-Admiral The Hon. Horace Hood, Captain Charles F. Sowerby, Captain Cecil I. Prowse, Captain Arthur

L. Cay, Captain Thomas P. Bonham, Captain Charles J. Wintour, and Captain Stanley V. Ellis, and those who perished with them, is a serious loss to the Navy and to the country. They led officers and men who were equally gallant, and whose death is mourned by their comrades in the Grand Fleet. They fell doing their duty nobly, a death which they would have been the first to desire.

The enemy fought with the gallantry that was expected of him. We particularly admired the conduct of those on board a disabled German light cruiser which passed down the British line shortly after deployment, under a heavy fire, which was returned by the only gun left in action.

THE PERSONNEL OF THE FLEET.

The conduct of officers and men throughout the day and night actions was entirely beyond praise. No words of mine could do them justice. On all sides it is reported to me that the glorious traditions of the past were most worthily upheld—whether in heavy ships, cruisers, light cruisers, or destroyers—the same admirable spirit prevailed. Officers and men were cool and determined, with a cheeriness that would have carried them through anything. The heroism of the wounded was the admiration of all.

I cannot adequately express the pride with which the spirit of the Fleet filled me.

Details of the work of the various ships during action have now been given. It must never be forgotten, however, that the prelude to action is the work of the engine-room department, and that during action the officers and men of that department perform their most important duties without the incentive which a knowledge of the course of the action gives to those on deck. The qualities of discipline and endurance are taxed to the utmost under these conditions, and they were, as always, most fully maintained throughout the operations under review. Several ships attained speeds that had never before been reached, thus showing very clearly their high state of steaming efficiency. Failures in material were conspicuous by their absence, and several instances are reported of magnificent work on the part of the engine-room department of injured ships.

The artisan ratings also carried out much valuable work during and after the action; they could not have done better.

The work of the medical officers of the Fleet, carried out very largely under the most difficult conditions, was entirely admirable and invaluable. Lacking in many cases all the essentials for performing critical operations, and with their staff seriously depleted by casualties, they worked untiringly and with the greatest success. To them we owe a deep debt of gratitude.

It will be seen that the hardest fighting fell to the lot of the Battle-cruiser Fleet (the units of which were less heavily armoured than their opponents), the Fifth Battle Squadron, the First Cruiser Squadron, Fourth Light-cruiser Squadron, and the Flotillas. This was inevitable under the conditions, and the squadrons and flotillas mentioned as well as the individual vessels composing them were handled with conspicuous ability, as were also the 1st, 2nd, and 4th Squadrons of the Battle Fleet and the 2nd Cruiser Squadron.

I desire to place on record my high appreciation of the manner in which all the vessels were handled. The conditions were such as to call for great skill and ability, quick judgment and decisions, and this was conspicuous throughout the day.

I beg also to draw special attention to the services rendered by Vice-Admiral Sir Cecil Burney (Second in Command of the Grand Fleet), Vice-Admiral Sir Thomas Jerram, Vice-Admiral Sir Doveton Sturdee, Rear-Admiral Hugh Evan-Thomas, Rear-Admiral Alexander L. Duff, Rear-Admiral Arthur C. Leveson, and Rear-Admiral Ernest F. A. Gaunt commanding squadrons or divisions in the Battle Fleet. They acted throughout with skill and judgment. Sir Cecil

Burney's squadron, owing to its position, was able to see more of the enemy Battle Fleet than the other battle squadrons, and under a leader who has rendered me most valuable and loyal assistance at all times the squadron did excellent work. The magnificent squadron commanded by Rear-Admiral Evan-Thomas formed a support of great value to Sir David Beatty during the afternoon, and was brought into action in rear of the Battle Fleet in the most judicious manner in the evening.

Sir David Beatty once again showed his fine qualities of gallant leadership, firm determination, and correct strategic insight. He appreciated the situations at once on sighting first the enemy's lighter forces, then his battle-cruisers, and finally his Battle Fleet. I can fully sympathize with his feelings when the evening mist and fading light robbed the Fleet of that complete victory for which he had manœuvred, and for which the vessels in company with him had striven so hard. The services rendered by him, not only on this, but on two previous occasions, have been of the very greatest value.

Sir David Beatty brings to my notice the brilliant support afforded him by Rear-Admiral Hugh Evan-Thomas; the magnificent manner in which Rear-Admiral The Hon. Horace Hood brought his squadron into action; the able support afforded him by Rear-Admiral William C. Pakenham and Rear-Admiral Osmond de B. Brock; and the good work performed by the Light-cruiser Squadrons under the command respectively of Rear-Admiral Trevylyan D. W. Napier, Commodore William E. Goodenough, and Commodore Edwyn S. Alexander-Sinclair. He states that on every occasion these officers anticipated his wishes and used their forces to the best possible effect.

I most fully endorse all his remarks, and I forward also the following extract from his report regarding the valuable services rendered by his staff :—

" I desire to record and bring to your notice the great assistance that I received on a day of great anxiety and strain from my Chief of the Staff, Captain Rudolf W. Bentinck, whose good judgment was of the greatest help. He was a tower of strength. My Flag-Commander, the Hon. Reginald A. R. Plunkett, was most valuable in observing the effect of our fire, thereby enabling me to take advantage of the enemy's discomfiture ; my Secretary, Frank T. Spickernell, who made accurate notes of events as they occurred, which proved of the utmost value in keeping the situation clearly before me ; my Flag Lieutenant-Commander, Ralph F. Seymour, who maintained efficient communications under the most difficult circumstances despite the fact that his signalling appliances were continually shot away. All these officers carried out their duties with great coolness on the manœuvring platform, where they were fully exposed to the enemy's fire."

I cannot close this dispatch without recording the brilliant work of my Chief of the Staff, Vice-Admiral Sir Charles Madden, K.C.B., C.V.O. Throughout a period of 21 months of war his services have been of inestimable value. His good judgment, his long experience in fleets, special gift for organization, and his capacity for unlimited work, have all been of the greatest assistance to me, and have relieved me of much of the anxiety inseparable from the conduct of the Fleet during the war. In the stages leading up to the Fleet Action and during and after the action he was always at hand to assist, and his judgment never at fault. I owe him more than I can say.

My special thanks are due also to Commodore Lionel Halsey, C.M.G., the Captain of the Fleet, who also assists me in the working of the Fleet at sea, and to whose good organization is largely due the rapidity with which the Fleet was fuelled and replenished with ammunition on return to its bases. He was of much assistance to me during the action.

Commander Charles M. Forbes, my flag-commander, and Commander Roger M. Bellairs, of my Staff, plotted the movements of the two Fleets with rapidity and accuracy as reports were received ; Commander the Hon. Matthew R. Best,

M.V.O., of my Staff, acted as observer aloft throughout the action, and his services were of value. These officers carried out their duties with much efficiency during the action.

The signals were worked with smoothness and rapidity by Commander Alexander R. W. Woods, assisted by the other signal officers, and all ships responded remarkably well under difficult conditions. The signal departments in all ships deserve great credit for their work. My Flag-Lieutenant, Lieutenant-Commander Herbert Fitzherbert, was also of much service to me throughout the action.

The high state of efficiency of the W/T arrangements of the Fleet, and the facility with which they were worked before, during, and after the action, is a great testimony to the indefatigable work carried out by Commander Richard L. Nicholson. His services have been invaluable throughout the war.

A special word of praise is due to the wireless departments in all ships.

My Secretaries, Fleet Paymasters Hamnet H. Share, C.B., and Victor H. T. Weekes, recorded with accuracy salient features of the action. Their records have been of much assistance.

To the Master of the Fleet, Captain Oliver E. Leggett, I am indebted for the accuracy with which he kept the reckoning throughout the operations.

In a separate dispatch I propose to bring to the notice of their Lordships the names of officers and men all of whom did not come under my personal observation, but who had the opportunity of specially distinguishing themselves.

I append the full text of Sir David Beatty's report to me, from which, as will be seen, I have made copious extracts in order to make my narrative continuous and complete.

I am, Sir,

Your obedient Servant,

J. R. JELLICOE, Admiral,
Commander-in-Chief.

List of Enemy Vessels put out of action, 31 May—1 June, 1916.

Battleships *or* Battle-cruisers.

2 Battleships, *Dreadnought* type.
1 Battleship, *Deutschland* type.
(Seen to sink.)

1 Battle-cruiser.
(Sunk—*Lutzow*, admitted by Germans.)
1 Battleship, *Dreadnought* type.
1 Battle-cruiser.
(Seen to be so severely damaged as to render it extremely doubtful if they could reach port.)

Light Cruisers.

5 Light Cruisers.
(Seen to sink ; one of them had the appearance of being a larger type, and might have been a battleship.)

Torpedo-boat Destroyers.

6 Torpedo-boat Destroyers.
(Seen to sink.)

3 Torpedo-boat Destroyers.
(Seen to be so severely damaged as to render it extremely doubtful if they could reach port.)

Submarines.

1 Submarine.
(Sunk.)

APPENDIX.

Lion,

19th June 1916.

Sir,

I have the honour to report that at 2.37 p.m. on 31st May 1916 I was cruising and steering to the northward to join your Flag.

The Light-cruiser Screen was disposed from E. to W.

At 2.20 p.m. reports were received from *Galatea* (Commodore Edwyn S. Alexander-Sinclair, M.V.O., A.D.C.) indicating the presence of enemy vessels. The direction of advance was immediately altered to S.S.E., the course for Horn Reef, so as to place my force between the enemy and his base. At 2.35 p.m. a considerable amount of smoke was sighted to the eastward. This made it clear that the enemy was to the northward and eastward, and that it would be impossible for him to round the Horn Reef without being brought to action. Course was accordingly altered to the eastward, and subsequently to north-eastward, the enemy being sighted at 3.31 p.m. Their force consisted of five battle-cruisers.

After the first reports of the enemy the 1st and 3rd Light-cruiser Squadrons changed their direction, and, without waiting for orders, spread to the east, thereby forming a screen in advance of the Battle-cruiser Squadrons and 5th Battle Squadron by the time we had hauled up to the course of approach. They engaged enemy light cruisers at long range. In the meantime the 2nd Light-cruiser Squadron had come in at high speed, and was able to take station ahead of the battle-cruisers by the time we turned to E.S.E., the course on which we first engaged the enemy. In this respect the work of the Light-cruiser Squadrons was excellent and of great value.

From a report from *Galatea* at 2.25 p.m. it was evident that the enemy force was considerable, and not merely an isolated unit of light cruisers; so at 2.45 p.m. I ordered *Engadine* (Lieutenant-Commander C. G. Robinson) to send up a seaplane and scout to N.N.E. This order was carried out very quickly, and by 3.8 p.m. a seaplane, with Flight Lieutenant F. J. Rutland, R.N., as pilot, and Assistant Paymaster G. S. Trewin, R.N., as observer, was well under way; her first reports of the enemy were received in *Engadine* about 3.30 p.m. Owing to clouds it was necessary to fly very low, and in order to identify four enemy light cruisers the seaplane had to fly at a height of 900 ft. within 3,000 yards of them, the light cruisers opening fire on her with every gun that would bear. This in no way interfered with the clarity of their reports, and both Flight Lieutenant Rutland and Assistant Paymaster Trewin are to be congratulated on their achievement, which indicates that seaplanes under such circumstances are of distinct value.

At 3.30 p.m. I increased speed to 25 knots and formed line of battle, the 2nd Battle-cruiser Squadron forming astern of the 1st Battle-cruiser Squadron, with destroyers of the 13th and 9th Flotillas taking station ahead. I turned to E.S.E., slightly converging on the enemy, who were now at a range of 23,000 yards, and formed the ships on a line of bearing to clear the smoke. The 5th Battle Squadron, who had conformed to our movements, were now bearing N.N.W., 10,000 yards. The visibility at this time was good, the sun behind us and the wind S.E. Being between the enemy and his base, our situation was both tactically and strategically good.

At 3.48 p.m. the action commenced at a range of 18,500 yards, both forces opening fire practically simultaneously. Course was altered to the southward, and subsequently the mean direction was S.S.E., the enemy steering a parallel course distant about 18,000 to 14,500 yards.

At 4.8 p.m. the 5th Battle Squadron came into action,

and opened fire at a range of 20,000 yards. The enemy's fire now seemed to slacken. The destroyer *Landrail* (Lieutenant-Commander Francis E. H. G. Hobart), of the 9th Flotilla, which was on our port beam, trying to take station ahead, sighted the periscope of a submarine on her port quarter. Though causing considerable inconvenience from smoke, the presence of *Lydiard* (Commander Malcolm L. Goldsmith) and *Landrail* undoubtedly preserved the battle-cruisers from closer submarine attack. *Nottingham* (Captain Charles B. Miller) also reported a submarine on the starboard beam.

Eight destroyers of the 13th Flotilla, *Nestor* (Commander the Hon. Edward B. S. Bingham), *Nomad* (Lieutenant-Commander Paul Whitfield), *Nicator* (Lieutenant Jack E. A. Mocatta), *Narborough* (Lieutenant-Commander Geoffrey Corlett), *Pelican* (Lieutenant-Commander Kenneth A. Beattie), *Petard* (Lieutenant-Commander Evelyn C. O. Thomson), *Obdurate* (Lieutenant-Cecil H. H. Sams), *Nerissa* (Lieutenant-Commander Montague C. B. Legge), with *Moorsom* (Commander John C. Hodgson) and *Morris* (Lieutenant-Commander Edward S. Graham) of 10th Flotilla, *Turbulent* (Lieutenant-Commander Dudley Stuart), *Termagant* (Lieutenant-Commander Cuthbert P. Blake), of the 9th Flotilla, having been ordered to attack the enemy with torpedoes when opportunity offered, moved out at 4.15 p.m. simultaneously with a similar movement on the part of the enemy's destroyers. The attack was carried out in the most gallant manner and with great determination. Before arriving at a favourable position to fire torpedoes, they intercepted an enemy force consisting of a light cruiser and 15 destroyers. A fierce engagement ensued at close quarters, with the result that the enemy were forced to retire on their battle-cruisers, having lost two destroyers sunk and having their torpedo attack frustrated. Our destroyers sustained no loss in this engagement, but their attack on the enemy battle-cruisers was rendered less effective owing to some of the destroyers having dropped astern during the fight. Their position was therefore unfavourable for torpedo attack.

Nestor, Nomad, and *Nicator,* gallantly led by Commander Hon. E. B. S. Bingham of *Nestor,* pressed home their attack on the battle-cruisers and fired two torpedoes at them, being subjected to a heavy fire from the enemy's secondary armament. *Nomad* was badly hit, and apparently remained stopped between the lines. Subsequently *Nestor* and *Nicator* altered course to the S.E., and in a short time, the opposing battle-cruisers having turned 16 points, found themselves within close range of a number of enemy battleships. Nothing daunted, though under a terrific fire, they stood on, and their position being favourable for torpedo attack, fired a torpedo at the second ship of the enemy line at a range of 3,000 yards. Before they could fire their fourth torpedo *Nestor* was badly hit, and swung to starboard ; *Nicator* altering course inside her to avoid collision, and thereby being prevented from firing the last torpedo. *Nicator* made good her escape, and subsequently rejoined the Captain D, 13th Flotilla. *Nestor* remained stopped, but was afloat when last seen. *Moorsom* also carried out an attack on the enemy's Battle Fleet.

Petard, Nerissa, Turbulent, and *Termagant* also pressed home their attack on the enemy battle-cruisers, firing torpedoes after the engagement with enemy destroyers. *Petard* reports that all her torpedoes must have crossed the enemy's line, while *Nerissa* states that one torpedo appeared to strike the rear ship. These destroyer attacks were indicative of the spirit pervading His Majesty's Navy, and were worthy of its highest traditions. I propose to bring to your notice a recommendation of Commander Bingham and other Officers for some recognition of their conspicuous gallantry.

From 4.15 to 4.43 p.m. the conflict between the opposing battle-cruisers was of a very fierce and resolute character. The 5th Battle Squadron was engaging the enemy's rear ships, unfortunately at very long range. Our fire began to tell, the accuracy and rapidity of that of the enemy depreciating considerably. At 4.18 p.m. the third enemy ship was seen to be on fire. The visibility to the north-eastward had become considerably reduced, and the outline of the ships very indistinct.

At 4.38 p.m. *Southampton* (Commodore William E. Goodenough, M.V.O., A.D.C.) reported the enemy's Battle Fleet ahead. The destroyers were recalled, and at 4.42 p.m. the enemy's Battle Fleet was sighted S.E. Course was altered 16 points in succession to starboard, and I proceeded on a northerly course to lead them towards the Battle Fleet. The enemy battle-cruisers altered course shortly afterwards, and the action continued. *Southampton*, with the 2nd Light-cruiser Squadron, held on to the southward to observe. They closed to within 13,000 yards of the enemy Battle Fleet, and came under a very heavy but ineffective fire. *Southampton's* reports were most valuable. The 5th Battle Squadron were now closing on an opposite course and engaging the enemy battle-cruisers with all guns. The position of the enemy Battle Fleet was communicated to them, and I ordered them to alter course 16 points. Led by Rear-Admiral Evan-Thomas in *Barham* (Captain Arthur W. Craig), this squadron supported us brilliantly and effectively.

At 4.57 p.m. the 5th Battle Squadron turned up astern of me and came under the fire of the leading ships of the enemy Battle Fleet. *Fearless* (Captain (D) Charles O. Roper), with the destroyers of 1st Flotilla, joined the battle-cruisers and, when speed admitted, took station ahead. *Champion* (Captain (D) James U. Farie), with 13th Flotilla, took station on the 5th Battle Squadron. At 5 p.m. the 1st and 3rd Light-cruiser Squadrons, which had been following me on the southerly course, took station on my starboard bow; the 2nd Light-cruiser Squadron took station on my port quarter.

The weather conditions now became unfavourable, our ships being silhouetted against a clear horizon to the westward, while the enemy were for the most part obscured by mist, only showing up clearly at intervals. These conditions prevailed until we had turned their van, at about 6 p.m. Between 5 and 6 p.m. the action continued on a northerly course, the range being about 14,000 yards. During this time the enemy received very severe punishment, and one of their battle-cruisers quitted the line in a considerably damaged condition. This came under my personal observation, and was corroborated by *Princess Royal* (Captain Walter H. Cowan, M.V.O., D.S.O.) and *Tiger* (Captain Henry B. Pelly, M.V.O.). Other enemy ships also showed signs of increasing injury. At 5.5 p.m. *Onslow* (Lieutenant-Commander John C. Tovey) and *Moresby* (Lieutenant-Commander Roger V. Alison), who had been detached to assist *Engadine* with the seaplane, rejoined the Battle-cruiser Squadrons, and took station on the starboard (engaged) bow of *Lion* (Captain Alfred E. M. Chatfield, C.V.O.). At 5.10 p.m. *Moresby*, being 2 points before the beam of the leading enemy ship, fired a torpedo at a ship in their line. Eight minutes later she observed a hit with a torpedo on what was judged to be the sixth ship in the line. *Moresby* then passed between the lines to clear the range of smoke and rejoined *Champion*. In corroboration of this *Fearless* reports having seen an enemy heavy ship heavily on fire at about 5.10 p.m., and shortly afterwards a huge cloud of smoke and steam.

At 5.35 p.m. our course was N.N.E., and the estimated position of the Battle Fleet was N. 16 W., so we gradually hauled to the north-eastward, keeping the range of the enemy at 14,000 yards. He was gradually hauling to the eastward, receiving severe punishment at the head of his line, and probably acting on information received from his light cruisers, which had sighted, and were engaged with, the Third Battle-cruiser Squadron. Possibly Zeppelins were present also. At 5.50 p.m. British cruisers were sighted on the port bow, and at 5.56 p.m. the leading battleships of the Battle Fleet, bearing north 5 miles. I thereupon altered course to east, and proceeded at utmost speed. This brought the range of the enemy down to 12,000 yards. I made a report to you that the enemy battle-cruisers bore south-east. At this time only three of the enemy battle-cruisers were visible, closely followed by battleships of the *Koenig* class.

At about 6.5 p.m. *Onslow*, being on the engaged bow of *Lion*, sighted an enemy light cruiser at a distance of 6,000 yards from us, apparently endeavouring to attack with torpedoes. *Onslow* at once closed and engaged her, firing 58 rounds at a range of from 4,000 to 2,000 yards, scoring a number of hits. *Onslow* then closed the enemy battle-cruisers, and orders were given for all torpedoes to be fired. At this moment she was struck amidships by a heavy shell, with the result that only one torpedo was fired. Thinking that all his torpedoes had gone, the commanding officer proceeded to retire at slow speed. Being informed that he still had three torpedoes, he closed the light cruiser previously engaged and torpedoed her. The enemy's Battle Fleet was then sighted, and the remaining torpedoes were fired at them, and must have crossed the enemy's track. Damage then caused *Onslow* to stop.

At 7.15 p.m. *Defender* (Lieutenant-Commander Lawrence R. Palmer), whose speed had been reduced to 10 knots while on the disengaged side of the battle-cruisers by a 12-inch shell, which damaged her foremost boiler, closed *Onslow* and took her in tow. Shells were falling all round them during this operation, which, however, was successfully accomplished. During the heavy weather of the ensuing night the tow parted twice, but was resecured. The two struggled on together until 1 p.m. 1st June, when *Onslow* was transferred to tugs. I consider the performances of these two destroyers to be gallant in the extreme, and I am recommending Lieut.-Commander J. C. Tovey of *Onslow* and Lieut.-Commander L. R. Palmer of *Defender* for special recognition. *Onslow* was possibly the destroyer referred to by Rear-Admiral Commanding 3rd Light-cruiser Squadron as follows :—

" Here I should like to bring to your notice the action of a destroyer (name unknown) which we passed close in a disabled condition soon after 6 p.m. She apparently was able to struggle ahead again, and made straight for the *Derfflinger* to attack her."

At 6.20 p.m. the Third Battle-cruiser Squadron appeared ahead, steaming south towards the enemy's van. I ordered them to take station ahead; which was carried out magnificently, Rear-Admiral Hood bringing his squadron into action ahead in a most inspiring manner, worthy of his great naval ancestors. At 6.25 p.m. I altered course to the E.S.E. in support of the Third Battle-cruiser Squadron, who were at this time only 8,000 yards from the enemy's leading ship. They were pouring a hot fire into her, and caused her to turn to the westward of south. At the same time I made a report to you of the bearing and distance of the enemy Battle Fleet.

By 6.50 p.m. the battle-cruisers were clear of our leading Battle Squadron then bearing about N.N.W. 3 miles from *Lion*, and I ordered the 3rd Battle-cruiser Squadron to prolong the line astern and reduced to 18 knots. The visibility at this time was very indifferent, not more than 4 miles, and the enemy ships were temporarily lost sight of. It is interesting to note that after 6 p.m., although the visibility became reduced, it was undoubtedly more favourable to us than to the enemy. At intervals their ships showed up clearly, enabling us to punish them very severely and establish a definite superiority over them. From the reports of other ships and my own observation it was clear that the enemy suffered considerable damage, battle-cruisers and battleships alike. The head of their line was crumpled up, leaving battleships as targets for the majority of our battle-cruisers. Before leaving us the 5th Battle Squadron was also engaging battleships. The report of Rear-Admiral Evan-Thomas shows that excellent results were obtained, and it can be safely said that his magnificent squadron wrought great execution.

· From the report of Rear-Admiral T. D. W. Napier, M.V.O., the 3rd Light-cruiser Squadron, which had maintained its station on our starboard bow well ahead of the enemy, at 6.25 p.m. attacked with the torpedo. *Falmouth* (Captain John D. Edwards) and *Yarmouth* (Captain Thomas D. Pratt) both fired torpedoes at the leading enemy battle-cruiser, and it is believed that one torpedo hit, as a heavy underwater explosion was observed. The 3rd Light-cruiser Squadron then gallantly attacked the heavy ships with gunfire, with impunity to themselves, thereby demonstrating that the fighting efficiency of the enemy had been seriously impaired. Rear-Admiral Napier deserves great credit for his determined and effective attack. *Indomitable* (Captain Francis W. Kennedy) reports that about this time one of the *Derfflinger* class fell out of the enemy's line.

At 7.6 p.m. I received a signal from you that the course of the Fleet was south. Subsequently signals were received up to 8.46 p.m. showing that the course of the Battle Fleet was to the south-westward. Between 7 and 7.12 p.m. we hauled round gradually to S.W. by S. to regain touch with the enemy, and at 7.14 p.m. again sighted them at a range of about 15,000 yards. The ships sighted at this time were two battle-cruisers and two battleships, apparently of the *Koenig* class. No doubt more continued the line to the northward, but that was all that could be seen. The visibility having improved considerably as the sun descended below the clouds, we re-engaged at 7.17 p.m. and increased speed to 22 knots. At 7.32 p.m. my course was S.W., speed 18 knots, the leading enemy battleship bearing N.W. by W. Again after a very short time the enemy showed signs of punishment, one ship being on fire, while another appeared to drop right astern. The destroyers at the head of the enemy's line emitted volumes of grey smoke, covering their capital ships as with a pall, under cover of which they turned away, and at 7.45 p.m. we lost sight of them.

At 7.58 p.m. I ordered the 1st and 3rd Light-cruiser

Squadrons to sweep to the westward and locate the head of the enemy's line, and at 8.20 p.m. we altered course to west in support. We soon located two battle-cruisers and battleships, and were heavily engaged, at a short range of about 10,000 yards. The leading ship was hit repeatedly by *Lion*, and turned away 8 points, emitting very high flames and with a heavy list to port. *Princess Royal* set fire to a three-funnelled battleship; *New Zealand* (Captain John F. E. Green) and *Indomitable* report that the third ship, which they both engaged, hauled out of the line heeling over and on fire. The mist which now came down enveloped them, and *Falmouth* reported they were last seen at 8.38 p.m. steaming to the westward.

At 8.40 p.m. all our battle-cruisers felt a heavy shock as if struck by a mine or torpedo, or possibly sunken wreckage. As, however, examination of the bottoms reveals no sign of such an occurrence, it is assumed that it indicated the blowing up of a great vessel.

I continued on a south-westerly course with my light cruisers spread until 9.24 p.m. Nothing further being sighted, I assumed that the enemy were to the north-westward, and that we had established ourselves well between him and his base. *Minotaur* (Captain Arthur C. S. H. D'Aeth) was at this time bearing north 5 miles, and I asked her the position of the leading Battle Squadron of the Battle Fleet. Her reply was that it was not in sight, but was last seen bearing N.N.E. I kept you informed of my position, course, and speed; also of the bearing of the enemy.

In view of the gathering darkness, and of the fact that our strategical position was such as to make it appear certain that we should locate the enemy at daylight under most favourable circumstances, I did not consider it desirable or proper to close the enemy Battle Fleet during the dark hours. I therefore concluded that I should be carrying out your wishes by turning to the course of the Fleet, reporting to you that I had done so.

The 13th Flotilla, under the command of Captain James U. Farie, in *Champion*, took station astern of the Battle Fleet for the night. At 0.30 a.m. on Thursday, 1st June, a large vessel crossed the rear of the flotilla at high speed. She passed close to *Petard* and *Turbulent*, switched on searchlights, and opened a heavy fire, which disabled *Turbulent*. At 3.30 a.m. *Champion* was engaged for a few minutes with four enemy destroyers. *Moresby* reports four ships of *Deutschland* class sighted at 2.35 a.m., at whom she fired one torpedo. Two minutes later an explosion was felt by *Moresby* and *Obdurate*.

Fearless and the 1st Flotilla were very usefully employed as a submarine screen during the earlier part of the 31st May. At 6.10 p.m., when joining the Battle Fleet, *Fearless* was unable to follow the battle-cruisers without fouling the battle-ships, and therefore took station at the rear of the line. She sighted during the night a battleship of the *Kaiser* class steaming fast and entirely alone. She was not able to engage her, but believes she was attacked by destroyers further astern. A heavy explosion was observed astern not long after.

The 1st and 3rd Light-cruiser Squadrons were almost continuously in touch with the battle-cruisers, one or both squadrons being usually ahead. In this position they were of great value. They very effectively protected the head of our line from torpedo attack by light cruisers or destroyers, and were prompt in helping to regain touch when the enemy's line was temporarily lost sight of. The 2nd Light-cruiser Squadron was at the rear of our battle line during the night, and at 9 p.m. assisted to repel a destroyer attack on the 5th Battle Squadron. They were also heavily engaged at 10.20 p.m. with five enemy cruisers or light cruisers, *Southampton* and *Dublin* (Captain Albert C. Scott) suffering severe casualties during an action lasting about 15 minutes. *Birmingham* (Captain Arthur A. M. Duff), at 11.30 p.m., sighted two or more heavy ships steering south. A report of this was received by me at 11.40 p.m. as steering W.S.W. They were thought at the time to be battle-cruisers, but it is since considered that they were probably battleships.

The work of *Engadine* appears to have been most praiseworthy throughout, and of great value. Lieutenant-Commander C. G. Robinson deserves great credit for the skilful and seamanlike manner in which he handled his ship. He actually towed *Warrior* for 75 miles between 8.40 p.m., 31st May, and 7.15 a.m., 1st June, and was instrumental in saving the lives of her ship's company.

It is impossible to give a definite statement of the losses inflicted on the enemy. The visibility was for the most part low and fluctuating, and caution forbade me to close the range too much with my inferior force.

A review of all the reports which I have received leads me to conclude that the enemy's losses were considerably greater than those which we had sustained, in spite of their superiority, and included battleships, battle-cruisers, light cruisers, and destroyers.

This is eloquent testimony to the very high standard of gunnery and torpedo efficiency of His Majesty's ships. The control and drill remained undisturbed throughout, in many cases despite heavy damage to material and personnel. Our superiority over the enemy in this respect was very marked—their efficiency becoming rapidly reduced under punishment, while ours was maintained throughout.

As was to be expected, the behaviour of the ships' companies under the terrible conditions of a modern sea battle was magnificent without exception. The strain on their *moral* was a severe test of discipline and training. Officers and men were imbued with one thought—the desire to defeat the enemy. The fortitude of the wounded was admirable. A report from the Commanding Officer of *Chester* gives a splendid instance of devotion to duty. Boy (1st class) John Travers Cornwell, of *Chester*, was mortally wounded early in the action. He nevertheless remained standing alone at a most exposed post, quietly awaiting orders till the end of the action, with the gun's crew dead and wounded all round him. His age was under $16\frac{1}{2}$ years. I regret that he has since died, but I recommend his case for special recognition in justice to his memory, and as an acknowledgment of the high example set by him.

In such a conflict as raged continuously for five hours it was inevitable that we should suffer severe losses. It was necessary to maintain touch with greatly superior forces in fluctuating visibility, often very low. We lost *Invincible*, *Indefatigable*, and *Queen Mary*, from which ships there were few survivors. The casualties in other ships were heavy, and I wish to express my deepest regret at the loss of so many gallant comrades, officers and men. They died gloriously.

Exceptional skill was displayed by the Medical Officers of the Fleet. They performed operations and tended the wounded under conditions of extreme difficulty. In some cases their staff was seriously depleted by casualties, and the inevitable lack of such essentials as adequate light, hot water, etc., in ships damaged by shell fire, tried their skill, resource, and physical endurance to the utmost.

As usual, the Engine Room Departments of all ships displayed the highest qualities of technical skill, discipline, and endurance. High speed is a primary factor in the tactics of the squadrons under my command, and the Engine Room Departments never fail.

I have already made mention of the brilliant support afforded me by Rear-Admiral H. Evan-Thomas, M.V.O., and the 5th Battle Squadron, and of the magnificent manner in which Rear-Admiral Hon. H. L. A. Hood, C.B., M.V.O., D.S.O., brought his squadron into action. I desire to record my great regret at his loss, which is a national misfortune. I would now bring to your notice the able support rendered to me by Rear-Admiral W. C. Pakenham, C.B., and Rear-Admiral O. de B. Brock, C.B. In the course of my report I have expressed my appreciation of the good work performed by the Light-cruiser Squadrons under the command respectively of Rear-Admiral T. D. W. Napier, M.V.O., Commodore W. E. Good-enough, M.V.O., and Commodore E. S. Alexander-Sinclair, M.V.O. On every occasion these officers anticipated my wishes, and used their forces to the best possible effect.

I desire also to bring to your notice the skill with which their respective ships were handled by the Commanding Officers. With such Flag Officers, Commodores, and Captains to support me my task was lightened.

The destroyers of the 1st and 13th Flotillas were handled by their respective Commanding Officers with skill, dash, and courage. I desire to record my very great regret at the loss of Captains C. F. Sowerby (*Indefatigable*), C. I. Prowse (*Queen Mary*), and A. L. Cay (*Invincible*)—all officers of the highest attainments, who can be ill spared at this time of stress.

I wish to endorse the report of the Rear-Admiral Commanding the 5th Battle Squadron as to the ability displayed by the Commanding Officers of his squadron.

In conclusion, I desire to record and bring to your notice the great assistance that I received on a day of great anxiety and strain from my Chief of the Staff, Captain R. W. Bentinck, whose good judgment was of the greatest help. He was a tower of strength. My Flag Commander, Hon. R. A. R. Plunkett, was most valuable in observing the effect of our fire, thereby enabling me to take advantage of the enemy's discomfiture ; my Secretary, F. T. Spickernell, who made accurate notes of events as they occurred, which proved of the utmost value in keeping the situation clearly before me ; my Flag Lieutenant, Commander R. F. Seymour, who maintained efficient communications under the most difficult circumstances, despite the fact that his signalling appliances were continually shot away. All these officers carried out their duties with great coolness on the manœuvring platform, where they were fully exposed to the enemy's fire.

In accordance with your wishes, I am forwarding in a separate letter a full list of Officers and Men whom I wish to recommend to your notice.

I have the honour to be, Sir,
Your obedient Servant,
DAVID BEATTY,
Vice-Admiral.

The Commander-in-Chief,
Grand Fleet.

APPENDIX VI.

ITALY'S CAMPAIGN UP TO JANUARY 31, 1916.

A SEMI-OFFICIAL STATEMENT.*

THE difficulties which the Italian offensive against Austria had to cope with at the beginning of the war were manifold and serious. We have only to consider the large extension of frontier (eight hundred kilomètres), the precipitous and alpine character of the theatre of operations, and especially the powerful defensive preparations made by Austria—preparations which in the long period of peace following the war of 1866 had been carried out with a view to permanency, while during the period of Italian neutrality, from August 1914 to the end of May 1915, they had assumed a semi-permanent and occasional aspect. The development and origins of the war are, in fact, strictly dependent upon the unfavourable conformation given to the frontier in 1866, entirely to the advantage of Austria, and a perpetual menace to Italy, represented by the Austrian military system, which was founded on the absolute superiority of their frontier positions. The peculiar situation of the Trentino in respect to North-Eastern Italy made it easy for Austria to strike a blow in the rear of an Italian army operating on the Isonzo.

The first task of the Italian Army was therefore to overcome the difficulties incident to this initial strategical situation, at the same time not neglecting to co-operate with the Allies in the most efficient way, especially at a moment when

* Reprinted by permission of the *Morning Post*.

the Russian Army was being severely tried, and relief from the pressure which had been brought to bear on it was urgently needed. And thus it was that while large contingents of Italian troops were operating on the Isonzo front, another important section of the army was fighting on the Trentino, Tyrolese, and Carnic fronts in order to cover the flank and rear of the army on the Isonzo and to seriously engage the enemy, and especially to rectify the defective conformation of the frontier line with lightning rapidity.

It is thus that the operations from the very beginning assumed a definitely offensive character on a vast front, and in necessarily divergent directions and on ground which was for the most part mountainous and difficult ; and the army undertook the arduous task with a courage and tenacity which has never lessened during the carrying out of the campaign, which has even increased with the increasing difficulties and hardships, dangers and sacrifices.

OPERATIONS IN TIROL AND TRENTINO.

The Italian troops at the beginning of hostilities, by means of powerful pressure on the advanced portion of the enemy's forces, succeeded in driving them away from the frontier, which they then notably rectified. Thus between the end of May and the beginning of July a great part of the right side of the Daone Valley, the Val Vestino group, between the Idro and the Garda Lakes, the valley of the Adige as far as Ala, the Vallarsa, the *conche* of Tesino in the Brenta Valley, of Fiera di Primiero in the Cismon Valley, and of Cortina d'Ampezzo in the Boite Valley, were occupied. These important positions were immediately strengthened, and some violent counter-attacks on the part of the enemy were repulsed.

In Cadore, after a period of preparation by means of artillery fire, the offensive operations were initiated in the high valleys from the Cordevole to the Padola. It was thus possible to occupy the whole region of Ampezzo between the